Russian Economic Policy
under Nicholas I

Russian Economic Policy under Nicholas I

Walter McKenzie Pintner

Cornell University Press
Ithaca, New York

First published 1967

Library of Congress Catalog Card Number: 67–23067

PRINTED IN THE UNITED STATES OF AMERICA

BY THE COLONIAL PRESS INC.

For Molly

PREFACE

The reign of Nicholas I was, in a sense, a breathing spell for Russia. After centuries of struggle, the nation's military efforts had been crowned with a brilliant success, the destruction of Napoleon's armies, and the once despised eastern empire had become the dominant power on the continent. Later in the nineteenth century, of course, after the defeat in the Crimea, it became clear that all was not right, that Russia's supremacy had been undermined by rapid economic development in western Europe, particularly in England. But during Nicholas' reign, Russia still trusted in the economic system that had made it powerful.

In the previous centuries, the primary responsibility for developing and mobilizing Russia's resources had belonged to the state. The process had involved much suffering by the population, but it had enabled Russia to reach the status of a great power. The obvious question is therefore whether the state under Nicholas I stopped trying or whether it failed simply because the task of keeping up had become too difficult. What were the substance and the goals of state economic policy? Was there, perhaps, a serious attempt to emulate the economic progress of western Europe that was frustrated by lack of physical resources or by the inability of gentrymen, peasants, and bureaucrats to change their traditional roles and perform new functions? Or was there simply complacent indifference or even a deliberate policy of discouraging economic change for fear of the social and political consequences that were already beginning to assume an ominous character in the West?

The answer, of course, is that a complicated mixture of

the various possibilities characterized Russian economic policy during this period. With respect to cultural and political matters, the beliefs of Nicholas, eventually elaborated in the doctrine of "Official Nationality," provided a reasonably clear guide to what actual policy ought to be. But the regime had no general theory of economic policy. Official Nationality had no economic content. There was no accepted view on whether factories were good or bad, what tariff policy should be, or how agriculture ought to be improved. Nicholas was fortunate in that he was not under severe external pressure to produce guns or uniforms by any means he could. Nevertheless, decisions had to be made and the sum of them was state policy, no less important for the fact that it was not clearly thought out by those who made it.

The major historians of the reign agree that it was "all of a piece," that Nicholas was a man consistent to the point of tedium.[1] There were, however, modest changes in economic policy that had important long-run implications, and they provide the basis for the chronological organization of the chapters that follow. Each chapter examines the various aspects of economic policy and the extent to which it was influenced by the major events of the day, wars and revolutions abroad and, perhaps most important, crop failures at home. The somewhat technical problem of monetary policy receives full consideration in a separate chapter, but brief discussions of the problem are included at appropriate points in the narrative.

One institution, the Ministry of Finance, with E. F. Kankrin, its head for twenty-one years, is particularly prominent in this study. With some significant but limited exceptions, the Ministry of Finance was responsible for all aspects of government economic policy, not simply for collecting and disbursing funds. As finance minister, Kankrin was the only individual with responsibility for economic policy as a whole.

[1] See Nicholas V. Riasanovsky, *Nicholas I and Official Nationality in Russia, 1825–1855* (Berkeley and Los Angeles, 1959), pp. 184–185, for references to the major writers on this point.

He was overruled on several occasions, but he was never rivaled or replaced, even after his retirement and death, by anyone with comparable general influence. Nevertheless, the focus of this investigation is state policy, not the Ministry of Finance or Kankrin, no matter how frequently they are mentioned.

The discussion of general economic policy and of industry relies heavily on archival material, particularly the annual reports of the Ministry of Finance and of its Department of Manufacturing and Trade. On many subjects the records, both published and unpublished, of the State Council, Department of the State Economy, were helpful. For monetary matters, there is ample published documentation and considerable secondary literature. In the sections dealing with the state peasantry and with the tariff, greater reliance has been placed on extensive secondary studies.

This study would not have been possible without the advice and support of many people and institutions. First of all I am indebted to my teachers in various fields, on both the graduate and undergraduate level: George Carson, the late Michael Karpovich, Alexander Gerschenkron, William L. Langer, Sterling Dow, and Richard Pipes. The friends who read all or parts of the manuscript, Philip E. Anderson, Arcadius Kahan, George Staller, and Mack Walker, provided both encouragement and needed criticism. William Benjamin and Serena Weaver were invaluable research assistants. The faculty of the History Department of Leningrad State University was most helpful. No work of this kind could be carried out without the assistance of many librarians and archivists. I would like to mention the staffs of the Harvard College Library, the Cornell University Library, the Library of Congress, the Saltykov-Schedrin State Public Library, and the Central State Historical Archive in Leningrad. My work has benefited from the financial support of the Ford Foundation's Foreign Area Training Program, the Inter-University Committee on Travel Grants, and the Cornell University Committee on Soviet Studies. The Russian Research Center at Harvard University kindly made its research facilities available to me. David Munford of the Inter-University Committee and Leslie Brady of the United States Information Agency deserve special mention for their devoted work in making the academic exchange program with the Soviet Union a success in its early years.

The editors of the *Slavic Review* have kindly consented to the inclusion of parts of an article first published in that journal.

It goes without saying that none of the persons or institutions who have helped me are in any way responsible for any mistakes or omissions in the text.

W. M. P.

Ithaca, New York
1966

CONTENTS

TABLES

ABBREVIATED TITLES

AGS — Russia, Gosudarstvennyi sovet, *Arkhiv Gosudarstvennago soveta, zhurnaly po delam departamenta gosudarstvennoi ekonomii.*

Chteniia — *Chteniia v Moskovskom obshchestve istorii i drevnostei rossiiskikh pri Moskovskom universitete.*

Materialy — Russia, Gosudarstvennaia kantseliariia, *Materialy po voprosu ob ustroistve denezhnoi sistemy (izvlechennye iz dela Gosudarstvennogo soveta, 1837–1839 g.).*

"Nastavlenie" — [Egor Frantsevich Kankrin], "Nastavlenie: O predpolozheniiakh i vidakh po finansovoi chasti." The unpublished manuscript of a memorandum prepared by Kankrin in 1840.

PSZ — *Polnoe sobranie zakonov rossiiskoi imperii. PSZ* I refers to the first series, from 1649 to December 12, 1825. *PSZ* II refers to the second series, from December 12, 1825, to February 28, 1881.

Rtb. — Egor Frantsevich Kankrin, *Aus den Reisetagebüchern des Grafen Georg Kankrin, ehemaligen kaiserlich russischen Finanzministers, aus den Jahren 1840–1845: Mit einer Lebensskizze Kankrin's nebst zwei Beilagen.*

Sbornik IRIO — *Sbornik Imperatorskago russkago istoricheskago obshchestva.*

TsGIAL — Tsentral'nyi Gosudarstvennyi istoricheskii arkhiv v Leningrade. Archival citations are given as follows: f. *(fond)* —, op. *(opis)* —, d. *(delo)* —, p. or pp. (for *list* or *listy)* — . The *list* number refers to both sides of the sheet of paper. The published *opis* of the State Council is cited thus: f. 1152, op. T. I. *(Tom* I), d. —, 1830. In this case the year is essential because *delo* numbers start over each year. The records of the State Council are cited as follows: f. 1263, kn. (*kniga*) 1572, Nov. 1843, *prilozheniia* (if the reference is to the volume of supplementary papers accompanying every volume of proceedings).

The titles, and in many cases the dates, following the formal reference are not part of the citation that is needed to locate the document and are included for purposes of general information. In many cases they refer not to the *delo* as a whole but to a single item in it.

NOTE ON
TRANSLITERATION
AND DATES

Except in the case of a few familiar names, such as Speransky and Tolstoy, the Library of Congress system of transliteration has been used throughout, without diacritical marks. For M. L. Tengoborskii, I have employed the spelling used in Russian documents, rather than using Tegoborski or other variants found in his writings published in western Europe.

All dates are old style unless otherwise noted. Add eleven days in the eighteenth century and twelve in the nineteenth century to get the new-style date.

Russian Economic Policy
under Nicholas I

Introduction

Russia is not a naturally rich land. The climate is severe, the growing season short. In the south, where the soils are fertile, the rainfall is unreliable; farther north, where moisture is more plentiful, the soils are poor. The rivers are useful for transport across the broad territory, but they are not nearly as satisfactory as those in western Europe, where the streams are largely ice-free and, most important, the sea is never far away. The poverty of the land in Russia always meant that the margin of wealth produced above the minimum necessary for survival was desperately small. But it was from this margin that the state had to derive its support, because it was impossible to tax or confiscate more heavily without destroying the producer or driving him away. Furthermore, the Russian state was always faced with severe and pressing demands on its resources engendered by centuries of steady conflict with neighbors to the east, south, and west. This combination of few materials and great need certainly contributed to the early emergence in Russia of a centralized autocratic state to mobilize the strength necessary for survival and expansion. The enserfed peasant supported his lord and paid taxes to the state; the lord in turn served the state directly. In theory, control was complete; in practice, it was greatly limited by the realities of a large and sparsely populated territory that made peasant flight a constant problem and allowed the landowner much independence.

Largely lacking the concentrated wealth that commercial development created in the towns of preindustrial western Europe, the Russian state of the post-Kievan era was almost totally dependent on the small and unreliable surpluses that the peasants could produce. Despite the universal predominance of agriculture as the occupation of most men throughout preindustrial Europe, the towns and cities of the West afforded their rulers some cushion of wealth that did not immediately disappear with the first crop failure. Western rulers could hope to tax or borrow something until the next good harvest. The grand prince of Muscovy, and later the emperor of imperial Russia, could not. Whatever the form of the levy—head tax, household tax, land tax, vodka tax, salt tax—virtually all of it had to come from the peasant, for there was no one else who could pay. The gentry's wealth, such as it was, was merely a share of what their peasants produced. Everything depended on the annual gamble on the weather made by the peasant when he sowed his seed. Russia was able to maintain its independence and even to compete successfully with the major powers of the West only because the government could extract the maximum amount of revenue, in money, in kind, and in services from all of the population, from the bottom to the top of the social ladder.

Only in the mid-eighteenth century, when the gentry were exempted from the obligation to render service to the state, did signs of breakdown in this comprehensive system appear. Not only did the gentry win exemption from compulsory service, but they became "westernized," at least to the extent of adopting a different and more expensive way of life. No longer were they content with the simple rural pleasures of the seventeenth-century lord. The gentry now expected to enjoy the costly luxuries that Peter I and his successors had introduced: wine, coffee, tea, sugar, fine cloth, works of art, and so forth. Thus, in the very years in which the expense of Russia's military effort increased because of the extensive adoption of Western techniques, the pressures on internal resources increased because of the effect of the same process on the most influential segment of the population. Both the state and the upper classes of Russian society required more and more real income to meet what came to be regarded as the minimum expenditure necessary for national

security and personal consumption. The increased needs
were largely met by increased domestic output. Manufacturing grew dramatically in some areas, and the gentry extracted additional income from their estates.[1]

Russia could, with effort, hold her own in preindustrial
Europe. Although the country was far less urbanized or technically advanced than western Europe in the eighteenth century, a relatively large population, an autocratic government,
and the availability of the appropriate raw materials enabled Russia to meet many of its own needs and even to become an important exporter of crude manufactures like pig
iron and sailcloth.[2] In the mid-nineteenth century, Russia's
population was larger than ever before and her territory continued to dwarf that of the Western powers. Population
statistics for the period, and particularly for Russia, are at
best approximations. In 1820, England had about twelve
million people, Austria fifteen, and France thirty, while
Russia probably had well over forty million. By 1850, England and Austria each had a population of about eighteen
million, France had thirty-five, and Russia was still ahead
with approximately fifty-five million.

In terms of other, more important, measures of economic
strength, the mid-nineteenth-century situation had become
highly unfavorable to Russia. A Russian statistician estimated in 1850 that Russia's total foreign trade in the mid-
forties was about 30 per cent of France's, 18 per cent of
England's, and about 5 per cent of the total for the major
European trading nations. According to these estimates, Russian trade was very slightly larger than Austria's, although
its population was about three times as great. In the early

---

[1] See Arcadius Kahan, "The Costs of Westernization, the Gentry and
the Russian Economy in the Eighteenth Century," *Slavic Review,* XXV
(1966), 40–66. Kahan argues that, in general, it was impossible to increase real rents and that increased revenues were the result of an
expanded area under cultivation.

[2] Roger Portal, "The Industrialization of Russia," *Cambridge Economic History of Europe,* ed. H. J. Habakkuk and M. Postan, IV (Cambridge, Eng., 1965), 802.

1820's, Russian pig-iron production of approximately 160,-
000 metric tons was still comparable to that of France, which
produced 113,000 tons in 1819, and even that of England,
which produced 364,000 tons in 1820. In 1850, however,
Russian output had grown only to 227,000 metric tons,
France produced 406,000, while England, well launched on
the industrial revolution, produced over 2,000,000 tons. Pig
iron is, of course, the outstanding example of a major eighteenth-century Russian industry that stagnated, but even the
development of cotton spinning, the Russian industry that
grew most rapidly, shows a similar lag. In 1820, when Russia
had no spinning industry, Britain consumed 55,000 metric
tons of raw cotton. By 1850, the Russian industry that had
grown up in the thirties and especially in the forties was
already using 20,000 tons, but by then France was using
60,000 and Britain 222,000 tons.[3]

Although the increasing economic backwardness of Russia
relative to western Europe was to prove crucially important
in time, it was not one of the obvious economic problems
that confronted the state in the first half of the century. The
state's perpetual problem of mobilizing enough resources for
current needs, either through the medium of money or di-

[3] Detailed statistics have been omitted in the foregoing discussion to
avoid giving a misleading appearance of precision to data that are very
uncertain. The sources used are as follows: for Russian population,
Vladimir Maksimovich Kabuzan, *Narodonaselenie Rossii v XVIII–
pervoi polovine XIX v. (po materialam revizii)* (Moscow, 1963), pp.
169–171, and Adol'f Grigorevich Rashin, *Naselenie Rossii za 100 let
(1811–1913 gg.)* (Moscow, 1956), pp. 28–29; for other population data,
Handwörterbuch der Staatswissenschaften (4th ed.; Jena, 1926), II,
688–689; for data on French and British iron production, *Handwörterbuch*, III, 550–552; for raw-cotton consumption outside Russia, David
S. Landes, "Technological Change and Development in Western
Europe, 1750–1914," *Cambridge Economic History,* ed. Habakkuk and
Postan, IV, 394; for all Russian commodity data, P. A. Khromov,
Ekonomicheskoe razvitie Rossii v XIX–XX vekakh, 1800–1917 (Moscow, 1950), pp. 436–439; for the estimates on comparative volumes of
international trade, Grigorii Nebolsin, *Statisticheskoe obozrenie vneshnei torgovli Rossii* (St. Petersburg, 1850), II, 472–474.

rectly by collections in kind and forced labor, remained the primary concern. Certain significant changes in attitude, however, differentiated the policy of this period from that of the previous century. The development of domestic manufacturing to satisfy most traditional military requirements removed the pressure on the state for direct involvement in developing strategic industries. Perhaps even more important was the increased complexity of policy-making largely resulting from the introduction of paper money, a new device first issued by Catherine the Great in 1769. The real wealth of the nation remained the same, but because the value of paper money depended in part on public trust, a psychological element was introduced into economic policy that had not been there before. Whether or not a given measure would weaken confidence in the currency was a problem of real importance. Even the conviction that the state had a moral obligation to maintain the face value of its currency came to have a role in determining policy.

When Nicholas I succeeded his brother Alexander I as emperor in 1825, he was faced with the same physical limitations on his supposedly absolute power that had confronted all his predecessors. The state's fiscal difficulties simply expressed graphically Russia's lack of productive farms and factories, skilled civil servants, craftsmen, and technicians. Nicholas was not, however, bound by any firmly established pattern of economic policy. There was ample precedent for active state participation in the economy. This mercantilist (or, perhaps better termed, cameralist) tradition in Russia certainly begins with Peter the Great, if not earlier.[4] Statesmen in the era of Nicholas I did not have to look exclusively to the precedent of Russian tradition for examples of state involvement in a wide range of economic activities. In England, and to a considerable extent in France, the doctrines of *laissez faire* were being put into practice, but in Austria and Prussia, the major European powers on Russia's own

[4] B. H. Sumner, *Peter the Great and the Emergence of Russia* (London, 1950), pp. 131–133.

borders, the state continued policies of direct intervention in the economy in a manner often thought more typical of the seventeenth or eighteenth century than of the nineteenth. The cameralist tradition of achieving the desired end through administrative action remained strong, although abolishing restrictions on private enterprise came to be seen, at times, as the most effective means to employ.[5]

The tradition of state action and state direction was not the only one, however, that could be drawn on by Nicholas and his advisers. The Tsar's own tutor in political economy, Heinrich Storch, was an exponent of Adam Smith's theories and saw Russia destined to be an agricultural nation under conditions of complete free trade. Others were unwilling to abandon the hope of a prosperous Russian economy combining both manufacturing and agriculture, and they believed that private enterprise with the aid of state credit and tariff protection was the way to achieve it. Speransky's financial plan of 1810 looked in this direction and so did Admiral Mordvinov's many projects. Later in Alexander's reign, Finance Minister Gurev and Interior Minister Kozodavlev took similar positions.

Nicholas was therefore bound neither by firmly established tradition nor by accepted doctrine to any particular economic policy. Though his conservative soul may have longed for some clearly established precedent for what was proper policy, there was none. The conservatism of Nicholas and his chief economic adviser, Kankrin, expressed itself in caution and timidity of policy rather than by adherence to a

[5] The exact nature of state economic policy in any of these countries requires as complex a discussion as does that in Russia and cannot be dealt with here. For further comments and references see: Landes, "Technological Change," pp. 363–366, 379–380, 385; W. O. Henderson, *The State and the Industrial Revolution in Prussia, 1740–1870* (Liverpool, 1958), esp. pp. xv–ixvii and chs. 3–4, 7–8; A. J. P. Taylor, *The Hapsburg Monarchy, 1809–1918* (London, 1948), p. 39; and Karl Uhlirz, *Handbuch der Geschichte Österreichs und seiner Nachbarländer Böhmen und Ungarn* (Graz, Vienna, and Leipzig, 1930), II, pt. 1, 576–594, esp. 578–582.

coherent economic ideology. Both were fully aware that many aspects of Russian life needed improvement. But, like the peasant on the margin of subsistence who will seldom risk the adoption of a potentially profitable innovation for fear of failure and total catastrophe, the Tsar and the Minister of Finance usually felt they could not risk temporary strain, either social or fiscal, for the sake of eventual economic improvement.

To suggest that more dynamic or imaginative policies on the part of the state could have enabled Russian economic development to equal that of western Europe would be absurd, but so too would be the contrary assertion that Nicholas and his government did everything possible to promote the development of the empire, given the means at their disposal. Russia could not avoid losing ground in the nineteenth century, but the degree of economic retardation was certainly not fixed. There were a limited number of options open to state policy-makers, and to assume that over a thirty-year period it made no difference how those options were used would be entirely unwarranted. The poverty of Russia determined the general nature of the economic problem that faced the state and restricted the range of possibilities open to it, but it did not make any specific program inevitable.

CHAPTER I

The Chief Policy-Maker

The basic approach to economic policy that characterized the reign of Nicholas I did not begin with his accession to the throne in December 1825, but had originated nearly three years earlier, with the appointment of Egor Frantsevich Kankrin as minister of finance. At that time Nicholas had no immediate expectation of becoming tsar. He had never shown an interest in anything except military matters and had nothing whatever to do with Kankrin's selection. Nevertheless Nicholas was to retain Kankrin as minister of finance for nearly twenty years, until the old Minister was physically unable to continue working.[1]

The two men eventually differed on a few important issues and the Tsar overruled his minister, but the basic features of economic policy as established by Kankrin were maintained by Nicholas throughout his reign, even in the decade between Kankrin's retirement and the Crimean War. The Tsar, although he held the ultimate authority, played no role in establishing overall policy. Imperial intervention was confined to a few specific issues that excited his interest: the state peasants, railroads, and certain aspects of currency reform. It is impossible to discuss the views of Nicholas in general except to say that he usually supported his minister of finance.

---

[1] *Rtb.*, I, 282, and II, 86.

FROM QUARTERMASTER TO MINISTER

Like so many other important figures in Russian society of the eighteenth and early nineteenth centuries, Kankrin was not a Russian by nationality or even a native of the empire. He was born Georg Ludwig Daniel von Cancrin in a small Hessian principality, in 1774.[2] Kankrin's father, Franz Ludwig, a well-known mining engineer and author of several technical books, was employed by the Langraviate of Hessen-Kassel. In 1783, he accepted the invitation of Catherine II to enter Russian service and departed for St. Petersburg the following year, leaving his ten-year-old son Georg behind, probably in Hanau. The senior Kankrin's talents were so highly regarded in Russia that after less than a year there he was permitted to return to Germany, at full pay, to pursue his scientific work. From late in 1784 until 1794 (or possibly 1796), Franz Ludwig lived in Giessen, but remained on the Russian payroll. A few years after his final return to Russia, Tsar Paul presented him with a house in St. Petersburg, and in 1800 he was made director of the salt works at Staraia Rossiia.[3]

Virtually nothing is known about the childhood of Franz Ludwig's son Georg, beyond the fact that he lived in his birthplace, Hanau, until about the age of ten, when the family

[2] His father, Franz Ludwig, also used the Latin form of the surname, "Cancrinus," which in turn had been derived in earlier generations from the German "Krebs." In Russia the Finance Minister's name was normally written as Egor Frantsevich Kankrin. Later German sources use either "Cancrin" or "Kankrin" and various combinations of the given names.

[3] On Kankrin's father see "Cancrin, Franz Ludwig," *Allgemeine Deutsche Biographie* (Leipzig, 1876), III, 740–742; Irene Grüning, "Graf Georg Kankrin," *Lebensbilder aus Kurhessen und Waldeck, 1830–1930*, III, ed. Ingeborg Schnack (*Veröffentlichungen der Historischen Kommission für Hessen und Waldeck*, Vol. XX) (Marburg, 1942), 21–23; and I. N. Bozherianov, *Graf Egor Frantsevich Kankrin, ego zhizn', literaturnye trudy i dvadtsatiletniaia deiatel'nost' upravleniia Ministerstva finansov* (St. Petersburg, 1897), pp. 5–11.

moved to Giessen, where they lived after his father's return from the brief first trip to Russia. In 1790, at the age of sixteen, the young Kankrin entered the University of Giessen.

In the 1790's, Giessen was a very inferior institution. Professorial salaries were low, the library was insignificant, and there were only about one hundred and fifty students. A visitor who surveyed the German universities in 1789 wrote of Giessen: "This university distinguishes itself in no way and belongs among the less significant universities. . . . The professors themselves say that a student cannot profitably finish his studies here." [4] Fifty years later, Kankrin recalled the "pedantry, arid professionalism, pettiness, and one-sidedness" of academic life at Giessen in his student days.[5] He left Giessen without receiving a degree, not long before the town was occupied by French troops in the middle of 1796.

The young man's last year in Germany was spent in Marburg. Although there is no record of his enrolling at Marburg University or receiving a degree there, he may well have attended lectures and participated in the wild student life for which the town was noted.[6] Through the influence of his father, Georg was given the rank of *Regierungsrat* of Anhalt-Bernburg, but the title was not accompanied by a job or a

[4] Richard Fester, *"Der Universitäts-Bereiser" Friedrich Gedike und sein Bericht an Friedrich Wilhelm II (Ergänzungsheft des Archivs für Kulturgeschichte,* Vol. I) (Berlin, 1905), pp. 42–43.

[5] *Rtb.,* I, 193.

[6] There is no record of Kankrin's activities at Giessen other than his signature on the matriculation papers. His biographers, Keyserling, Bozherianov, and Sementkovsky assume that he did study and graduate from Marburg University, but there seems to be no solid basis for this assumption. In his travel diaries Kankrin described a visit to Marburg and Giessen and only in the latter case did he mention the university. Nolcken reports finding Kankrin's name in records at Giessen, but nothing whatever at Marburg. I am indebted to Dr. I. Schnack of the Marburg University Library for checking the records there with the same result (*Rtb.,* II, 28–29; Michael Herman Freiherr von Nolcken, *Der russische Finanzminister Graf Georg Kankrin und seine Handelspolitik* [Riga, 1909], p. 32).

salary. Unable to find any suitable employment in Germany,
he left for Russia in 1797, at the age of twenty-three.

St. Petersburg did not impress the young German student
when he first arrived. The customhouse seemed shabby,
everything was dirty and disorderly, and the uniforms of
soldiers and civilians alike looked forty years behind the
times.[7] The years that followed were the most trying of his
entire life. He knew no Russian and his unfinished university training did not give him any special skill that might
have eased the task of finding employment. Tsar Paul I gave
Kankrin the rank of court councillor, the seventh from the
top in the table of ranks and the equivalent of the German
rank that he already held, but again no pay went with the
honor and the situation became all the more difficult since
he was not qualified for posts commensurate with his rank.
Georg's father was a stern man, and he did little or nothing
to help his son. The two, it seems, were not on very good
terms with each other, and the young Kankrin may have
rejected his father's aid. An unsuccessful attempt to obtain a
position in a *gymnasium* is recorded, but how he actually
earned his living during his first three years in Russia is unknown. Poverty forced him to develop the habits of personal
thrift that in later years made him a conspicuous figure in
the extravagant St. Petersburg society. As the Tsar's minister
he still wore an old army coat and an old watch.[8]

Relations with his father evidently improved enough so
that in January 1800 he accepted a position as assistant to his
father at the salt works in Staraia Rossiia. The post was not
obtained for him by Franz Ludwig Cancrin, but by the influential I. A. Ostermann. The twenty-five-year-old Georg
had prepared a project for the improvement of sheep breeding that had aroused Ostermann's interest.[9] It was the first of
a series of studies on widely differing topics that played an

[7] *Rtb.*, I, 3–4.

[8] Alexander Keyserling, "Lebensskizze Kankrin's," *Rtb.*, I, 2, 7–10;
Rtb., I, 3. Kankrin's diaries and the biographical sketch by Keyserling,
Kankrin's son-in-law, are bound together, but paged separately.

[9] I. I. Lazhetnikov, "Neskol'ko zametok i vospominanii po povodu

important part in advancing Kankrin's career in both civil and military service. From 1803 to 1809, as an official of the salt section of the Ministry of Interior, he traveled widely on state business. For the first time, the young German had the opportunity of becoming well acquainted with his adopted country and its problems and of perfecting his knowledge of the Russian language. He learned to speak and write Russian effectively, but he never lost his German accent or manner of speaking.

One of the tasks assigned to Kankrin during this period was to assist Count Arakcheev in planning the park on his estate. When Kankrin first went to Arakcheev's office, the Count used the familiar form of address; Kankrin took offense and started to leave, but Arakcheev was impressed by the young man's independence, soothed his feelings, and they proceeded to discuss the task at hand.[10] The friendship with Arakcheev that developed after this meeting was a crucial factor in Kankrin's subsequent career and ultimately led to the appointment as minister of finance.

In August of 1809, Kankrin became inspector of the foreign colony in St. Petersburg. The job was not a demanding one and he had time for other activities, including reviewing current productions at the German theatre.[11] His main interests, however, were more serious. He wrote in his diary over thirty years later:

Little busied in my then unimportant post, without pretensions and significant possibilities and connections, I studied military science with great zeal, and indignation drove me to write a small book in 1809: *Fragmente über die Kriegskunst.*

The book was published anonymously, like all his other works that appeared during his lifetime, and came to the attention of the Prussian General Pfuel then in Russian service. Pfuel took an interest in Kankrin, and the two men

stat'i 'Materialy dlia biografii A. P. Ermolova,' " *Russkii vestnik,* LI (1864), 802; Keyserling, "Lebensskizze," p. 12.

[10] Keyserling, "Lebensskizze," p. 9.

[11] *Ibid.,* p. 13.

spent evenings discussing the problems of a war using delaying tactics, which both were convinced were the only means of opposing Napoleon. Kankrin adds in his reminiscences, "I believe also, but have not heard it said, that General Pfuel suggested me to the Tsar as *General-Intendant* and intentionally received me so well and sought to instruct me." [12] Pfuel enjoyed the confidence of Alexander I and played a major role in the early stages of the campaign of 1812. He is criticized by military historians as being overly theoretical and for serious strategic and tactical errors. [13]

The publication of *Fragmente* and acquaintance with Pfuel were most important in determining the course of Kankrin's career. In February 1811, he was appointed aide to the quartermaster general with the civil rank (fourth from the top) of actual state councillor. This was the beginning of a highly successful military career. In 1812, Kankrin was named *general-intendant* of the Western Army and in April 1813 *general-intendant* of the entire active army in Germany and France. As *general-intendant*, he was in charge of both the quartermaster and financial functions of a major part of the Russian army during the great war. He accompanied the victorious Russian armies to Paris in both 1814 and 1815 and was awarded full military rank as a lieutenant general of infantry in 1815, a distinction of which he was particularly proud.

Without influential family connections, Kankrin must have shown considerable ability in performing his duties to have achieved such rapid promotion. Pfuel's influence at court declined after his strategic plan was abandoned in 1812. Kankrin himself recalled that he was consulted and assisted by Kutuzov. After the battle of Bautzen in May 1813, Kankrin's success in obtaining badly needed supplies reportedly

12 *Rtb.*, I, 238–239.
13 See, for example, Hereford B. George, *Napoleon's Invasion of Russia* (London, 1899), p. 109. Eugene Tarle is more severe (*Napoleon's Invasion of Russia, 1812*, trans. "G. M." [New York, 1942], pp. 71–73). In *War and Peace*, Bk. IX, chs. 10 and 11, Tolstoy presents Pfuel as a dogmatic and unrealistic theorist of the worst sort.

impressed Tsar Alexander himself, who was then with the army.[14] After the end of hostilities, Kankrin negotiated with the French regarding contributions they were to make toward supplying the Russian army.[15]

The end of the war naturally reduced the opportunities for advancement in the military service. From 1816 to 1820, when he left active service, Kankrin served with the army in western Russia and was not involved in any major public activity. During the years of his peacetime military service and subsequent retirement, Kankrin devoted much of his time to writing. His first work was a project for gradually abolishing serfdom which he gave to Nesselrode in February 1818 for submission to the Tsar. Nothing came of the proposal and in later years Kankrin never mentioned it.[16] It was simply another attempt to establish his reputation as an expert in a field of current general concern.

A more substantial work written during this same period was *Über die Militairökonomie im Frieden und Krieg und ihr Wechselverhältniss zu den Operationen,* which appeared in three lengthy volumes in St. Petersburg from 1820 to 1823. It was a technical military study containing virtually nothing of a general nature on economic problems. Much less bulky but of far greater interest was *Weltreichthum, Nationalreichthum, und Staatswirtschaft, oder Versuch neurer Ansichten der politischen Oekonomie,* published in Munich in 1821, which developed Kankrin's ideas on political economy. In 1809, in *Fragmente über die Kriegskunst,* he had written, "The author is no economist trained in financial affairs." [17]

[14] *Rtb.,* I, 243, 283–285; Aleksandr Vasilevich Nikitenko, *Moia povest' o samom sebe i o tom "chemu svidetel' v zhizni byl," zapiski i dnevnik (1804–1877 gg.)* (2nd ed.; St. Petersburg, 1905), I, 503–504.

[15] Bozherianov, *Kankrin,* pp. 31–32.

[16] P. B. [Peter Bartenev], "Graf Egor Frantsovich Kankrin," *Russkii arkhiv,* no. 1 (1866), p. 126; [E. F. Kankrin], "Zapiska ob osvobozhdenii krest'ian v Rossii ot krepostnoi zavisimosti, sostavlennaia v 1818 godu," trans. S. A. Sobolevskii, *Russkii arkhiv,* nos. 10–11 (1865), pp. 1360–1373. The original text was in French, but has not been published.

[17] *Fragmente über die Kriegskunst, nach Gesichtspunkten der militärischen Philosophie* (St. Petersburg, 1809), p. 14.

Ten years of practical labor had evidently changed his mind, and with *Weltreichthum* he set out to establish a reputation as an expert in economics as well as in military matters. The publication of *Weltreichthum* may have helped to pave the way for his appointment as minister of finance just as *Fragmente* had pulled him out of his quiet life in the St. Peters-burg German colony.[18] In 1821, Kankrin accompanied the Tsar to the Laibach conference, but the anticipated military campaign in Italy did not take place and his advice was not needed. Shortly thereafter he was appointed to the State Council, Department of the National Economy.[19] Only a year and a half later he became minister of finance.

How did this relatively obscure retired general of foreign birth suddenly come to be appointed to the State Council and soon thereafter to be minister of finance? Retired gen-erals were plentiful in the years following the Napoleonic Wars, and Kankrin was not the only person in Russia who had written on military affairs or political economy. In 1823, there were several obvious reasons for a change in financial administration. The state budget was in very bad shape. The program sponsored by the incumbent minister of finance, Count Gurev, to restore the depreciated paper money to its face value had failed. Gurev's proposal to abolish the State Loan Bank can hardly have been popular with gentrymen anxious to borrow money on their estates. There were also the usual complaints about high taxes, and charges of cor-ruption were widespread.[20] Shortly after Gurev's replace-ment, Admiral Mordvinov wrote:

The former Minister of Finance knew no other rule, no other method, except to weaken and destroy capital; thus he left pov-erty behind him in the state treasury, exhaustion in the private

[18] Keyserling, "Lebensskizze," p. 24.

[19] Bozherianov, *Kankrin,* pp. 42–44, 55.

[20] M. M. Fok, "Pis'ma M. M. Foka k A. Kh. Benkendorfu," *Russkaia starina,* XXXII (1881), 190; N. M. Longinov to S. R. Vorontsov, St. Petersburg, May 15, 1823, *Arkhiv kniazia Vorontsova,* ed. Peter Bar-tenev, XXIII (Moscow, 1882), 467–469.

estates, and the dejection and indignation of the citizens toward the government.[21]

Count D. A. Gurev was an aristocrat and prominent in the gay social life of the capital, the personal antithesis of his successor, the frugal and antisocial Kankrin. St. Petersburg society, however, approved of the change. According to Speransky, "the joy over the dismissal was general and in my opinion even indecent." [22] It was the Easter season and some used a variation of the traditional Easter greeting, replying to *Khristos voskres* (Christ has risen) with *Gurev izchez* (Gurev has vanished).[23]

There is absolutely no evidence, however, that issues of financial policy or public opinion had anything to do with Gurev's removal. All contemporary sources agree that Count Arakcheev had simply been successful in ousting a personal opponent. Arakcheev's influence had been growing rapidly in the early twenties and his primary aim was certainly to get Gurev out; that his choice for a successor was Kankrin was a secondary consideration.[24] The new finance minister was regarded as a technician and a protégé of Arakcheev and was not well known in the salons of St. Petersburg. Few of the contemporary commentators ventured an opinion, except for General A. P. Ermolov, who probably had known Kankrin during his army careeer: "How sudden is the fall of Gurev

[21] N. S. Mordvinov to the Minister of Finance, July 12, 1823, *Arkhiv grafov Mordvinovykh,* ed. V. A. Bilbasov, V (St. Petersburg, 1902), 617.

[22] *V pamiat' grafa Mikhaila Mikhailovicha Speranskago, 1772–1872,* ed. A. F. Bychkov (St. Petersburg, 1872), p. 635.

[23] Osip Antonovich Przhetslavskii, "Beglye ocherki," *Russkaia starina,* XXXIX (1883), 388; P. V. Dolgorukov, *Peterburgskie ocherki,* ed. P. E. Shchegolev (Moscow, 1934), p. 150.

[24] No source gives much detail, but all mention Arakcheev's role: Aleksandr Ivanovich Riboper, "Zapiski," *Russkii arkhiv,* no. 5 (1877), p. 5; A. I. Mikhailovskii-Danilevskii, "Zapiski," *Istoricheskii vestnik,* XLIX (1892), 275–276; F. F. Vigel', "Vospominaniia," *Russkii vestnik,* XLIX (1864), 559; V. I. Panaev, "Vospominaniia," *Vestnik Evropy,* IV (1867), 79; N. I. Grech, *Zapiski o moei zhizni* (Moscow and Leningrad, 1930), p. 561.

and many, I think, are suprised at the designation of Kankrin. But finances without doubt well be in better condition, judging from his knowledge and abilities." [25]

Although Kankrin was not appointed to undertake major changes in economic policy, his administration does mark the beginning of an era that was to last well beyond the twenty-one years Kankrin himself remained in office. His views had great influence on the development of state policy because Nicholas I, who soon succeeded to the throne, retained Kankrin and generally deferred to his judgment. Kankrin was never cowed by Nicholas' dominating personality. P. F. Brok, minister of finance from 1850 to 1857, recalled that Nicholas once asked him if funds were available for a certain project. Brok replied that for the fulfillment of the Tsar's will means could always be found, at which Nicholas reportedly smiled and said, "I am very glad, Brok, that I do not find in you that perpetual opposition to which Kankrin trained me. He would come to me in his slippers and stand with his back to the stove and warm himself and no matter what I said he had only one answer, 'Impossible, your majesty, quite impossible.' " [26] In personal matters Nicholas was liberal toward his finance minister, who was the only member of the cabinet ever permitted to smoke in the Tsar's presence. Kankrin received generous financial rewards and was given the distinguished title of count.

Despite these favors, Kankrin was not one of the Tsar's intimate associates. Their relationship was based not on friendship but on mutual respect, devotion to duty, and a basic similarity in outlook. Nicholas was thirty when he became tsar and had little knowledge or interest in economic affairs. The strong-willed and self-assured Kankrin was fifty-

[25] A. P. Ermolov to A. A. Zakrevskii, Tiflis, June 8, 1823, *Sbornik IRIO,* LXII (1890), 417.

[26] M. A. Korf, "Imperator Nikolai v soveshchatel'nykh sobraniiakh: (Iz sovremennykh zapisok stats-sekretaria barona Korfa)," *Sbornik IRIO,* XCVIII (1896), 183; I. S. Bliokh, *Finansy Rossii XIX stoletiia* (St. Petersburg, 1882), I, 242. Bliokh attributes the story to Brok, but gives no source.

two, and in addition to extensive practical knowledge of finance he had the military background that Nicholas favored so strongly in his advisers. The result was that in the early years of the reign Kankrin was in complete control and his influence dominated the entire reign.

To his contemporaries he was neither a colorful nor attractive person; perhaps few finance ministers are. He was self-confident to the point of conceit and ridiculed his opponents with crude and biting sarcasm, but even critics admit that he was extremely intelligent and well informed in many fields, not only in finance. Kankrin was cold and reserved even with his own family, saw little of his children, and seldom took part in the gay social life of the capital. The day and much of the night were spent at the ministry, and all commentators agree that he worked tirelessly, inspiring respect and loyalty in some subordinates and fear and dislike in others. Although he rewarded an aide who won an Academy of Science essay contest, and encouraged the playwright N. V. Kukolnik and the poet V. G. Benediktov, who were on his staff, he must have been a difficult man to work for.[27]

THE ECONOMIST

Policy, not personality, made Kankrin a figure of historical importance. Given the generally low level of higher education and professional training at the time in Russia, Kankrin was unquestionably well qualified technically for his position. He had studied at Giessen for five years. Even though the institution was a weak one and he left without a degree, he had more formal education than many other important officials, and subsequent state service had given him extensive

[27] The most detailed personal description of Kankrin is that in Korf, "Imperator Nikolai," pp. 139–140. See also Keyserling, "Lebensskizze," pp. 10, 39, 51–52; Przhetslavskii, "Beglye ocherki," p. 389; and V. I. Safonovich, "Vospominaniia," *Russkii arkhiv*, no. 4 (1903), pp. 506–510. For a survey of other comments see Bozherianov, *Kankrin*, pp. x–xxii, 241.

practical experience in economic and financial matters. He was never an important theorist; the two books he published on economic questions do not present a consistent theoretical approach or contribute to the development of economics as a science. His general views are best understood in the light of the immediate problems with which he was trying to deal.

Most commentators have recognized that Kankrin was not really a theorist, but nevertheless some have felt it necessary to classify him under one general heading or another, as an "eclectic mercantilist, influenced by physiocratic and Smithian thought," or as an economist "reacting against mercantilism, physiocracy, and Smith," or as simply a "mercantilist with eccentric ideas." [28] These labels are simply meaningless. Wilhelm Roscher's description of Kankrin's economic work as "a reaction against the teachings of Smith from the point of view of a man not basically learned, but gifted and well-educated, a very superior man of the world, who conducted the affairs of a people who were little developed compared with England" [29] is sound, but Roscher is not convincing when he attempts to group Kankrin with several essentially Smithian economists, Schlözer, Jakob, and Storch, into a German-Russian school of economics.[30]

Kankrin's only consistent guiding standard or principle was the extent to which a given policy contributed to the strength of the state as an independent entity, separate not

[28] Georg Schaulis, *Graf Georg Kankrin in nationalökonomischer und finanzwirtschaftlicher Beziehung: Ein Beitrag zur Geschichte der N.-Ökonomie und der Finanzwissenschaft* (Tilsit, 1914), pp. 28–29, 32–33, 112–113; Nolcken, *Russische Finanzminister*, pp. 31, 36; V. P. Bezobrazov, *O vliianii ekonomicheskoi nauki na gosudarstvennuiu zhizn' v sovremennoi Evrope* (St. Petersburg, 1867), pp. 56–57.

[29] "Über die deutsch-russische Schule der Nationalökonomik," *Berichte über die Verhandlungen der königlichen sächsischen Gesellschaft der Wissenschaften zu Leipzig: Philologisch-historische Classe,* XXII (1872), 170. Also in Roscher, *Geschichte der National-Oekonomik in Deutschland* (Munich, 1874), p. 815.

[30] Hans-Jürgen Seraphim, "Die Deutsch-russische Schule, eine kritische Studie," *Jahrbücher für Nationalökonomik und Statistik,* ser. 3, LXVII (1924), p. 330.

only from other states but from the welfare or happiness of
the population itself. This emphasis is clear even in *Dagobert*, a romantic novel written during his student days. The
central characters are loyal but disillusioned officers of the
French Republic who see the revolution as a failure and want
to make a new beginning, emphasizing national greatness
(*Volksgrösse*), rather than national happiness, (*Volksglück*).[31]
   The national economy was the focus of Kankrin's first
work on economic affairs, *Weltreichthum*, published more
than twenty years after *Dagobert*. The pessimism evident in
the novel has deepened. The total wealth of the world is a
virtually fixed quantity and one nation can increase its share
only at the expense of another. Trade can be useful for exchanging surpluses for what is lacking locally, but it cannot
increase the total prosperity of all nations involved. Self-
sufficiency in necessities is essential for reasons of national
security, a point Adam Smith did not deny, but for Kankrin
war was a more normal situation than peace.[32] His political
outlook was no more cheerful. Absolute monarchy is the best
form of government for raw, uneducated people, but no form
of government can truly protect a nation from "misfortune,
unrest, and catastrophe," or even assure the maintenance of
tolerable conditions, because human institutions are built of
contradictory elements and cannot withstand the slightest
pressure.[33] At the close of his career, in the early 1840's,
Kankrin deplored what he saw to be an abandonment of the
"great spirit of 1812, the spirit of national freedom" and a
turning to thoughts of purely personal freedom.[34] His view
of the problem of national wealth as the struggle among na-

---

[31] *Dagobert; eine Geschichte aus dem jetzigen Freiheitskriege: Als
Gegenstück zum Graf Donomar, eine Geschichte aus dem siebenjährigen Kriege* (Altona, 1797–1798), II, 157–158, 233–234.
   [32] *Weltreichthum, Nationalreichthum, und Staatswirtschaft, oder Versuch neurer Ansichten der politischen Oekonomie* (Munich, 1821), pp.
28–30, 105, 116–120; Roscher, "Über die deutsch-russische Schule," pp.
168–169.
   [33] *Weltreichthum*, pp. 28–30, 200–201.
   [34] *Rtb.*, I, 19.

tions for a share of a fixed quantity remained unchanged.[35]

The doctrines of the Smithian school did not satisfy those who, like Kankrin, were devoted to strengthening the state and the social *status quo*. But for them there was no satisfactory alternative economic theory that enjoyed widespread prestige. The teachings of the seventeenth- and eighteenth-century cameralists had lost much of their former status as the accepted doctrine in the universities. Compared to the more rigorous analysis of the classical economists, cameralist theory was weak.[36] Many European states continued to follow traditional economic policies with little modification, although there was no generally recognized theoretical leadership until the time of List. In the 1840's, Kankrin commented favorably on some of List's work, but he never shared the famous economist's enthusiasm for vigorous industrial growth. Kankrin's own position, in any case, was well developed long before List was well known.[37]

So little information is available on the content of Kankrin's formal education and the course of his intellectual development that the specific sources of his thought on economic policy must remain uncertain. Educated at a time when the ideas of Adam Smith had just begun to penetrate the German universities, he escaped without liberal infection. At Giessen, political economy was taught by August Friedrich Wilhelm Crome, noted primarily as a statistician. In his later years, Crome was influenced by Smith, but during Kankrin's days at Giessen, he taught in the tradition of the famous cameralist Sonnenfels.[38] At Marburg, Kankrin could have

[35] [E. F. Kankrin], *Die Oekonomie der menschlichen Gesellschaften und das Finanzwesen—von einem ehemaligen Finanzminister* (Stuttgart, 1845), pp. 8–9.

[36] Joseph A. Schumpeter, *History of Economic Analysis* (New York, 1954), pp. 173, 501.

[37] Kankrin, *Die Oekonomie,* p. 245. List's first book, *Outlines of American Political Economy,* was published in Philadelphia in 1827 and was almost certainly unknown to Kankrin. List's major work, *Das Nationale System der Politischen Oekonomie,* appeared in Stuttgart in 1841.

[38] Roscher, *Geschichte,* p. 650.

heard lectures by Johann Heinrich Jung, an opponent of the physiocrats, who also was largely unaffected by Smith.[39]

Almost nothing is known of the people and the books that influenced Kankrin after he completed his formal education. In Russia the most influential economists in the early nineteenth century were the German Heinrich von Storch, tutor to the imperial family and member of the Academy of Sciences, and Ludwig H. von Jakob, Speransky's adviser and a professor at Kharkov University. Kankrin may have known them but he need not have, for both occupied far more important positions in society than did the young German bureaucrat in the early years of the century. In any case, both Storch and Jakob were supporters of Smithian liberalism, which Kankrin rejected.

Although he must have been trained, at least to some extent, in the tradition of eighteenth-century European cameralism, and he too emphasized the central importance of the state, he did not subscribe to one essential feature of its teaching: a belief in the duty and confidence in the ability of the state to provide for the economic and even for the general welfare of the population. Cameralism tended to be optimistic, but Kankrin never was. He accepted some of the specific policies advocated by the prominent cameralists Justi and Sonnenfels, but rejected others on practical grounds. Banks and the use of credit, for example, useful tools for Justi or Sonnenfels, were regarded with suspicion by Kankrin, ever fearful of the dangers arising from their misuse. If cameralist theory was too optimistic for Kankrin, *laissez faire,* with its assumption of a basic harmony of interests and peace as the normal state of affairs, was pure nonsense. Some traces of physiocratic thought can be discerned in *Weltreichthum,* the first of his two treatises on economics. In it agriculture is seen as productive and factory work as purely reproductive. The difference, however, had no practical implications for

[39] *Ibid.,* pp. 552–553; Wilhelm Stieda, *Die Nationalökonomie als Universitätswissenschaft (Abhandlungen der philologisch-historischen Klasse der koniglichen sachsischen Gesellschaft der Wissenschaften,* Vol. XXV) (Leipzig, 1906), pp. 222–223.

Kankrin, since for an individual nation anything that increased its share of the world's total wealth is productive.[40]

The emphasis on the central importance of the national economy was not peculiar to Kankrin and could have been derived from sources other than the cameralist texts that he presumably studied in his youth. Fichte, notably in *Der Geschlossene Handelsstaat* (1800), emphasized the importance of the national unit and the advantages of minimizing economic dependence on other states. The rest of Fichte's socialistic, utopian, and thoroughly impractical outline, however, can have contributed little to Kankrin's pessimistic practicality. Among the more strictly economic writers of the early nineteenth century, the German romanticist Adam Müller (1779–1829) was the foremost critic of Smithian liberalism. Although Kankrin never refers to him in writing, he was undoubtedly familiar with Müller's work. General Pfuel, Kankrin's friend and sponsor in his early years in Russia, was interested in Müller, and it can be assumed that Pfuel introduced Kankrin to Müller's works if he did not already know of them.[41]

Certain of Müller's specific notions, particularly his emphasis on the importance of "mental capital," that is, ideas, laws, and scientific knowledge, as well as land, labor, and material resources, were also important to Kankrin, who used virtually the same term in his own writings. On other specific points the two men are in sharp conflict. Müller looked with great favor on paper money because it made a state independent of foreign-controlled stocks of precious metals, while Kankrin regarded the printing press with fear and distrust. Nor can anything of Müller's attempt to introduce religious elements into economic theory be found in Kankrin, whose thoughts were always too close to immediate problems to permit him to be drawn into any general theoretical sys-

---

[40] Kankrin, *Weltreichthum*, pp. 24–27.

[41] [Ernst von] Pfuel, "Kurze Darstellung der National Ökonomie, nach Adam Müller," *Archiv für Geografie, Historie, Staats- und Kriegskunst*, nos. 80–81 (July 5 and 8, 1811), pp. 341–346; *Rtb.*, I, 238–239.

tem, whether it was based on a rational or a spiritual foundation.[42]

Kankrin's devotion to a national point of view did not lead him to attempt to construct a general theory of national economic policy. Whether or not to encourage industry, eliminate or maintain the use of paper money, loan money to the gentry, establish banks, build railroads, encourage technical education, and so forth, were all questions to be decided on the basis of the immediate situation and the possibilities of the moment. Kankrin admitted that almost any policy could be justified under the proper circumstances.

Although he had no comprehensive theory, it was Kankrin who determined the character of economic policy for the entire reign of Nicholas I. Other men, Speransky, Kiselev, Drutskii-Liubetskii, Tengoborskii, and a few others, offered advice and had a major part in deciding certain specific questions, but they never came to have a continuing role in determining overall policy. The views and background of these men will be noted at the appropriate points. None of them were sufficiently influential to justify special consideration here.

The major figures of the age who might have commanded the respect of Nicholas and exerted a major influence in the years following Kankrin's retirement in 1844 disappear along with the old Finance Minister. Admiral Mordvinov, the tolerated radical and perpetual critic, already an elder statesman in the 1820's but active throughout the thirties, died in 1845 at the age of ninety-one. The two major figures of Kankrin's own generation prominent in general economic affairs were Speransky and Prince Drutskii-Liubetskii. The last of Speransky's many contributions was in connection with the monetary reform that began in 1839, the year of

[42] Adam H. Müller, *Die Elemente der Staatskunst* (Berlin, 1809); Jakob Baxa, ed., *Ausgewählte Abhandlungen* (2nd ed.; Jena, 1931). See also Roscher, *Geschichte,* pp. 770–778; Othmar Spann, *The History of Economics,* trans. Eden and Cedar Paul (New York, 1930), pp. 158–169; and Schumpeter, *History of Economic Analysis,* pp. 421–422, 428.

his death. Prince Drutskii-Liubetskii, minister of finance of Congress Poland until the revolt of 1830, was a major critic of Kankrin within the government during the 1830's and was Mordvinov's candidate to replace Kankrin.[43] Drutskii-Liubetskii might have had considerable influence on the Emperor once Kankrin had left the scene, but like Mordvinov and Kankrin himself, he died in 1845. Kiselev confined his activity to the Ministry of State Domains and various aspects of the peasant question. Perovskii, who had introduced reforms in the administration of the appanage peasants, became minister of the interior in 1841 and was never active in matters outside its jurisdiction. Thus there was no familiar figure with stature and experience in general economic affairs who could have replaced Kankrin as a powerful influence on the Emperor. The two succeeding ministers of finance, Vronchenko and Brok, were career bureaucrats without influence. Nicholas had been tsar for a long time and felt that he had become familiar with a field once strange to him. He said to a special committee on monetary reform in 1843:

In former times I had to confirm everything presented to me on financial matters blindly and absolutely, because I knew nothing about them. But now, after seventeen years of activity, I should be ashamed not to have acquired some practical knowledge on these matters and to have continued to accept everything without question as before.[44]

His teacher had been Kankrin, and now that the pupil had grown up he was not really going to change the pattern he had learned.

---

[43] *Arkhiv grafov Mordvinovykh,* VII (1903), 265–267.
[44] Korf, "Imperator Nikolai," p. 176.

CHAPTER II

The Establishment of the New Regime

The accession of Nicholas I to the throne in 1825 was accompanied by the brief and pitifully ineffective attempt of a group of guards officers to carry out a *coup d'état* and establish a constitutional government. The incident, known as the Decembrist revolt, had great importance for the development of dissident political thought in Russia. Herzen and later opponents of the autocracy felt that they were continuing a struggle that the Decembrists had begun. Nicholas himself was profoundly shocked. Not only had the rightful authority of the tsar been challenged in an armed uprising, but the rebels were officers of the élite guards regiments. Many came from the highest circles of Russian society. If these men could not be trusted, who could? The educated upper class from which the major officials of the state were drawn was small. When the ringleaders of the Decembrist organization were hanged, and the rest were shipped off to exile in Siberia, almost every leading family in St. Petersburg must have been affected in some way. Even the trusted and loyal advisers of the Tsar who were responsible for economic policy had personal ties with the Decembrists.[1] Kiselev, for example, was a

[1] The only exceptions were the two Poles, Drutskii-Liubetskii and Tengoborskii.

friend and former commander of the radical Pestel'. The impeccably conservative Kankrin, it turns out, was married to a Murav'ev, sister of a minor conspirator and cousin of major ones.

The revolt undoubtedly had much to do with Nicholas' repressive political and cultural policies. Wide-ranging investigations were carried out under the new tsar's personal supervision, and they may have aroused his interest in the problems of the Russian peasantry. Economic policy, however, was affected neither by the revolt itself nor by the accession of a new tsar. There was no break, no change in direction, not even a shift in emphasis after December 1825. Nicholas left economic affairs in the hands of Kankrin, who had been minister of finance since the spring of 1823.

The years immediately following Kankrin's appointment are particularly important because it is in the early part of a reign or an administration that the development of new policies, reforms, or changes seems most natural. The new man is anxious to bring affairs into line with his own wishes. In later years either the changes have been made or he has learned to live with the customs or institutions that are impossible to alter. The new minister of finance did not come in as a reformer but as the protégé of the conservative Arakcheev. Nevertheless, the most interesting feature of economic policy in the twenties is that it had two distinct and contradictory tendencies. One was to maintain the *status quo:* collect revenues, minimize expenses when possible, and support the interests of the gentry. The other was to undertake, or at least to consider, measures to make the economy more productive. These were the only years during the entire reign of Nicholas when there was serious concern about the overall development of the economy.

In the end, very little was actually accomplished, but an optimistic observer in 1830 would have seen much suggesting that for the past seven years the state had been seriously interested in modernizing the economy. If pressed, such an observer could have pointed to the extended discussion of how to encourage the growth of the urban population, new legislation purportedly designed to aid the commercial classes in the towns, and the projected law on "Honored citizens" to give the successful merchant greater legal security and social prestige. There was also a whole series of measures furthering technical education and the dissemination of technical information, the vigorous program begun by Perovskii to improve the administration of the appanage peasants (those on the estates of the imperial family), and discussion of reforms affecting the state peasants.

A skeptic could argue that most of these measures were actually undertaken for fiscal reasons and that the state was more concerned with the welfare of the rural gentry than with that of the towns. If that was not the case, why did the State Loan Bank extend credit to serf owners but not to factory owners? Furthermore, what could be expected of an administration that refused to act positively toward the bulk of the peasantry and was forced to admit it could not even run the state vodka monopoly? Both the sceptic and the optimist were correct, but each recognized only one of the two tendencies present in state policy in the twenties. By 1830, the state had neither moved decisively in the direction of innovation nor firmly committed itself to the *status quo*. It was not until the early thirties that severe fiscal pressure caused by poor harvests and war in Poland, plus the realization that towns and manufacturing created problems as well as benefits, tipped the scales in favor of leaving everything as it was.

THE IMMEDIATE PROBLEM: FINANCE

Despite the disturbance made by the Decembrists, the 1820's were years of relative calm and no extraordinary strains were imposed on the state's resources by major wars or crop failures. The desire to increase revenue and reduce expenditure was nevertheless a determining factor in many decisions. The administration of finance under Count Gurev had not been noted for its devotion to strict economy or careful management. Unspent funds were not returned to the treasury and unbudgeted expenditures were common. The Ministry of Finance did not even make a comprehensive annual report.[2] If Kankrin had any special mission assigned to him when he replaced Gurev in the spring of 1823, it was undoubtedly to improve management and save money, tasks that admirably suited his personality and training.

Virtually the first action of the new minister of finance was to stop Gurev's expensive and unsuccessful attempt to restore the depreciated paper rubles (assignats) to their full face value by withdrawing them from circulation. The action was a *de facto* acceptance of the devaluation of the ruble, although this was not admitted at the time. The final reform of the money system on the basis of this devaluation was not to come for sixteen years.[3] By shoving monetary problems under the rug, Kankrin was able to cover the budget deficit with forty-three million silver rubles that had already been borrowed by Gurev. Had the retirement of assignats continued, there would not have been sufficient funds to cover expenditures.

The year 1824 was the first for which Kankrin prepared the budget. He cut the estimate substantially, and, more important, expenditures stayed within the estimates, producing a 13 per cent reduction (62.1 million assignat rubles) in actual expenditures from 1823 to 1824. Much of the reduc-

[2] The confused and decentralized budgetary system was not significantly altered during the reign of Nicholas I. Kankrin did little more than introduce the custom of a regular annual report. The most detailed discussion of the subject is in L. N. Iasnopol'skii, *Ocherki russkago biudzhetnago prava,* I (Moscow, 1912), ch. 5. See also Ia. I. Pecherin, *Istoricheskii obzor rospisei gosudarstvennykh dokhodov i raskhodov s 1803 po 1843 god vkliuchitel'no* (St. Petersburg, 1896), pp. 87–88; *AGS,* IV, pt. 1, 246–247, 252–254; and S. M. Seredonin, *Istoricheskii obzor deiatel'nosti Komiteta ministrov,* I (St. Petersburg, 1902), 35–36.

[3] A full discussion of monetary policy will be found in Chapter V.

tion was in the military accounts, which took about 45 per cent of total revenue, and some from the Ministry of Finance itself. Kankrin's inclination was to solve budgetary problems by limiting expenditure, not through increasing taxes or seeking to expand the economy. He rejected the notion that the state should borrow in poor times and repay in good times, for he believed that the good times would never come.[4]

The available statistics suggest that he was right and the good times did not come. According to figures published in 1909 by the Ministry of Finance, there was a deficit in almost every year during Nicholas' reign, despite Kankrin's own claim that he had to resort to "extraordinary measures" only six times during his administration.[5] Data on total state debt (Table 1) shows that the policy of economizing was successful only until 1828–1829, when war with Turkey required a modest increase in both foreign and internal debt. From 1823 to 1827, despite an apparent total budget deficit of over a million silver rubles, debt fell by over eleven million. Eight million came from a reserve fund set aside by Gurev for the retirement of paper money, but two to three million represent a net reduction that must have come from savings in the current budget. It was a substantial achievement, but one that was not to be repeated during Nicholas' entire reign. In subsequent years not even Kankrin could hold expenditures down and he resorted to borrowing. It is noteworthy that in the twenties, a period without major crises, the Minister of Finance was trying very hard to increase government receipts and hold expenses down. In 1828, he was even able to get the military estimate reduced from 71.8 million to 59.0

[4] [E. F. Kankrin], *Weltreichthum, Nationalreichthum, und Staatswirtschaft, oder Versuch neurer Ansichten der politischen Oekonomie* (Munich, 1821), p. 181; TsGIAL, f. 560, op. 38, d. 213, "Obshchii otchet . . . za 1826," pp. 1–2.

[5] *Rtb.*, I, Supp. II, 70; Russia, Ministerstvo finansov, *Ministerstvo finansov, 1802–1902* (St. Petersburg, 1902), I, 626–639. Budget data are most unreliable because of the exclusion of major items from the regular accounts.

Table 1. Outstanding state debt, 1820–1856
(in thousands of silver rubles)

Year	Total state debt	Total borrowed abroad	% of state debt borrowed abroad	Total borrowed from State Loan Bank	% of state debt borrowed from State Loan Bank
1820	159,026	118,797	75	23,280	15
1821	180,120	143,310	80	21,840	12
1822	200,600	166,657	83	20,720	10
1823	213,623	181,223	85	20,470	10
1824	207,491	177,436	86	19,500	9
1825	208,317	173,101	83	17,960	9
1826	204,206	168,717	83	19,200	9
1827	202,129	171,513	85	20,390	10
1828	203,375	169,614	83	24,000	12
1829	232,713	191,429	82	31,980	14
1830	245,959	189,655	77	43,850	18
1831	277,807	201,064	72	47,840	17
1832	291,047	208,164	72	50,050	17
1833	314,907	227,175	72	54,860	17
1834	326,621	226,530	69	63,110	19
1835	335,734	225,243	67	67,920	20
1836	342,805	224,153	65	76,250	22
1837	346,739	222,977	64	81,290	23
1838	349,132	221,772	64	85,310	24
1839	358,665	220,555	61	95,030	26
1840	371,721	219,279	59	110,090	30
1841	396,789	241,139	61	115,560	29
1842	405,544	249,582	62	115,110	28
1843	431,765	257,278	60	131,900	31
1844	458,165	267,695	58	143,760	31
1845	467,683	265,324	57	151,970	32
1846	478,764	262,586	55	163,680	34
1847	505,593	273,609	54	178,270	35
1848	517,226	270,697	52	190,550	37
1849	546,769	267,241	49	210,550	39
1850	619,269	298,072	48	234,260	38
1851	651,923	293,762	45	252,530	39
1852	665,743	289,436	43	265,440	40
1853	696,424	284,946	41	279,900	40
1854	774,448	330,080	43	299,030	39
1855	868,873	375,286	43	336,770	39
1856	867,423	370,668	43	346,680	40

Source: Calculated from data in N. Brzheskii, *Gosudarstvennye dolgi Rossii* (St. Petersburg, 1884), table 17, p. 25 of the appendix; I. I. Kaufman, "Statistika russkikh bankov," pt. 1, *Statisticheskii vremennik rossiiskoi imperii*, ser. 2, no. 9 (1872), pp. 2–3.

million rubles only a few months before the war with Turkey began.[6] Although the cuts had to be restored, they show how vigorous was the drive for economy. More than at any other time during the reign of Nicholas, state expenditures in the twenties were limited by voluntary action rather than the pressure of famine or war. The limitation applied as much to the small amounts spent on economic development as to the major budget items.

There are two basic approaches to state finance, plus innumerable possible variations and partial combinations. One is the policy, adopted in practice by Kankrin, which concentrates on minimizing expenses and collecting as much revenue as possible from existing sources. The other puts primary emphasis on increasing the wealth of the revenue producer to enable him to pay more to the state. Speransky in his financial plan of 1810 had emphasized the importance of this approach when he suggested more rational taxation, the encouragement of private enterprise by abolishing state monopolies, and the provision of credit through private banks. The most persistent advocate of this approach in later years was Admiral N. S. Mordvinov, an influential adviser on economic affairs early in the century and a continual critic of both Gurev and Kankrin. Although a supporter of autocracy and serfdom, Mordvinov corresponded with Jeremy Bentham and accepted the classical liberal doctrine of the basic harmony of individual and general interests. He firmly believed that if the state would remove restrictions on individual enterprise and provide the needed capital and technical advice Russia's great but untapped wealth could rapidly be exploited and the state's financial problems would be ended. Throughout the twenties and thirties Mordvinov bombarded the Tsar with projects designed to increase the productivity of the economy and subjected government poli-

[6] N. Epanchin, *Ocherk pokhoda 1829 g. v Evropeiskoi Turtsii* (St. Petersburg, 1905), I, 351–357, cited in John S. Curtiss, *The Russian Army under Nicholas I, 1825–1855* (Durham, 1965), p. 55.

cies to scathing criticism.[7] In answering Mordvinov, Kankrin made his own position explicit. He virtually denied the possibility of rapid economic growth and firmly rejected Mordvinov's potentially inflationary proposals for easier credit. The supply of metal money would, he believed, last for thousands of years.[8] As minister of finance, Kankrin was perpetually confronted with the immediate need for funds, not several years hence when the fruits of a proposed project might be available, but at once, so that the expenses of the state could be met. To one of Mordvinov's numerous memoranda suggesting ways to develop the national economy and thus increase revenues, Kankrin replied with irritation:

The law of the enrichment of the nation does not relate directly to the state budget. Nikolai Semenovich [Mordvinov] begins with expenditures and their increase for useful enterprises; this increases the wealth of the people, and then they can pay more. It is true, but there is a mistake in chronology! The state budget's goal is to cover the actual needs of the state; where [in Mordvinov's proposal] is the reduction of expenditures and the increase of revenue considered? Future wealth leads neither to the one nor to the other.[9]

The quotation shows Kankrin reacting sharply to criticism. Not every decision he made was based solely on short-run fiscal considerations. Particularly in the twenties, other factors played an important role. The hope of fostering industrial development through the improvement of technical education was one. On another important occasion, reasons of social policy alone determined the state's decision as to what

[7] Mordvinov was a fascinating man, but since he never occupied a position with executive responsibility and few of his proposals were ever adopted, he must remain a peripheral figure here. For an excellent study of Mordvinov, see Helma Repczuk, "Nicholas Mordvinov (1754–1845)" (unpublished Ph.D. diss., Columbia University, 1962), esp. pp. 78–119, 146–174.

[8] Kankrin, *Weltreichthum,* pp. 66–72.

[9] TsGIAL, f. 560, op. 22, d. 58, "Zapiska admirala N. Mordvinova i ministra finansov E. F. Kankrina . . . ," p. 13.

group was to get long-term credit. Neither fiscal expediency nor economic improvement were involved.

WHO DESERVES A LOAN?

The rural gentry class had long been the main support of the Russian state. It had been created by the granting of land and serfs in exchange for military service rendered to the Tsar, but in the mid-eighteenth century the gentrymen were relieved of the obligation to render service. The government of Russia in the late eighteenth and early nineteenth centuries was essentially an alliance of the autocracy and the gentry. There was occasional friction, but each side seemed to accept the mutually beneficial nature of the existing system. Not until the autocracy, in the reign of Alexander II, became convinced that the emancipation of the serfs was unavoidable did any serious divergence of interests develop.

An excellent example of the central government's devotion to the interests of the rural gentry is the credit policy established by Kankrin and followed throughout Nicholas' reign. Kankrin was the son of a German civil servant and had a low opinion of the spendthrift Russian gentry.[10] But he did not let his feelings affect his judgment of what was wise from the standpoint of the state and vigorously supported the extension of credit to the gentry, even when it was clearly unjustified on economic grounds. Kankrin's opponent on this issue was his predecessor Count Gurev, a Russian gentryman with a reputation for extravagant habits.

In 1821, while still Minister of Finance, Gurev had proposed that the State Loan Bank be abolished and the State Commercial Bank provide loans for industrial development.[11] According to Gurev, the Loan Bank, established in

[10] [E. F. Kankrin], *Die Oekonomie der menschlichen Gesellschaften und das Finanzwesen—von einem ehemaligen Finanzminister* (Stuttgart, 1845), pp. 32–33, 205.

[11] Gurev may well have been acting at the urging of Balugianskii, Speransky's former adviser on economic affairs, or even as a result of

1754 as the Bank of the Nobility, had been originally designed to promote both agriculture and industry but had failed to achieve its aims. In 1811, it suspended the granting of loans to individuals, and its activity was subsequently limited to safekeeping functions and the shipment of funds between cities. With the exception of loans granted by special imperial decree, the Loan Bank's role with respect to agriculture had been taken over by the *sokhrannye kazny,* especially since 1817, when the terms of their loans were considerably liberalized.[12] Agriculture, said Gurev, did not need a new source of capital, and commerce had the existing Commercial Bank, leaving only industry unprovided for. There was no limit to the demand for credit by manufacturers, because the market for their products depended on the current level of education, tastes, and prices, and therefore could be greatly expanded. In Gurev's view there were two requirements for the growth of industry: capital and demand. The presence of adequate demand in Russia was proved by the consumption of foreign goods, while the supply of capital was limited only by the Ministry of Finance. He therefore urged that the Commercial Bank grant loans of 5,000 to 500,000 rubles at 5 or 6 per cent interest to all who were permitted to operate factories, except serfs. The Loan Bank was to be closed by the end of 1822.[13]

The proposal was submitted for discussion to the State Council's Department of the Economy and the reaction was generally favorable. Prince Lobanov-Rostovskii II suggested, with Kankrin's support, that if the Loan Bank were to be

Speransky's own prompting. The idea, however, was put forward by Gurev as his own proposal as minister of finance (*Ministerstvo finansov,* I, 32–33).

[12] The *sokhrannye kazny* were credit offices attached to orphanages in St. Petersburg and Moscow. They used the endowment funds of these institutions plus deposits to make their loans. On their history see S. Ia. Borovoi, *Kredit i banki Rossii (seredina XVII v.–1861 g.)* (Moscow, 1958), pp. 119–121.

[13] *AGS,* IV, pt. 1, 319–329.

abolished, a section in the Commercial Bank be set up in its stead to make loans to the gentry for agricultural use. Otherwise, according to the Prince, the gentry would be cut off from the state aid to which they had been accustomed for over fifty years.[14] Gurev insisted that if the excess of deposits in the Loan Bank were used by the Commercial Bank for loans to industry, the main beneficiaries would still be the gentry, because they were the major owners of mines and factories. The state auditor, Baron Kampenhausen, strongly supported him, arguing that available capital was insufficient to meet all demands and that it was more important to aid industry than agriculture because the country needed facilities to process materials required in wartime. Agricultural loans, complained Kampenhausen, were not used to improve agriculture anyway, but were spent on luxuries.[15]

No final decision was reached during Gurev's administration, but in May 1824, a year after becoming minister of finance, Kankrin proposed to do almost the complete reverse of what his predecessor had advocated. His plan did not, as might be expected, save money or reduce the administrative burden on the bureaucracy. Kankrin's idea was to reopen the inactive Loan Bank, provide it with new capital, and make new loans, not to manufacturers and merchants, but to the rural gentry on the security of their serfs. In summing up his position, Kankrin said in the State Council:

Agriculture still demands from us many improvements, and if the money is not always used purposefully, at least the larger part is, and the support of the gentry estates is unavoidable for us. On the other hand, the attempts of the past year have demonstrated the difficulty of loans on factories, if they are not limited with great circumspection. In general it can be said that the excessive amplification of monetary capital in this area can hardly fail to lead to large losses when the capital of knowledge in the population has not yet received a corresponding expansion.[16]

[14] *Ibid.*, pp. 343, 352–353.
[15] *Ibid.*, pp. 353–354.
[16] *Ibid.*, pp. 365–366.

One could hardly ask for a clearer statement on the question of credit for industry or for gentry agriculture. Loans to the gentry are "unavoidable" whether or not they are used productively, but loans to industry are undesirable because of the danger of large losses. A subsequent provision of the same proposal even called for the transfer of funds from the Commercial Bank to the Loan Bank. According to Kankrin, the Commercial Bank did not have an opportunity to fully utilize its capital through short term loans to merchants and discounting obligations of the *sokhrannye kazny* and the State Treasury. The Loan Bank was to lend on inhabited estates and stone houses in St. Petersburg and on serfs of factory and mining establishments if they had some land. The income produced by the estate was not to be considered in determining the size of the loans. Progressive landowners who used hired labor were therefore ineligible, since only land with serfs could be used as security for loans.[17]

Kankrin's proposal was accepted by the State Council and approved by the Tsar. The Loan Bank renewed large-scale operations. Borrowing rose sharply, from about 700,000 rubles in 1823 to 7,700,000 rubles in 1824 and 13,000,000 in 1825.[18] Almost simultaneously with the increase in credit granted by the Loan Bank, there was a sharp increase in the transfer of funds to it from the Commercial Bank. In 1822, private deposits in the Loan Bank represented 82 per cent of the total, the remainder coming from the state (see Table 2). In 1825, when deposits of the Commercial Bank in the Loan Bank first reached a significant level, they amounted to 12 per cent while private deposits had fallen to 68 per cent. The importance of deposits of Commercial Bank funds continued to rise sharply and virtually without interruption until 1839, when they stabilized at slightly over 50 per cent of total deposits in the Loan Bank and remained at approximately this level throughout the reign of Nicholas I. Correspondingly, the share represented by private deposits fell

17 *Ibid.*, pp. 367–370; Borovoi, *Kredit,* pp. 185–190.
18 Borovoi, *Kredit,* p. 191.

steadily and, after 1839, remained at about 25 per cent of the total. Deposits by the state also declined in importance, falling from about 20 per cent before the transfers were first made to about 14 per cent in the later years.

This movement of funds means that the official policy of the state was to transfer funds from the potentially dynamic commercial sector of the economy to the landed gentry. The Commercial Bank was not only weakened by the transfer of funds to the Loan Bank, but was strictly limited in its operations to discounting notes on a short-term basis. Kankrin viewed it with suspicion and wrote in his first major report to Nicholas that it could produce "repugnant speculation" as easily as "advantageous consequences for commerce," for the merchants were all too easily led into speculation.[19] In one of his few recorded public speeches, he took a similar view and said that credit institutions must not supply capital to those who have none themselves, since their proper goal is simply to help capitalists in temporary need.[20]

There is no doubt that Kankrin favored loans to the gentry primarily for reasons of social policy without regard to strict economic calculations. This interpretation is supported not only by the statement made in 1824 and quoted above but by Kankrin's subsequent actions. In 1828, Count Stroganov requested a loan of 3.2 million rubles, but sources within the government claimed that the value of the estates offered in security did not approach this figure. The Ministry of Finance, however, made no attempt to refute these assertions and the loan was granted.[21] In 1830, Kankrin rejected a sug-

[19] TsGIAL, f. 560, op. 38, d. 213, "Obshchii otchet . . . za 1826," pp. 91–92.

[20] *Zhurnal manufaktur i torgovli*, no. 7 (1827), p. 158.

[21] TsGIAL, f. 560, op. 22, d. 49, 1828, "Materialy o vydache gr. Stroganovu ssudy pod zalog imenii . . . ," pp. 7, 14, 22. Unfortunately, there is no indication of the critic's identity in the documents preserved. He must, however, have been a high government official, because he felt free to criticize Kankrin harshly and had access to confidential documents. This transaction, like all other financial matters, was secret and not a matter of public record.

Table 2. Major sources of deposits in the State Loan Bank, 1822–1856 (in millions of silver rubles)

Year	Total deposits	From the Commercial Bank	From the Commercial Bank, % of total	From individuals	From individuals, % of total	From the state	From the state, % of total
1822	30.39			25.04	82	5.29	17
1823	31.03			24.70	80	6.32	20
1824	32.08			25.27	79	5.98	19
1825	40.32	5.03	12	27.49	68	6.77	17
1826	46.73	7.61	16	26.55	57	8.14	17
1827	52.94	11.75	22	26.66	50	8.15	15
1828	60.87	16.53	27	27.52	45	9.02	15
1829	74.12	25.44	34	30.62	41	10.22	14
1830	78.79	27.76	35	33.45	42	11.52	15
1831	81.10	30.75	38	32.75	40	11.31	14
1832	85.37	32.14	38	34.33	40	11.41	13
1833	93.45	37.58	40	35.08	38	13.28	14
1834	100.02	41.56	42	35.77	36	14.32	14
1835	109.12	46.57	43	37.03	34	15.68	14
1836	115.44	51.83	45	37.41	32	16.19	14
1837	122.83	54.81	45	38.06	31	19.72	16

1838	133.60	62.10	46	38.93	29	22.92	17
1839	150.89	78.86	52	39.74	26	21.13	14
1840	160.77	87.25	54	39.89	25	22.72	14
1841	163.31	87.21	53	41.85	26	22.58	14
1842	178.73	96.31	54	44.36	25	24.67	14
1843	187.37	100.71	54	44.38	24	26.95	14
1844	198.26	103.33	52	44.48	22	30.73	15
1845	207.26	107.98	52	50.65	24	29.83	14
1846	222.81	120.44	54	52.05	23	30.21	14
1847	234.13	125.86	54	53.27	23	33.09	14
1848	252.08	140.23	56	54.58	22	32.89	13
1849	275.21	159.19	58	56.48	21	33.19	12
1850	292.76	170.87	58	57.58	20	34.63	12
1851	307.68	178.56	58	59.57	19	35.82	12
1852	319.25	186.59	58	58.12	18	37.59	12
1853	338.51	194.99	58	59.70	18	41.61	12
1854	349.40	203.31	58	59.87	17	38.23	11
1855	369.12	212.46	58	62.86	17	39.82	11
1856	400.16	222.02	56	63.88	16	42.70	11

Source: I. I. Kaufman, "Statistika russkikh bankov," pt. 1, *Statisticheskii vremennik rossiiskoi imperii*, ser. 2, no. 9 (1872), p. 2.

gestion that mortgaged estates be liquidated for cash because, he said, the well-being of the gentry depended on the continuity of family estates.[22] Foreclosure was indeed rare. Between 1824 and 1837, twenty-five estates with 3,696 souls were sold, and three, with 13,336 souls, became state property.[23] It is hardly surprising then that gentry indebtedness rose rapidly. Exact figures are unavailable, but the general upward trend is unquestionable (see Table 3). The bulk of

Table 3. Gentry indebtedness, 1823–1856

Year	Outstanding debt of the gentry (millions of silver rubles)	Mortgaged serfs (millions of male souls)	Number of serfs mortgaged as % of total number, according to latest revision
1823	90	2.1	20.2
1833	205	4.5	43.2
1843	340	6.4	52.4
1856	398	6.6	61.7

Source: S. Ia. Borovoi, *Kredit i banki Rossii (seredina XVII v.–1861 g.)* (Moscow, 1958), p. 197.

the credit was supplied by the *sokhrannye kazny,* and the Loan Bank was definitely a source of supplementary credit. Such a supplementary program could have been directed primarily at landlords or members of other classes interested in new ventures and techniques, either agricultural or industrial, but instead loans were made on serfs already mortgaged elsewhere, while landlords using hired agricultural or industrial labor were ineligible and credit limitations on factory serfs were tight.[24]

22 TsGIAL, f. 560, op. 38, d. 117, 1830, "Zapiska neustanovlennogo avtora . . . ," p. 35. Kankrin's views are expressed in his comments on this anonymous project submitted to the Tsar and referred to the Minister of Finance.

23 Borovoi, *Kredit,* p. 187, quoting TsGIAL, f. 583, d. 232, p. 420.

24 In 1823, the Loan Bank provided 12.55 million silver rubles of credit to the gentry, or about 14 per cent of the estimated total; in

Thus even before the reign of Nicholas began, one major aspect of his economic policy was firmly established. The state would continue and even expand its support of the rural gentry for social and political reasons. The modest program providing credit for industry through the state banking system, suggested by Gurev, was firmly rejected. It was soon made clear that it was not simply because the new minister of finance felt that the banking system was an inappropriate institution. Direct loans from the state treasury to aid industry were also firmly rejected, even though there was ample precedent in Russia, from the time of Peter I and earlier, for such loans. Under Russian conditions with the banks operating as agencies of the Ministry of Finance, there was no essential difference between bank credit and state credit and Kankrin's action in 1824 was, in effect, a rejection of both. In 1826, he explicitly stated his opposition to direct loans to industry by the state.[25] There were a few minor exceptions, but the general position was not changed subsequently.[26] In reports prepared in the 1840's covering his

---

1833, 35.94 million, about 18 per cent; and in 1843, 52.71 million or 16 per cent. The remainder came from the *sokhrannye kazny* in Moscow and St. Petersburg and to a limited extent from the provincial *Prikazy obshchestvennogo prizreniia* (D. Filimonov, "Kreditnye uchrezhdeniia Moskovskogo vospitatel'nogo doma," *Russkii arkhiv*, no. 1 [1876], pp. 265–267; I. I. Kaufman, "Statistika russkikh bankov," pt. 1, *Statisticheskii vremennik rossiiskoi imperii*, ser. 2, no. 9 [1872], pp. 2–3).

25 TsGIAL, f. 560, op. 38, d. 213, "Obshchii otchet . . . za 1826," p. 82.

26 The largest of these exceptions was a loan of 80,000 silver rubles made in 1827 to a French entrepreneur to establish a silk-spinning mill in Georgia. The project was short-lived and a total failure and can hardly have encouraged Kankrin to modify his attitude toward industrial loans. The Demidov mining interests received 1.75 million rubles in 1832, even though 5,884 of the 7,005 serfs offered in security were on state land. Kankrin justified this on the grounds that it was necessary to save the plant from abandonment. There were less than half-a-dozen other substantial industrial loans made during Kankrin's administration. In addition, a dozen or so small loans were made each year, largely to victims of natural disasters. The total amount varied sharply, but

entire tenure in office, Kankrin maintained that the policy was correct and should be continued in the future because direct loans did more harm than good.[27]

The willingness of the government to make loans to gentrymen and not to urban factory owners does not mean that it was opposed to manufacturing in the towns. The gentry simply had first call on credit at the disposal of the state because their welfare was felt to be essential. In the 1820's, there is not the slightest evidence of any antagonism to the growth of manufacturing on social, sanitary, aesthetic, or any other grounds. Industrialization in the modern sense and the problems associated with it, troublesome workers, and noisy, dirty factories had not, as yet, appeared in Russia. Two features of state policy in these years show that industry was regarded as good, although perhaps not very important. A highly protective tariff was maintained, and a whole series of projects was begun by the Ministry of Finance to develop and spread technical knowledge.

Russia had long had a protective and often prohibitive tariff system in the tradition of European mercantilism. Early in the nineteenth century, the inclusion of Russia in

---

from 1826 through 1838 it only once exceeded 25,000 rubles (assignats). From 1839 through 1843 the total was close to 60,000. On the silk fiasco see M. K. Rozhkova, *Ekonomicheskaia politika tsarskogo pravitel'stva na srednem vostoke vo vtoroi chetverti XIX veka i russkaia burzhuaziia* (Moscow and Leningrad, 1949), p. 135; TsGIAL, f. 560, op. 38, d. 226, "Obshchii otchet . . . za 1827 god," p. 42; and *Sbornik svedenii i materialov po vedomstvu Ministerstva finansov*, III, no. 9 (1866), 12–13. On the Demidov loan see TsGIAL, f. 583, op. 4, d. 228, 1833, "Vsepoddanneishie dokladnye zapiski," pp. 194–195. The other information on loans is from the annual "Otchet Departamenta manufaktur i vnutrennei torgovli," TsGIAL, f. 560, op. 38; each year's volume has a different *delo* number.

[27] "Nastavlenie," pp. 87–88; *Rtb.*, I, Supp. II, 92–93.

the French "Continental System" strengthened the effective level of protection. In 1816 and 1819, the Russian tariff was lowered as part of the international settlement at the end of the Napoleonic Wars. The influence of Novosiltsev and other strongly pro-Polish advisers of Alexander I and the desire to maintain close cooperation with Prussia in international affairs resulted in major tariff reductions on key items, especially those imported from Poland or from Prussia via Poland.[28]

Gurev had vigorously, but unsuccessfully, opposed the reductions of 1819, but the impact on Russian manufacturing, particularly woolen textiles and sugar refining, was such that in 1822 a severely protective tariff law was promulgated that included the total prohibition of the import of a wide range of goods.[29] Gurev, and especially his contemporary Kozodavlev, minister of the interior from 1810 to 1819, had supported protection as a device to stimulate industrial growth, Kozodavlev favoring total prohibition of imports and Gurev leaning to high duties since, as finance minister, he also had the revenue problems in view.[30]

[28] On eighteenth-century tariff policy and economic development in general see Arcadius Kahan, "Continuity in Economic Activity and Policy during the Post-Petrine Period in Russia," *Journal of Economic History*, XXV (1965), 77–78. On the tariff of 1819 see G. G. Proshin, "Tamozhennyi tarif 1819 goda," *Nauchnye doklady vyshei shkoly— Istoricheskie nauki*, no. 4 (1961), pp. 102–113.

[29] Proshin, "Tamozhennyi tarif 1819 goda," pp. 114–115; Konstantin Lodyzhenskii, *Istoriia russkago tamozhennago tarifa* (St. Petersburg, 1886), pp. 186–191; see also A. V. Predtechenskii, "Bor'ba protektsionistov s fritrederami v nachale XIX v.," *Uchenye zapiski Leningradskogo Gosudarstvennogo Universiteta, seriia istoricheskikh nauk*, no. 5 (1939); M. Tugan-Baranovskii, *Russkaia fabrika v proshlom i nastoiashchem*, I (3rd ed.; St. Petersburg, 1907), ch. 8. The actual circumstances of the enactment of the tariff of 1822 are far from clear, and I have been unable to determine exactly who was against it and who favored it. Evidently enough of the injured industries were owned by influential gentrymen to produce very substantial and effective complaints.

[30] A. V. Predtechenskii, *Ocherki obshchestvenno-politicheskoi istorii Rossii v pervoi chetverti XIX veka* (Moscow and Leningrad, 1957), pp. 299–300.

Kankrin was not involved in the elaboration and enactment of the 1822 tariff.[31] He nevertheless accepted it, giving the principle of tariff protection for industry firm support throughout his administration, and there was no relaxation of protection until the very last years of Nicholas' reign. The relatively low duties of 1819 had, he wrote, "forced the government to issue the tariff of 1822, based on the system of protection of internal industry," because a flood of foreign goods was driving Russian factories into bankruptcy. The progress of Russian industry was due to the existence of the protective tariff and its firm enforcement.[32]

During the 1820's, Kankrin resisted both the requests of Moscow woolen manufacturers for increased protection from Polish competition and the proposal of the Prince Drutskii-Liubetskii, the Polish minister of finance, to abolish all customs barriers between imperial Russia and the autonomous Polish state established at the Congress of Vienna. In opposition to Drutskii-Liubetskii, he argued that Russian industries could not withstand Polish competition and must be protected if they were not to be destroyed. In rejecting the request of Moscow manufacturers for total prohibition of woolen cloth and thread imports, the argument was more complex. To halt cloth imports entirely would cut state revenue, stimulate smuggling, and further protests against the system. Prohibition of thread imports would not only reduce revenue but might well injure the existing Russian weaving industry by denying it needed raw material. Both the weaving and spinning industries were, in any case, adequately protected, and changes in the existing system were not desirable.[33] Despite Kankrin's general rejection of the manufacturers' petition, some small changes were made in

[31] Kankrin, *Die Oekonomie*, p. 243.

[32] TsGIAL, f. 560, op. 38, d. 354, "Obshchii otchet . . . za 1835," pp. 30–31; and similar statements in *Rtb.*, I, Supp. II, 66–67; TsGIAL, f. 560, op. 38, d. 213, "Obshchii otchet . . . za 1826 g.," p. 81.

[33] On the manufacturers' petition see TsGIAL, f. 1152, op. T. I, d. 84, 1827, "O novoi poshline s shersti," pp. 2–8; on Drutskii-Liubetskii's proposal, *Ministerstvo finansov*, I, 325.

1828 to restrict the practice of importing and redyeing cloth to avoid higher duties on certain colors.[34]

The only significant tariff revisions of the 1820's were designed to increase revenues. The import prohibitions of the 1822 law were so sweeping that in many cases the result was simply to stimulate smuggling of luxury goods not produced in Russia. In 1824, 1825, and 1826, prohibitions were ended on some luxury items, particularly high-quality textiles, and they were admitted subject to high duties. Duties on other luxury items already admissible were increased.[35] These adjustments did not change the nature of the system. It went far beyond the limits of rational protection in a manner reminiscent of both the sumptuary laws of earlier centuries in western Europe and the import controls of modern nations with balance of payments problems. The effectiveness of the tariff was severely limited by smuggling, which is impossible to measure but was certainly most extensive. Efforts to solve the problem were strenuous but by no means fully successful despite strengthened border patrols and repeated adjustment of rates designed to reduce the incentive.[36] The customs duties were the only major source of state revenue that came primarily from the upper classes, but despite the sometimes bitter complaints there was no inclination on the part of the state to alter its policy.[37]

The maintenance of the protective tariff required no positive action or even a decision. The system that existed was simply allowed to continue in effect. Much more startling, in the light of the inclination of both the Tsar and his min-

[34] TsGIAL, f. 1152, op. T. I, d. 111, 1827, "O zapreshchenii rossiiskim krasil'niam . . . ," p. 1; *ibid.*, f. 560, op. 42, d. 3, "Otchet Departamenta manufaktur . . . za 1828 g.," p. 7.

[35] Lodyzhenskii, *Istoriia russkago tamozhennago tarifa*, pp. 209–215; Michael Herman Freiherr von Nolcken, *Der russische Finanzminister Graf Georg Kankrin und seine Handelspolitik* (Riga, 1909), pp. 39–43.

[36] *Rtb.*, I, Supp. II, pp. 103–105; Nolcken, *Russische Finanzminister*, pp. 46–48.

[37] For example, see criticism of Kankrin for raising the price of nutmeg mentioned in a letter, F. V. Rastopchin to A. A. Zakrevskii, Jan. 3, 1824, *Sbornik IRIO*, LXXIII (1891), 472–473.

ister of finance to leave well enough alone, was the state's interest in technical education and the diffusion of technical and commercial information. Probably not since the time of Peter the Great had the state been as active in that area.

Technical education and related functions were not the responsibility of the Ministry of Education nor of any other single agency. The existing institutions providing technical education had been established to meet specific state needs. The oldest was the Finance Ministry's Institute of Mining, established as the Corps of Mining Cadets in 1773. In 1809, the Institute of Transport Engineers was opened by the Chief Administration of Transport. On a less advanced level, the Ministry of War established an engineering school and a school for artillery engineers in the last year of Alexander's reign. The Department of State Domains of the Ministry of Finance supported the Institute of Forestry, established in 1811, and the Ministry of Justice maintained a school for surveyors that dated from 1779. The most important of these specialized institutions were those in mining and transport. The others were not only smaller in size, but operated on a much lower academic level and gave little more than a basic education with emphasis on arithmetic.[38]

In the early 1820's, the Institute of Transport Engineers produced about ten graduates a year. Alumni who transferred from military service to civil service were given a rank equal to that granted to university graduates. The state paid the expenses of more than half the student body (seventy-two in 1823) and the school was open to students of all free classes.[39] The Corps of Mining Cadets was larger, with about three hundred students. Graduates also had the privilege of transferring to the civil service on a basis of equality with university graduates.[40]

[38] [A. G. Nebolsin, ed.], *Istoriko-statisticheskii ocherk obshchago i spetsial'nago obrazovaniia v Rossii* (St. Petersburg, 1883), pp. 176–241.

[39] Russia, Institut inzhenerov putei soobshcheniia, *Spisok lits okonchivshikh kurs nauk v Institute inzhenerov putei soobshcheniia Imperatora Aleksandra I, s 1811 po 1882 g.* (St. Petersburg, 1883), pp. 1, 30.

[40] Nebolsin, *Istoriko-statisticheskii ocherk,* p. 196.

These institutes and the schools were small, and they were designed exclusively to prepare their graduates for state service, usually in the army. There was no establishment that provided technical training for persons likely to seek private employment. A gentry family of limited means would send its sons to one of the state institutes or schools so they could earn adequate incomes and reach appropriate ranks more quickly than the untrained. The son of a merchant or other freeman went not only to obtain the skills with which to earn a living, but also to gain admission to the higher levels of state service, which would make him a member of the gentry and enable him to have legal privileges and at least some of the social prestige enjoyed by those who inherited the rank. The few individuals who might have wished to hire a man with technical training could not readily find one trained in Russia willing to take private employment. The need was undoubtedly small, but if industry were to develop outside state-owned enterprises, the demand would certainly grow, and would have to be met.

The Minister of Finance was fully aware of this problem and gave every indication of being ready and anxious to take steps to improve the situation. He knew as well as any foreign aid administrator today that more than machines and buildings are needed for industrial development. Kankrin, following Müller, called the additional factor the "capital of knowledge." In 1824, he had argued against extending credit to industry because that kind of capital was lacking. The first issue of the *Journal of Manufacturing and Trade* included an introductory statement by Kankrin to the effect that money capital was not all that was necessary for industry and that frequently great sums were wasted because of the lack of the "capital of knowledge," which was needed to put hoarded money to proper use.[41] Kankrin clearly recognized one of the most important obstacles to economic progress in

---

[41] *AGS*, IV, pt. 1, 365–366; *Zhurnal manufaktur i torgovli*, no. 1 (1825), pp. i–ii (also in TsGIAL, f. 560, op. 38, d. 213, "Obshchii otchet . . . za 1826," pp. 81–82).

Russia. He was certainly not the only man who did, but his position enabled him to take positive steps to improve the situation. The final report that he submitted to the Tsar in 1843 listed some thirty-odd projects carried out during his administration "for the strengthening and improvement of factories." [42] Almost all of them were in one way or another designed to contribute to the "capital of knowledge" through specialized training or the diffusion of information. The responsibilities of the Ministry of Finance also acted as a limitation on Kankrin's activities in this field. His primary duty remained the financing of the state's major activities, military and administrative. If he was to discharge his overall responsibilities properly he could not give single-minded attention to technical education or any other special project. Nevertheless the activity in this field in the twenties was varied, imaginative, and of great potential importance.

Some added support was given to existing institutions, particularly the Corps of Mining Engineers, which received a 440,000-ruble loan in 1824, to be repaid from its annual appropriation over twenty-four years. For the most part, however, they continued their work as before.[43] The Institute of Transport Engineers received no special help, because Nicholas did not approve of the unruly student body. He may even have considered their behavior a sign of disloyalty.[44]

By far the most important project in the area of technical education in the entire first half of the nineteenth century was the Practical Technological Institute, which was formally established in 1828 and actually opened its doors in the fall of 1831. The mere opening of another small school was not as important as the new goal that was set for it. It was the first institution in Russia designed to provide private industry with qualified personnel. Graduates of the institute were specifically forbidden to enter government service, and al-

[42] *Rtb.,* I, Supp. II, 92–97.

[43] Gornyi Institut, *Nauchno-istoricheskii sbornik* (St. Petersburg, 1873), p. 75.

[44] A. I. Del'vig, *Polveka russkoi zhizni* (Moscow, 1930), I. 115.

though they enjoyed, while they were enrolled, the personal privileges of members of the merchant guilds—exemption from the head tax, corporal punishment, and recruitment—they reverted to their class of origin on graduation. The school was thus, as Kankrin himself said, not to be just another route to improved social status and possibly permanent entry into the gentry class, but was to provide the mechanics, foremen and perhaps eventually the engineers needed by privately owned industry.[45]

In 1826, the military governor of Moscow had proposed the establishment of a society of manufacturers including a technological institute. Kankrin approved in principle, but "felt the obligation to point out that such an enormous undertaking, because of its very newness for us, cannot be immediately brought to fulfillment, and therefore it is necessary at first to lay firm foundations, and then in the light of the circumstances and needs make further decisions." What this bureaucratic double talk meant was that Kankrin had already decided to build a technical institute, but in St. Petersburg, where he could run it as he chose, despite the fact that most of Russia's existing manufacturing industry was in the Moscow area.[46] The institute was his pet project, and he wrote to Alexander von Humboldt in 1828 that "I will not let the war stop me from building a large practical technological institute. We lack a middle class with moderate theoretical knowledge for a thousand uses."[47]

A substantial building (still in use) was constructed, and the institute opened in the fall of 1831 with thirty-three students in the lowest class and nineteen in the second of what was to be a six-year program. The numbers were not large

---

[45] TsGIAL, f. 1152, op. T. I, d. 99, 1828, "Ob uchrezhdenii v St. Peterburge Prakticheskago Tekhnologicheskago Instituta," pp. 7–8, 27–30.

[46] *Ibid.*, p. 3.

[47] [E. F. Kankrin], *Im Ural und Altai: Briefwechsel zwischen Alexander von Humbolt und Graf Georg Kancrin aus den Jahren 1827–1832* (Leipzig, 1869), p. 39.

and it was, in fact, very difficult to find students with sufficient primary education. Ambitious parents preferred to send their children to a school that would prepare them to climb higher on the social ladder, and less fortunate children seldom learned to read and write.[48]

The Practical Technological Institute was but one of several modest, but intelligent and realistic efforts made in the twenties to increase and spread technical knowledge. In 1829, the Commercial Marine School was opened in St. Petersburg to train personnel for Russia's small merchant fleet. A whole series of publications were founded to influence those who had completed their formal education: the *Journal of Manufacturing and Trade* (1825), the *Commercial Gazette* (1825), the *Mining Journal* (1825), the *Transport Journal* (1826), and later the *Agricultural Journal* (1834). The *Journal of the Ministry of the Interior* (1829) also contained much material of technical and commercial interest. All were solid publications containing official announcements, lengthy technical articles with plans and drawings, and many translations from western-European languages. The informed reader could have learned much from them; but there were few who could make use of this new flood of information. The Department of Manufacturing and Trade ruefully admitted in 1828 that after three years of publication their journal did not circulate widely.[49] The mining journal probably had the largest circulation, with a subscription list of 1,093, reflecting the old and well-established mining industry in Russia, both private and state owned.[50]

To supplement the printed word, the Ministry of Finance arranged for foreign experts to visit Russia. The most memorable of these visits was the remarkable journey by coach

[48] Tekhnologicheskii Institut imeni Leningradskogo Soveta rabochikh, krest'ianskikh i krasnoarmeiskikh deputatov, *Sto let (1828–1928)* (Leningrad, 1928), I, 17.

[49] TsGIAL, f. 560, op. 42, d. 3, "Otchet Departamenta manufaktur . . . za 1828 g.," p. 4.

[50] Gornyi Institut, *Nauchno-istoricheskii sbornik*, p. 84.

to the Altai and the Urals made by Alexander von Humboldt in 1829, paid for by the Ministry of Finance.[51] Less spectacular, but possibly of more immediate value to the Russian economy, were the visits of such other figures as the Saxon sheep-breeding expert Maximilian von Shpek, who traveled widely in 1825, addressed the Free Economic Society, and was decorated by the Russian government. In 1828, a few years after his visit, a state-subsidized wool-sorting establishment was opened in Moscow to serve domestic consumers of Russian wool, and throughout the 1820's the problem of wool growing and handling received extensive attention in the *Journal of Manufacturing and Trade* and the *Commercial Gazette*.[52]

In an attempt to improve communication between manufacturers and bureaucrats, the state encouraged the establishment of a manufacturing council composed of representatives of the manufacturers, merchants, gentry, and scientists. Specifically Kankrin wanted to collect statistics on existing industry and to spread information on the causes of the success or failure of various enterprises. The council was also to advise on requests for exclusive rights to the production of new products.[53] The idea was not a new one; such an organization had been proposed as early as 1816 by Senator Arshenevskii, after an inspection trip of Russian factories, but no action was taken until the plan was revived in 1827. The body finally established was supposed to advise the Ministry of Finance on all legislation dealing with private manufacturing,

---

[51] Kankrin, *Im Ural und Altai*, pp. 19–32.

[52] *Zhurnal manufaktur i torgovli*, no. 4 (1825), pp. 152–161, and no. 8 (1825) in particular, and many subsequent articles in issues through 1834; *Kommercheskaia gazeta*, nos. 83, 88 (1825), and 74, 75 (1826); TsGIAL, f. 560, op. 42, d. 4, "Otchet . . . Departamenta manufaktur . . . za 1829," p. 131; on sheep raising in general see Jerome Blum, *Lord and Peasant in Russia from the Ninth to the Nineteenth Century* (Princeton, 1961), pp 341–342.

[53] TsGIAL, f. 1152, op. T. I, d. 39, "Ob uchrezhdenii manufakturnogo soveta . . . ," p. 4; *Zhurnal manufaktur i torgovli*, no. 7 (1828), pp. 159–168.

and it received a state subsidy of 17,500 rubles (assignats) for its first year of operation.[54] The Manufacturing Council was established in St. Petersburg and Moscow and began its statistical work with enthusiasm. In 1828, the Moscow branch reported the existence of 3,981 manufacturing enterprises with 47,052 workers where only 290 enterprises with 19,493 workers had been known before. The new organization was obviously trying to get off to a good start by reporting every shoemaker and blacksmith as a "factory." [55] A year after the establishment of the Manufacturing Council, a commercial council was established with similar functions.[56]

More spectacular but closely related to the Manufacturing and Commercial Councils was the staging of the first Russian National Industrial Exhibition in St. Petersburg in 1829. In November 1828, Kankrin devoted a major portion of one of his rare public speeches to plans for the forthcoming exhibition.[57] It occupied the impressive neoclassical building of the St. Petersburg bourse and was opened with great fanfare by the Tsar himself. The *Journal of Manufacturing and Trade* filled two entire issues with reports on it, including a list of goods on display covering over one hundred pages. An en-

[54] A. V. Predtechenskii, "Istoriia osnovaniia manufakturnogo soveta," *Izvestiia Akademii Nauk, otdelenie obshchestvennykh nauk,* ser. 7, no. 5 (1932), pp. 375–393; *Zhurnal manufaktur i torgovli,* no. 7 (1828), pp. 159–168; TsGIAL, f. 1152, op. T. I, d. 39, "Ob uchrezhdenii manufakturnogo soveta . . . ," p. 12. I see no real evidence to support Predtechenskii's contention that the creation of the Manufacturing Council was a victory for the bourgeoisie over the gentry-bureaucracy represented by Kankrin. The plan is perfectly consistent with Kankrin's interest in encouraging the spread of technical knowledge. His insistence on a dominant role for the Ministry of Finance in the new council is consistent with the natural tendency of any official to want to avoid creating a rival agency and does not mean he opposed the aims of the Manufacturing Council.

[55] TsGIAL, f. 560, op. 38, d. 242, "Obshchii otchet . . . za 1828," p. 5.

[56] *Ibid.,* f. 1152, op. T. I, d. 97, 1829, "Ob uchrezhdenii kommercheskogo soveta," pp. 1–5.

[57] *Zhurnal manufaktur i torgovli,* no. 10 (1828).

thusiastic reporter for this government publication claimed that "even foreigners found items that were worth purchasing." The official goal of the exhibition was not only to acquaint the local population and foreign visitors with the achievements of Russian industry, but to give the manufacturers the public respect they deserved. The *Journal* observed that the exhibition was doing much to increase the prestige accorded to successful enterprise and also urged gentrymen who were unsuccessful in agriculture to take up industrial pursuits.[58]

None of these many educational projects undertaken in the 1820's could have, or were expected to have, dramatic or immediate results. They were necessarily of a rather small scale, funds were limited, and at best their impact could only be gradual, as the graduates of the various schools went to work and the information, spread through the journals, visitors, councils, and exhibitions, was received and absorbed by those in a position to make constructive use of it. Taken together, the various parts of the program added up to a vigorous attack by the state, largely by the Ministry of Finance, on one of the major obstacles to economic development in Russia. Above all, they clearly show the direction in which the government hoped that the economy would move. The basis for more extensive educational projects and progress was certainly laid in the 1820's. That these were not, in fact, undertaken does not mean that the work of the 1820's is unimportant. It does suggest that the attitude of the state toward economic development changed in later years.

THE DREAM OF A MIDDLE CLASS

When Kankrin wrote to Alexander von Humboldt about his plans for the Technological Institute, he referred sadly to Russia's lack of a middle class.[59] The reason for his sadness

[58] *Ibid.*, no. 5 (1829), pp. 20–33.
[59] Kankrin, *Im Ural und Altai*, p. 39.

was probably fiscal. A prosperous urban middle class would have been a most convenient source of revenue for the state. Not only would it be close at hand in a few centers of population, but its income would be far less dependent on the weather than that of the peasantry.

There was genuine interest within the government during the 1820's in encouraging the growth of the urban population and particularly the commercial middle class. There was also much uncertainty about what was actually involved and even about exactly what the state's goal should be. Was it really to increase revenue collections or was it, perhaps, to bolster grain prices by expanding the urban market? Which categories of urban residents should be encouraged? Were all the merchants, artisans, petty traders, and peasants who lived in towns and engaged in trade equally desirable? All these people did help maintain the price of grain. Or was it only a specific group within the town population that would be really beneficial to the state—possibly the prosperous merchants, who could conveniently be made to pay substantial taxes?

In a rather confused picture, three separate themes can be isolated: the attempt by the state to increase the amount of revenue collected from the existing urban population; the attempt to favor, and give increased prestige to, the upper strata of this existing population; and the desire to increase the total urban population in order to raise the price of grain. All three are closely related. Tax preferences or tax discrimination were a way of favoring one segment of the urban population over another. The wish to increase total urban population tended to come in conflict with the concern over the welfare and status of the most prosperous. What was lacking throughout the period, except for Kankrin's long-range educational projects, was any serious attention to the problem of developing the economic basis of either a larger town population or a more prosperous upper stratum. Neither was there any evidence of concern over possible social or political problems associated with large-scale urban growth.

When Kankrin took over the Ministry of Finance in 1823,

tax receipts from the merchant guild had been falling steadily for ten years, and it is hardly surprising that an attempt to restore these revenues, at least to their previous level, was one of the new minister's first actions. The Russian merchant guild was established by Peter the Great as part of his new system of local administration and soon came to be used almost exclusively for the convenience of the state in collecting taxes from the urban population, rather than for serving the particular interests of its members. During the eighteenth century, the state made some attempts to protect the guild members from the competition of peasants engaged in trade, but the serf-owning gentry had a personal interest in the financial success of their peasants and successfully prevented the enforcement of statutes limiting commercial activity to merchants.[60] Members were classified in one of the three grades of the merchant guild according to the amount of capital they possessed. Those who had less than required for the third guild were assigned to the burgher class (*meshchanstvo*).[61] Guild members paid a tax on their capital, but they were exempt from the head tax, army recruitment, and corporal punishment and were permitted to engage in various forms of business activity that were theoretically forbidden to burghers and trading peasants.

Guild tax revenues had fallen in the early nineteenth century because it was no longer worthwhile to belong to the guilds. Restrictions on the activity of burghers and peasants were not enforced and when the rate of taxation on merchant capital was increased almost fivefold in 1812, the prestige and special privileges of membership ceased to be sufficiently attractive. It was almost always possible to conceal capital assets and transfer to the burgher class.[62] Either the government

[60] Blum, *Lord and Peasant,* pp. 289–290.

[61] "Burgher" is the term used for the Russian *meshchanin.* The English term suggests a more solid and prosperous group than does the Russian. "Petty traders and artisans" would be clumsy, but a more accurate translation.

[62] *Ministerstvo finansov,* I, 73–74, 82–84; Russia, Ministerstvo finan-

could make membership in the guilds worthwhile by strengthening their privileged position in some way or it could move in the direction of some sort of general sales-tax or licensing system that would be levied on all businessmen without regard to their legal status.

Kankrin chose to retain the existing system and the new guild law of 1824 increased the tax burden and the restrictions on the burgher and the trading peasant in order to make general membership more attractive. All urban residents and peasants who engaged in any sort of trade were henceforth required to have special certificates, the cost depending on the size of their business. The type of goods to be sold and the location of the shop or stand was specified.[63] The taxes on the guild merchants were not lowered, as they had requested, but at least their competitors were now subject to equal or greater levies. Kankrin's justification for increased restrictions was that small-scale trade, especially when it was undertaken on a part-time basis by peasants, did not aid in developing the towns or general prosperity. In his first major report to Nicholas I, he said of the 1824 revisions of the guild law:

Some measures were taken for the gradual reduction of petty trade in the cities and in the country in order, on the one hand, to concentrate industry in the cities, and on the other that people without capital would occupy themselves more with productive activities, especially in factories, rather than with worthless petty trade. It is well known that from the time that the

---

sov, Departament torgovli i manufaktur, *Istoricheskii ocherk oblozheniia torgovli i promyslov v Rossii, s prilozheniem materialov po torgovopromyshlennoi statistike* (St. Petersburg, 1893), pp. 116–118; Vladimir Potekhin, "O gil'deiskom sbore v Rossii," *Promyshlennost', zhurnal manufaktur i torgovli*, III (1861), 243–246; "Predlozheniia Moskovskago kupecheskago obshchestva," *Sbornik svedenii i materialov po vedomstvu Ministerstva finansov*, III (1865), 306.

[63] For details see *PSZ* I, statute 30115; Ministerstvo finansov, *Istoricheskii ocherk oblozheniia*, pp. 120–132; P. G. Ryndziunskii, "Gil'deiskaia reforma Kankrina 1824 goda," *Istoricheskie zapiski*, no. 40 (1952), pp. 118–120, 132; and *Ministerstvo finansov*, I, 85–86.

peasants intensified their trading, our cities began to decline noticeably. Ancient Russia had better cities, for then the peasants had freedom to become real city residents, not uniting agriculture with trade.[64]

In other words, to have prosperous towns one needs a prosperous upper commercial class that will provide employment for a permanent urban population that has severed its ties with the countryside and whose independent commercial activities are taxed and strictly regulated. Just a decade later the official attitude was very different.[65]

The guild law of 1824 was a step away from the traditional gentry view that favored peasant trade as a means of indirectly strengthening the landlords' own financial position. Gentry opposition to Kankrin's proposals, however, may have been reduced because some landowners had come to the conclusion that the use of the *obrok* system and the relative independence that a trading peasant had might lead to increased pressure for total emancipation.[66] In the State Council, Prince S. N. Saltykov expressed the gentry viewpoint and opposed Kankrin's suggested increase in taxes on trade, supporting instead the restriction on the burghers, the group most directly competing with the trading peasants. The most carefully developed opposition to Kankrin came from Speransky, who had only recently returned to official life in the capital after almost ten years' enforced residence outside Petersburg. Speransky's position was not inconsistent with the gentry's interest in the trading peasant, but his argument was based on the benefits that would be reaped by the state and the nation as a whole if trade were freed from useless restriction and from heavy and discriminatory taxation. According to Speransky, members of all classes should be free to engage in trade and the revenue should be raised by a simple fee

[64] TsGIAL, f. 560, op. 38, d. 213, "Obshchii otchet . . . za 1826 g.," p. 27. Also see Kankrin, *Weltreichthum,* pp. 91–92, for his negative view of small-scale trade in general.

[65] See below, pp. 100–102.

[66] Ryndziunskii, "Gil'deiskaia reforma Kankrina," p. 120.

charged to all shop owners. The governor general of Moscow, I. V. Tutolmin, took a similar position, emphasizing that agricultural Russia needed to develop trade and industry and that this could not be accomplished by increased regulation.[67]

Both the opponents and the proponents of the guild law of 1824 favored urban and commercial development. The debate was on how to achieve it, what the character of the urban population should be, and how trade was to be regulated. Speransky advocated an open-door policy, insofar as it was possible without changing the legal position of the privately owned serfs. The official position was to exercise much stricter control, to favor the more prosperous town classes, the guild merchants, and to discourage commercial and craft activity by peasants, particularly the peasants of the gentry who could never become true townsmen. State policy, however, was not directed against urban growth. In the summer of 1824, Kankrin sponsored measures that eliminated the double taxation of state peasants who moved to towns, and which made it easier for state peasants to enter the burgher or even the merchant class.[68]

There was nothing logically inconsistent in the policies that Kankrin pursued. He wanted a prosperous upper class and a growing lower class that supported but did not complete with their betters. The freedom of opportunity that Speransky and Mordvinov favored is not the only possible basis for urban growth, as the history of innumerable towns in western Europe shows.[69] What the state did not do was provide the necessary economic basis for the growth of prosperous towns. The merchants could be favored at the expense of the burghers and the peasants, but state peasants would

[67] *Ibid.,* pp. 120–131.

[68] *Ministerstvo finansov,* I, 78–79; N. M. Druzhinin, *Gosudarstvennye krest'iane i reforma P. D. Kiseleva,* I (Moscow and Leningrad, 1946), 82; *PSZ* I, statute 29846; Seredonin, *Istoricheskii obzor,* I, 316.

[69] For an eloquent appeal for equality of opportunity by Mordvinov see *Arkhiv grafov Mordvinovykh,* ed. V. A. Bilbasov, IV (St. Petersburg, 1902), 189.

not come to the cities unless they had a chance of making a better living there than on the land.

While the revisions of the guild statutes were being considered and put into effect, the state came to take an interest in general urban growth for a reason that had no direct connection with taxation or the status of the merchant class. Between 1822 and 1825, the price of grain fell sharply, and it was argued that a larger urban population would increase the domestic demand for grain. The most seriously concerned were those members of the gentry whose income came from the sale of grain produced on their estates.[70] The state's interest was not easy to determine. As a substantial purchaser of food for the army, it benefited from low prices. Low prices also helped the large number of peasants who had to buy grain to meet their needs, making it easier for them to pay their taxes, but peasants who sold grain to meet their tax and *obrok* obligations suffered and were more likely to fall into arrears. In periods of severe crop failures, revenues always fell drastically because the population simply could not meet its obligations. The ideal combination of good crops and high prices depended on two factors beyond the state's control, weather and foreign demand. In the early 1820's, it was foreign demand that failed.

In January 1825, a special committee was established, "On the Finding of Ways to Improve the Conditions in the Cities." In a memorandum addressed to the committee, Kankrin emphasized his belief that the best way to increase the general welfare of the nation was to stimulate the growth of the town population so that internal demand would equal agricultural output and thereby decrease the nation's dependence on the export market for grain. Every district (*uezd*) should have a significant city, and several trading centers as well, to provide for profitable exchange between the city and the country. The measures suggested to achieve this

[70] For gentry complaints about low prices see Repczuk, "Mordvinov," pp. 181–182, citing *Severnaia Pchela*, Feb. 16, 1826, p. 4; March 1, 1827, p. 4; and Dec. 18, 1828, p. 4.

goal included: concentrating taverns and craft activity in the towns, inducing the gentry to live in towns, separating town activities from rural ones; and improving regulations on the billeting of troops, which frequently resulted in virtual confiscation of private homes. Tax privileges were proposed for persons building new houses, and certain local taxes and the expenses of towns should be reduced. Finally, fire protection and insurance could be improved and direct loans and other special privileges could be granted to towns. The loans and privileges, Kankrin added, with his eye on costs, must be granted with great circumspection.[71]

In 1826, Alexander Fomin, an official of the Ministry of Finance, won a prize offered by the Academy of Sciences for an essay on the cause of the fall in grain prices. He attributed the decline to the conclusion of peace in Europe and improved harvests there, the disruption of the Black Sea trade caused by the Greek uprising, and the protectionist policies of other countries. To increase domestic demand he favored the movement of the population from the country to the cities, the development of technical education to aid industry, and, with considerable realism, the increased consumption of vodka.[72]

Despite all the talk, there was no real force behind the idea of encouraging overall urban growth. Fomin's essay was published, but rapidly forgotten. The committee "on the improvement of conditions in the cities" soon got bogged down in an attempt to compile statistical data. It despatched requests for information to the provinces, but received few answers. While it waited, nobody really cared that no action was being taken. By 1828, the committee was inactive, and it was formally abolished in 1830.[73] The price of grain went

71 TsGIAL, f. 560, op. 10, d. 220, "O sostavlenii osobogo komiteta dlia uluchsheniia gorodov," pp. 2–5, 147–153.

72 Aleksandr Fomin, *O ponizhenii tsen na zemledel'cheskiia proizvedeniia v Rossii* (St. Petersburg, 1829), pp. vii–xi, 7–28.

73 TsGIAL, f. 560, op. 10, d. 220, "O sostavlenii osobogo komiteta dlia uluchsheniia gorodov," p. 147; Russia, Ministerstvo vnutrennykh del, *MVD, Istoricheskii ocherk* (St. Petersburg, 1901), I, 72. The law

its own independent way, staying low throughout the twenties
and rising, with marked fluctuations, in later years.

The guild-tax statute of 1824, although it had been formally enacted, had little more success than the committee on
the cities. It proved impossible to tax and regulate petty
trade. The peasants persisted in selling their cabbages and
handicrafts wherever and whenever they could find a buyer
and saw no reason to get a permit to do it. In a series of
changes in 1825, 1826, and 1827, most of the taxes and restrictions on the burghers and peasants were removed.[74] After
this experience Kankrin had little faith in the ability of the
bureaucracy to carry out any but the simplest tasks, and his
entire policy in the years that followed was formed with this
severe limitation in mind.

In the mid and later twenties, attention shifted from the
ambitious attempt to tax more of the urban population to a
modest effort to give increased prestige and security to the
most prosperous segment of it. Instead of squeezing the lower
groups to help the upper, Kankrin now favored giving special advantages to the top stratum and ignoring the lower.
The implicit assumption was that the total wealth of the
community could not be increased, only redistributed. The
educational program contradicts this assumption, but it was
regarded as too long-range a matter to be of immediate significance. Kankrin suggested in 1826 that the wealthier merchants be transformed into a new category called "hereditary
citizens." Cities, he argued, "cannot flourish without that
solidity of status, which, although we have tried to introduce
it, actually does not exist." Membership in the merchant class
as it then existed, continued Kankrin, was conditional on
financial success. In the case of misfortune, any member of
the class would automatically fall back into the burgher class

---

of December 22, 1832, on the movement of state peasants to the towns
closely followed some of the committee's recommendations. See below,
Chapter III, pp. 101–102; Pavel Grigor'evich Ryndziunskii, *Gorodskoe
grazhdanstvo doreformennoi Rossii* (Moscow, 1958), pp. 176–177.

[74] Ministerstvo finansov, *Istoricheskii ocherk oblozheniia*, pp. 132–138.

and become subject to the soul tax, military service, corporal punishment, and be generally held in contempt. Guild merchants therefore strove to enter government service or, at least, to enable their children to do so in order to achieve permanent gentry status. The developing commercial bourgeoisie thus constantly lost its most energetic and capable members.[75]

Opposition to this new proposal of Kankrin's was not based on the argument that it would injure the burgher or trading peasant. On the contrary it was seen by some to be an overly democratic step. The State Council approved the project in July 1826, but at the urging of Prince Kurakin, president of the council's Department of the Economy, the plan was dropped, at least until after the coronation of Nicholas I. Kurakin cited the recent Decembrist uprising as evidence that dangerous ideas were circulating and continued:

It is better to postpone the publication of such a law which contains such a valuable privilege as freedom from military service and corporal punishment, and which, bringing the lower class of people closer to the upper, in itself gives birth, first to the wish and then to the determined intention in the former, to use all possible means to be equal to the latter, without regard for the consequences. France, above all, can serve as an example.[76]

Despite the opposition of Prince Kurakin, Kankrin continued to press for the creation of some kind of an élite status for the most successful merchants. He saw it as a simple way of raising some additional revenue and of strengthening a useful social group. In 1829, when he was particularly pressed for money, he proposed that anybody, even state peasants or burghers, be permitted to purchase permanent exemption from the head tax, army service, and corporal punishment for a stated sum of money. Socially this was a far more radical proposal than the one that Kurakin had attacked in 1826.

[75] *AGS*, V, pt. 1, 189–192; TsGIAL, f. 1152, T. I, d. 44, 1828, "Ob ustroistve gos. promyshlennosti . . . ," pp. 56–58.

[76] *AGS*, V, pt. 1, 194–195; Ryndziunskii, *Gorodskoe grazhdanstvo*, pp. 169–170.

It was considered by a secret committee and rejected on the grounds that the result would be to impoverish large numbers of burgher and peasant families who would sacrifice too much of their capital to gain the coveted privileges.[77]

When the new class of what had come to be called "honored citizens" was finally created by a manifesto of April 10, 1832, it was little more than a token of what had been discussed in the late twenties. Membership was limited to merchants with the rank of commercial or manufacturing councillor and those with ten years of continuous membership in the first guild or twenty years in the second. Scholars and artists certified by a university or the Academy of Art, and children of the nonhereditary nobility were also eligible. The right of exemption from military service, corporal punishment, and the head tax was hereditary and independent of commercial privileges associated with guild membership.[78] It did not replace the traditional merchant guilds, but was a small élite group added on top of them. The new type of citizenship had little impact on Russian society. In 1840, there were only 4,800 "honored citizens," 0.1 per cent of the estimated total town population. This was an insignificant number compared to the 219,400 merchants (4.5 per cent), 2,284,200 burghers (46.8 per cent), and 2,078,900 peasants (42.5 per cent).[79] In 1853, a commission reported that the class of honored citizen had introduced "a weak, but nevertheless constant element" into urban life, and the commission hoped that with the spread of education in the empire that it would be able to strengthen itself, "and in the end, form the basis for the formation of a middle class in the full meaning of that word, a status that not only in name, but in action and in its influence could be called middle, between the

[77] TsGIAL, f. 560, op. 38, d. 116, 1829, "Vsepoddanneishaia dokladnaia zapiska Ministra finansov," p. 607; Russia, Komitet uchrezhdennago vysochaishim reskriptom 6 dekabria 1826 goda, "Zhurnaly Komiteta 6 Dekabria 1826 goda," *Sbornik IRIO,* LXXIV (1891), 397–400.

[78] *PSZ* II, statute 5284.

[79] Adol'f Grigorevich Rashin, *Naselenie Rossii za 100 let (1811–1913 gg.)* (Moscow, 1956), p. 119.

higher gentry and the lower burgher and rural resident." [80]

The significance of the "honored citizens" project lies not in the practical consequences of the legislation but in the fact that in the middle and late 1820's it was the only matter affecting urban development that received serious attention. As yet there was no anxiety about the growth of the lower classes in the towns, but after the minor measures affecting state peasants and burghers taken in 1824, no further moves were made to encourage the increase of the lower strata of the town population. Instead, the state looked at the top and tried to create a commercial bourgeoisie in the image of western Europe, wealthy, secure, and reliable. The state sought to reach this goal by improving the legal and social position of the merchant, but did not provide any concrete assistance—loans, tax exemptions, or the like—that could have helped to develop the economic basis needed if "honored citizens" were to flourish. None of the recommendations Kankrin made to the committee on the improvement of the cities were acted on, except his warning to be circumspect in granting loans and tax privileges. Even the creation of the class of "honored citizens" was a prolonged and difficult task that raised suspicions among gentrymen and became entangled with the immediate fiscal needs of the state.

Never in the discussion of the various issues of the period did the state's attitude toward the towns become clearly defined. One reason for interest in urban growth was that grain prices had suddenly fallen and increased urban demand might raise them. That was clearly a long-range project and of much greater interest to a segment of the gentry than to the state itself and nothing was actually done. The other focus of attention was the "middle class," which, it turned out, was to be developed by protecting the prosperous merchant from the lower classes and by concentrating a larger share of the available wealth in a few hands rather than spreading it out among a large number of people. It was a pessimistic approach to the problem and contrasted sharply

[80] *Ministerstvo finansov,* I, 273–276.

with the positive approach of the educational program underway at the same time. Kankrin had found it to be administratively impossible to collect taxes from the small-scale traders, and he saw no hope of increasing the total wealth of the urban community in the immediate future. The only alternative left was to favor the group that was most useful to the state, the prosperous merchant, at the expense of the rest.

REALITY AND THE PEASANTRY

A prosperous middle class in towns was a dream, and however much statesmen of the day may have wished they had one in Russia, they knew perfectly well that it was not going to materialize very quickly. The peasantry, however, was there and everybody knew it. Peasant agriculture produced most of the country's wealth, and some economists, like Nicholas' tutor, Academician Heinrich Storch, felt that Russia should specialize in agriculture and concentrate on improving it. Others, notably Mordvinov, believed that substantial industrial development was required if agriculture was to become truly prosperous. The state itself was directly concerned with the peasant economy because every crop failure brought it to the brink of bankruptcy.

Agriculture and the peasantry were not, and could not be, viewed primarily in economic terms. By the early nineteenth century, the existence of serfdom was recognized as the most serious problem confronting Russian society. For some it was a question of right and wrong. More and more educated Russians were coming to feel that the system was morally indefensible. It was also a social question of the broadest significance. Any change in the status of the serfs meant a change in the position of the gentry, and the gentry were the most influential group in Russian society, the group which had been created by and helped so much to create the Muscovite state and which had come to dominate the state in the eighteenth century. There were also strictly economic aspects of the serf system, and they too were discussed, especially in the first quarter of the nineteenth century. Some questioned the profitability of serf labor as compared to free labor or, more frequently, the comparative virtues of the *obrok* and *barshchina* systems.[81] Changing the system of private serf ownership meant a radical change in the basic political and administrative system of the state, because the landlords dispensed justice and collected taxes for the state. It is hardly surprising that rulers approached the question of emancipation with trepidation, although apparently both Alexander I and Nicholas I were convinced that the step eventually would be necessary. Nor is it surprising that the alleged economic advantages of a free-mobile labor force were not sufficient to produce prompt action.

All these considerations applied to the privately owned serfs. They were applicable to a much lesser degree, or not at all, to the state peasants, who comprised almost half the total rural population. These people did not live on private estates, but on land administered by the Department of State Domains of the Ministry of Finance. Of varied origin and with an uncertain legal position, they were in practice permanent tenants on state land who paid a rent (*obrok*) as well as the regular head tax. Both the tax and the rent were levied on a per capita basis and then reapportioned by the peasant commune, which was responsible for the payment of the total tax for the group. Although the land legally belonged to the state, the peasants regarded it as virtually their own and frequently bought, sold, or bequeathed it as if it were private property.[82]

Until the late eighteenth century, the state lands and the peasants on them were treated as capital that could be expended by the state to reward its servitors. The whole *pomestie* system of Muscovite Russia was based on the practice of

---

[81] Blum, *Lord and Peasant*, pp. 563, 571–574.

[82] For a general description of the state-peasants' status see Olga Crisp, "The State Peasants under Nicholas I," *Slavonic and East European Review*, XXXVII (1959), 387–412.

giving away land and assuring the new owner that labor would be available to exploit it. During the reign of Catherine the Great, vast areas of land with large populations had been bestowed on the ruler's favorites. In the early nineteenth century, although the alienation of state land did not entirely cease, the prevailing view changed. When the general attitude toward private serfdom became more critical, the state peasantry came to be regarded as a group that could serve as an example and testing ground for policies that might subsequently be applied to the privately owned serfs. The state could deal more freely with its own peasants than with those belonging to private individuals.

Some members of the gentry, including Admiral Mordvinov, favored the continued transfer of state peasants to private ownership, which, it was argued, would benefit both the peasant and the economy in general because of the superior administrative ability of the lord and his greater knowledge of local problems.[83] Even Speransky had supported this position in his financial plan of 1810, although he was concerned primarily with the possibility of raising large sums of money through the sale of state lands. The practical difficulties of selling, as opposed to giving away, land were great, and after 1816 the state abandoned the attempt.[84] In 1816, Alexander established a system of military agricultural colonies on a large scale. These settlements of state peasants were a curious mixture of barracks, concentration camp, and utopian community. The continued development of the project would have had major implications for the state peasantry but it proved to be a costly and unpopular failure. Under Nicholas the colonies continued to exist, but as a part of the military establishment they played no positive role in agricultural or general economic policy.[85]

[83] See Druzhinin, *Gosudarstvennye krest'iane*, I, 125–130, and Repczuk, "Mordvinov," pp. 215–216, for detailed references on this topic.

[84] Druzhinin, *Gosudarstvennye krest'iane*, I, 148–153.

[85] For a discussion and additional references see Richard Pipes, "The Russian Military Colonies, 1810–1831," *Journal of Modern History*,

In 1818, Alexander I requested Count Gurev to prepare proposals for the emancipation of privately owned serfs and for reform in the administration of the state peasantry. The first part of the project was soon abandoned, but in 1823, Alexander requested that Gurev complete his plans for the state peasants. The work was finished in July 1824, and the newly appointed minister of finance, Kankrin, was faced with proposals for major changes in his own ministry prepared by his predecessor. The Gurev plan called for a new administrative system and new civil, criminal, and economic statutes for the state peasants. The aim was to establish a firm legal basis for the state peasants in a "free taxed condition," just as the gentry had received a written guarantee of its rights during the reign of Catherine II. Tenure was to be hereditary and based on individual holdings not subject to periodic redivision.

On the administrative level Gurev's proposals envisaged greater responsibility for officials of the central government at the expense of the local gentry and the peasant's own village organizations. The basic economic reform suggested by Gurev was the institution of a rent based on land values rather than a per capita levy. The plan called for extensive surveys and measures to raise the level of agricultural technique and encourage trade and crafts.[86] It was a program designed to promote the independence of the peasant family from its fellows and to stimulate improvement of individual holdings. At the same time, bureaucratic supervision by the state was to be increased and applied at a lower level.

Kankrin vigorously opposed Gurev's proposals:

The sudden and universal introduction without any trial of a completely new system not only in administration, but in the actual civil life of the state peasant, as proposed in this project,

---

XXII (1950), 205–219; and Alan D. Ferguson, "The Russian Military Settlements, 1825–1866," *Essays in Russian History: A Collection Dedicated to George Vernadsky,* ed. Alan D. Ferguson and Alfred Levin (Hamden, Conn., 1964).

[86] Druzhinin, *Gosudarstvennye krest'iane,* I, 156–161.

presents insurmountable obstacles, by tying up the revision of tax rolls and essential changes in the present tax system, and it even shocks the general established order.[87]

When Alexander died in December 1825, no final decision had been made, but the Finance Minister's position was clear and for nearly a decade Nicholas was to support him.

To block Gurev's plan, Kankrin proposed to introduce changes on an experimental basis in a few provinces. The specific changes to be made in the rural economy were vaguely defined. Kankrin's main suggestion was to put the state peasants under the direct control of a new section of the Ministry of Finance, thus removing them from the jurisdiction of the existing local authorities. The State Council's Department of the National Economy rejected the idea in January 1826, but Kankrin was able to persuade Nicholas to permit a trial in Pskov and St. Petersburg provinces. The experimental program became law in July 1826, although the State Council agreed to it only because Nicholas had already approved the plan.[88] The change was unpopular with the gentry because it increased direct government control of the state lands and reduced their influence in local affairs. The practical results were negligible, for the system was found to be expensive and unwieldy. Within two years a special commission was designated to investigate charges of corruption in the new administration.[89]

The failure of the new administrative system for the state peasants in Pskov and St. Petersburg provinces came immedi-

[87] Quoted in *ibid.*, p. 166.

[88] *PSZ* II, statute 423; Druzhinin, *Gosudarstvennye krest'iane*, I, 166–169; A. P. Zablotskii-Desiatovskii, *Graf P. D. Kiselev i ego vremia* (St. Petersburg, 1882), II, 33–35; and *Ministerstvo finansov*, I, 353–354. Druzhinin's suggestion that the program of L. A. Perovskii for the appanage peasants was the model or the source of stimulation for Kankrin's plan seems unlikely, since Perovskii did not join the appanage department until late in 1826. See Russia, Glavnoe upravlenie udelov, *Istoriia udelov za stoletie ikh sushchestvovaniia, 1797–1897* (St. Petersburg, 1902), I, 66.

[89] Druzhinin, *Gosudarstvennye krest'iane*, I, 170.

ately after the breakdown of the guild law of 1824. Both programs were attempts to accomplish something through administrative action requiring more extensive and direct contact with the population. The new guild law had called for the collection of taxes from thousands of peasants; the experimental program for the state peasants required bureaucrats to do things that had previously been left to the peasants themselves. Both attempts failed and Kankrin never again tried anything that increased the administrative burden on the state. The desire to reduce this burden became a governing principle of his administration and the principal focus of controversy between him and statesmen, like Kiselev, who were more optimistic about the ability of the bureaucracy to get things done.

The two principal methods of improving the lot of the state peasants that were suggested in the 1820's were accurate land surveys and the resettlement of those living in overpopulated areas. Surveying would permit the introduction of taxes and rents based on land values, the demarcation of individual holdings, and the prevention of encroachments on peasant land by the gentry. Kankrin was not opposed to either of these measures in principle. Early in 1824, he had pointed out in the Committee of Ministers that in some provinces the state peasants had no more than two or three, or even as little as one, desiatin per soul and under such circumstances they could hardly feed themselves, much less pay their taxes. To remedy the situation he favored the allotment of state land to the needy peasants, whenever possible within their province.[90] Also in 1824, of course, movement to the cities had been made somewhat easier through the elimination of double taxation.[91]

Land surveys, however, were more important than resettlement for the state peasants as a whole. Kankrin admitted in

[90] Seredonin, *Istoricheskii obzor*, I, 386–387; *Ministerstvo finansov*, I, 158–159.

[91] See above, p. 60.

1826 that the latter was a good idea, but too difficult and costly to put into practice.

It would be desirable to convert the soul tax and especially the rent of state peasants into a land tax, but for this it is necessary to have a *cadastre* (the surveying and evaluation of land by field) or, at least, villages must be divided by survey with a general evaluation of the quality of the land for the determination of its grade, permitting the internal distribution of taxes by the inhabitants themselves. But either one is very difficult.

Even France, he continued, had had to abandon the system because of its complexity.[92]

In practice, the Ministry of Finance blocked all proposals for resettlement, surveying, indeed any significant changes in the condition of the state peasantry. From the ministry's point of view, the peasants were a major source of revenue, and it was too risky to tamper with anything that provided substantial receipts. The only change carried out in the 1820's was a measure designed solely to increase state revenue. The rent paid per peasant varied from province to province according to which one of four categories the province belonged. The peasants in the more prosperous provinces paid a higher rent. In December 1823, revisions in the classification of provinces were made which called for the addition of three provinces to the first class (the most heavily taxed), seven to the second class, and five to the third. Most provinces moved up one class but a few jumped two classes, causing a really substantial increase in the rent. Kankrin maintained that new settlements and improvements in the techniques of cultivation had made the twenty-six-year-old system of classification obsolete, but the temptation to use the reclassification as nothing more than a method of raising the rent must have been very great.[93]

The case of the appanage (*udel'*) peasants was quite dif-

[92] *Ministerstvo finansov*, I, 284; the parentheses are in the original.
[93] *AGS*, IV, pt. 1, 1767–1769; *Ministerstvo finansov*, I, 81–82.

ferent. They lived on estates assigned to the support of the imperial family and they were not under the jurisdiction of the Ministry of Finance. Although there were less than 600,000 of these peasants, they played an important role in determining future policy for the far larger population of state peasants.[94] It was easier to institute changes for a smaller group, and if they were not successful the consequences were less serious. The Minister of Finance, struggling to make ends meet, felt he could not take any risks that might produce even a temporary fall in income. The imperial household, although just as interested in increased revenues, was less hard-pressed financially than the state as a whole and knew that other resources could be made available if its own estate revenues failed. Under the leadership of the energetic L. A. Pervoskii, vice-president of the Department of Appanages of the Ministry of the Imperial Court, a series of measures was begun in the late 1820's designed to increase revenue from appanage lands and to benefit the peasantry as well.

Perovskii was one of four illegitimate sons of the prominent and wealthy Courtier A. K. Razumovskii. His grandfather was Kiril Razumovskii, who had risen from poverty and total obscurity, in the reign of Elizabeth, to be the last hetman of the Ukraine and the president of the Academy of Sciences. The surname Perovskii was derived from the name of a family estate, and the boys were given gentry status during the reign of Alexander I. They received a first-class education at home, and L. A. Perovskii studied at the University of Moscow, graduating in 1811. He entered military service, worked in the Foreign Ministry, and had some brief connection with the Decembrist movement, for which he was not prosecuted. It was a typical career for a man of his social station.

Perovskii's first proposal, made in 1826, was to set aside certain fields in each appanage village to be cultivated in

<hr>

[94] Glavnoe upravlenie udelov, *Istoriia udelov,* I, graph opp. p. 664. For an excellent general discussion of the various groups of nonseigniorial peasants, see Blum, *Lord and Peasant,* ch. 23.

common by the peasants. The harvest from these fields would provide a grain reserve for use in case of future crop failure. The successful operation of such a system would have been of obvious benefit to the peasants in time of need and would also have reduced the pressure on the state in periods of famine. The program enjoyed only limited success because of the peasant's tendency to neglect the cultivation of fields from which he drew no immediate benefit.[95] In 1829, Perovskii began a sweeping change in the system of taxing the appanage peasants, designed to shift the basis of taxation from a per capita basis to a rent based on the productivity of the land. According to Perovskii, this would show the peasant that the land was not his personal property but belonged to the imperial household and was simply rented by them. Secondly, it would increase revenues, since the current level of payments was set as the minimum and additional rent was to be demanded from those peasants with more or better-quality land.[96] The reform did relate the tax burden to the ability to pay, since only the more favored peasants were expected to pay more, but it was primarily a fiscal measure and, in fact, produced very significant additional revenues. It was fiscal success that made the Perovskii program such an influential example, and Nicholas became more and more insistent in the early 1830's that a similar program be carried out for the state peasants.[97] Additional administrative effort produced increased revenues from the appanage peasants and thus undermined Kankrin's basic argument that changing the condition of the state peasants was too expensive and risky. The analogy was a dubious one, for there were only 600,000 appanage peasants and millions of state peasants. The increase in scale would inevitably tend to reduce the effectiveness of an operation controlled by a single central agency.

[95] Glavnoe upravlenie udelov, *Istoriia udelov,* II, 143–146.
[96] *Ibid.,* I, 76–79, II, 98–100. For details of assessment method, see Blum, *Lord and Peasant,* pp. 496–497.
[97] Glavnoe upravlenie udelov, *Istoriia udelov,* I, 79–84.

Two important people learned opposite lessons from the experience with peasant problems in the 1820's. Kankrin, after his unsuccessful attempt to tax the trading peasant and the failure of the administrative changes in Pskov and St. Petersburg provinces, virtually abandoned hope of change through positive state action. Nicholas I, with the example of the Perovskii program before him, was to become increasingly impatient with his trusted minister of finance.

VODKA AND THE FAILURE
OF STATE ADMINISTRATION

The most decisive evidence of Kankrin's despair over the inability of the Russian bureaucracy to get anything done came with the abolition of the state monopoly on the manufacture and sale of spirits in 1827. The revenue derived from alcohol, in one way or another, normally produced nearly as much and in some years more, than direct taxation (see Table 4). The alcohol monopoly was certainly not an area where a cautious man would act unless he was firmly convinced of the urgency of the problem at hand. Furthermore, there was more outspoken opposition to the return to the farming-out system than to anything else that Kankrin ever proposed.

In 1819, the system of farming out the right to make and sell vodka to the highest bidders had been abolished, and the business was made a government monopoly administered by state officials. The purchasers of the vodka-selling privilege for a given area, the *otkupshchiki*, had become so powerful and influential that the government did not even know how much alcohol was being sold. At first the abolition of the farming-out system brought the desired result and revenues rose sharply, but this was in large part due to a temporary spurt of sales in anticipation of increased prices. The

Table 4. Major sources of state revenue, 1820–1856
(in thousands of assignat rubles)

Year	Direct taxes and rents	Alcohol revenues	Customs revenues	Total ordinary revenues
1820	132,321	157,281	52,483	447,048
1821	119,117	151,720	49,733	409,739
1822	125,083	138,578	40,776	391,084
1823	133,887	131,205	41,214	398,565
1824	118,042	120,984	50,226	379,940
1825	120,758	117,413	54,353	397,003
1826	117,591	116,601	56,968	390,244
1827	126,095	105,135	62,915	393,031
1828	119,280	106,672	62,852	384,220
1829	123,513	112,129	66,614	403,753
1830	115,930	108,629	66,411	393,216
1831	118,005	115,329	68,403	406,519
1832	141,995	118,155	81,515	450,661
1833	120,990	116,851	81,759	428,717
1834	115,172	122,058	80,653	430,465
1835	156,775	131,281	78,307	495,127
1836	159,451	138,664	81,684	519,563
1837	161,942	139,644	89,514	526,630
1838	163,487	146,718	87,280	542,825
1839	162,262	152,885	89,181	557,776
1840*	145,674	152,929	92,309	544,159
1841*	149,369	164,052	92,974	561,991
1842*	156,509	173,575	104,219	606,077
1843*	161,777	190,901	103,257	627,333
1844*	163,506	200,718	111,611	651,595
1845*	155,092	205,954	106,519	647,181
1846*	158,102	219,985	106,158	672,388
1847*	162,505	224,672	101,941	686,322
1848*	152,775	225,190	103,558	682,563
1849*	159,019	223,167	104,783	693,143
1850*	158,907	221,735	105,311	706,111
1851*	157,444	261,898	107,394	742,434
1852*	168,154	277,095	112,217	775,558
1853*	166,355	287,203	97,905	768,302
1854*	161,175	269,762	70,822	743,806
1855*	151,308	277,326	62,699	730,901
1856*	163,110	309,291	104,538	811,072

* Data given in silver rubles in the source; here converted to assignats at
3.5 to 1.
Source: Russia, Ministerstvo finansov, *Ministerstvo finansov, 1802–1902* (St.
Petersburg, 1902), I, 618–619, 624–627, 632–633.

actual volume of alcohol sold and the total revenues received declined rapidly from the high point reached in 1819.[98]

The old system of farming out had been abandoned because of corruption, but the new system of state administration was almost immediately subjected to the same charge. State officials were reputed to have special cellars in which to store stolen vodka.[99] In each province the vice-governor was in charge of the alcohol monopoly and the post became notoriously profitable. In discussing the state administration, Kankrin cited the popular anecdote about the man who asked, "Why has the provincial governor come to St. Petersburg?" and received the answer, "To request a vice-governorship for himself." [100]

Kankrin first proposed changes in the system of state administration of the alcohol monopoly in February 1825 and a year later, in May 1826, specifically recommended the reinstitution of the farming-out system used until 1819:

Although under state administration treasury receipts increased, despite the decline in the sale of spirits, and were above the last years of the farming-out system by several million rubles a year, the state administration has exhibited the important fault that all corruption in this area was attributed directly to the government, the bureaucrats were corrupted, and the public blamed the difficult times and the cheapness of grain on the abolition of the farming-out system. Although the latter was not the exclusive reason for the fall of private income, the amount of grain used for spirits in 1826 compared to 1819 was at least one million chetverts less, and thus contributed to the fall in the price of grain. If drunkenness has declined since that time, it has resulted largely from changes in morals; but one must wish that the moderate use of spirits among the simple people should increase, for after the extreme contraction of the overseas grain trade in a

---

[98] Gosudarstvennaia kantseliariia, *Svedeniia o piteinykh sborakh v Rossii* (St. Petersburg, 1860), I, 81–82; *Ministerstvo finansov*, I, 298.

[99] Gosudarstvennaia kantseliariia, *Svedeniia*, I, 82.

[100] *Rtb.*, I, Supp. II, 68.

country where agriculture is the main activity and cities are few, grain can only find use by transformation into spirits.[101]

It was the elimination of corruption on the part of state officials and stimulation of the market for grain that Kankrin stressed as the main reasons for abandoning the state administration of vodka sales. The statement was prepared at the height of the discussion of low grain prices and that aspect of it can probably be discounted. The hope of obtaining increased revenues was, along with the problem of administration, the compelling reason for change. Kankrin admitted this ten years later in his lectures on finance prepared for the Crown Prince.[102] The cause of temperance was clearly not one that interested the Ministry of Finance. Few contemporary observers would have agreed that the "moderate" increase in the use of spirits by the simple people was to be desired. A few years later, Kiselev found that drunkenness was one of the most serious obstacles to improvement of peasant agriculture.

To replace the state monopoly there were two alternatives, an excise tax or a return to the farming-out system. The excise tax was rejected on the grounds that it would not produce sufficient revenue and would create as great an administrative burden as the state monopoly. The farming-out system was not an attractive alternative and even Kankrin had to admit it, but he gamely asserted that the profits of the men who bought the monopoly rights (*otkupshchiki*) were moderate and that the capital was put to good use.[103] Those who

[101] Gosudarstvennaia kantseliariia, *Svedeniia*, I, 84–85.

[102] [E. F. Kankrin], "Kratkoe obozrenie rossiiskikh finansov, grafa E. F. Kankrina. 1838 god," *Sbornik IRIO*, XXXI (1881), 29.

[103] Gosudarstvennaia kantseliariia, *Svedeniia*, I, 85–87; TsGIAL, f. 560, op. 38, d. 117, "Zapiska neustanovlennogo avtora . . . ," pp. 21–22 (The reference is to Kankrin's comments on the unknown author's memorandum); and "O raznykh sposobakh dlia vzimaniia piteinogo dokhoda," *Sbornik svedenii i materialov po vedomstvu Ministerstva finansov*, I (1866), 66–67.

opposed the change actually had little of a practical nature to suggest. Mordvinov was for free enterprise in everything including distilling. If free distilling were to be introduced, he said, the price of vodka would fall so low that the populace would scorn the beverage, the business would become unprofitable, and capital would be diverted into more productive enterprises. Such nonsense is Mordvinov at his worst, and for once it is easy to understand Kankrin's immediate rejection of the plan.[104] After all, there were bills to pay, next week, and next year. He could not wait until the peasants got tired of drinking vodka, if they ever would.

The results of the changed system did not come up to expectations. Increased revenues did not materialize until the third round of four-year contracts were let in the mid-thirties, and it is most doubtful if the *otkupshchiki* were any more virtuous than they had been prior to 1819. The number of state officials involved in the liquor business was greatly reduced, and at least to that extent the number of persons exposed to severe temptation was smaller than before. The reestablishment of the farming-out system in 1827, however, has an importance that exceeds the immediate fiscal and moral aspects. It was the first major action that reflected Kankrin's growing discouragement and his conviction that the state could do little more than maintain itself. After 1827, only the technological institute and one or two other educational projects continued to hold his interest for a few more years. Every other forward-looking step taken by the state in economic policy was to be made over Kankrin's opposition. Even the tobacco tax that was introduced in 1839, the last positive measure Kankrin sponsored, was carefully constructed to minimize the amount of administrative effort involved in collecting it. When a state salt monopoly was pro-

---

104 N. S. Mordvinov, "Zapiska admirala Mordvinova o sredstvakh protiv neumerennogo upotrebleniia v narode vina," *Sbornik svedenii i materialov po vedomstvu Ministerstva finansov*, I (1865), 341–342. Kankrin's comments on Mordvinov's proposals are included.

posed he rejected it on the grounds of the additional effort involved.[105]

In 1829, after six years as minister of finance, Kankrin wrote to Alexander von Humboldt about the problems he faced and concluded simply that "good goes slowly, evil quickly." [106] Whether this statement is to be regarded as a confession of failure or a realistic assessment of the true situation, it is certainly a summation of the resigned, almost despairing attitude that Kankrin had for the remainder of his tenure in office.

[105] "Nastavlenie," p. 119; *Ministerstvo finansov*, I, 305–306; Ilarion I. Kaufman, *Kankrinovskaia sistema tabachnago oblozheniia v Rossii* (St. Petersburg, 1912), pp. 7–10; *Rtb.*, I, Supp. II, 75.

[106] Kankrin, *Im Ural und Altai*, p. 80.

Holding the Line

The 1830's did not start off well for the Russian Empire. The revolutions in France and Belgium that summer were most upsetting for Nicholas I, the ardent defender of legitimacy, but a much more immediate threat was the rebellion that broke out in Poland in November 1830 (new style). Kankrin had opposed Nicholas' plan to send troops to Belgium because of the expense, but there was no disagreement about the necessity of crushing the Polish revolt, whatever the cost. To make matters worse, there had been serious crop failures and cholera epidemics in 1830 that greatly reduced normal revenue collections, and the Moslem tribesmen of the Caucasus began a major uprising that was to be a constant drain on the treasury throughout the rest of Nicholas' reign.

A new phase in state economic policy begins in the 1830's, and it would be convenient to attribute it to the dramatic events, the financial pressures of 1830–1831, and Nicholas' "determination to fight the spirit of revolution and to come to the aid of monarchic principles." [1] To do so, however,

---

[1] The phrase is Polievktov's description of Nicholas' reaction to the events of 1830 (see M. Polievktov, *Nikolai I* [Moscow, 1918], p. 113). For other comments supporting this view see Theodor Schiemann, *Geschichte Russlands unter Kaiser Nikolaus I*, III (Berlin, 1913), 223; N. K. Schilder, *Imperator Nikolai Pervyi; ego zhizn' i tsarstvovanie* (St. Petersburg, 1903), II, 396; and Alexander Kornilov, *Modern Russian History*, trans. Alexander S. Kaun (New York, 1943), p. 252.

would be an oversimplification. The change in mood or attitude, and it was that more than one of actual policy, had begun in the late twenties with Kankrin's increasing discouragement about the possibility of effective action by the state bureaucracy. In the early thirties, increased attention was given to agriculture and doubts about the value of urban growth and industrial development began to be expressed, but these were based as much or more on fear of overproduction as on any concern about the social or political consequences of economic change.

THE FIRST FISCAL CRISIS

In the preparation of the state budget for 1831, Kankrin was faced for the first time with a real financial crisis.[2] The wars with Persia (1826–1828) and Turkey (1828–1829) had called for only a modest increase in state debt (see Table 1). The problem late in 1830 was far more grave. Normal revenues had fallen because of famine and epidemic, and the Polish revolt presented a far more serious problem than the wars with Persia or Turkey.

The cardinal principle of Kankrin's approach to financial affairs was to avoid foreign debt when possible, but above all to avoid issuing additional paper currency.[3] In theory he saw little objection to paper money and even recognized that the increased availability of money might lead to added productive investment and greater wealth for a country. The great drawback, however, was that whenever paper money was used there was no natural limit to state expenditures and thousands of deserving projects cropped up at once. Kankrin realized that the important issue was not the substitution of

[2] Ia. I. Pecherin, *Istoricheskii obzor rospisei gosudarstvennykh dokhodov i raskhodov s 1803 po 1843 god vkliuchitel'no* (St. Petersburg, 1896), pp. 133–138.

[3] TsGIAL, f. 560, op. 38, d. 213, "Obshchii otchet . . . za 1826," pp. 1–2; *ibid.*, d. 354, "Obshchii otchet . . . za 1835," p. 5.

intrinsically worthless paper for precious metals, but the control of the total amount of money, of whatever material. The scarcity of gold and silver provided a natural limit on metal currency, while only the "wisdom and restraint of statesmen" could keep the emission of paper within bounds, despite attempts to provide backing and convertibility into metal. In the wisdom of statesmen Kankrin had little faith: "It is just as unwise to advise a state to adopt paper money as to advise a youth to enter a gambling den." [4]

The possible policies actually open to Kankrin, or to anyone else in his unenviable position, were strictly limited. Revenues could not be significantly increased in the short run. They came from the heavily taxed peasant population, and its ability to pay depended on the weather and the price of grain, both factors beyond the control of St. Petersburg officials. Kankrin was severely criticized by Mordvinov for failing to take the proper measures for the long-range improvement of both agriculture and industry, but even Mordvinov would have had to admit that none of his pet projects for education, bank loans, and so forth could meet the immediate needs of a crisis like that of 1830–1831. Indeed Kankrin's usual reply to Mordvinov was, in effect: That's all very well in the long run, but how will it help us now? [5]

[4] [E. F. Kankrin], *Weltreichthum, Nationalreichthum, und Staatswirtschaft, oder Versuch neurer Ansichten der politischen Oekonomie* (Munich, 1821), pp. 58, 62–63. This was written before he became minister of finance, but his views are not essentially different in a work published the year after his resignation. Paper currency is still a "dangerous venture" and certainly should never be used to cover budget deficits ([E. F. Kankrin], *Die Oekonomie der menschlichen Gesellschaften und das Finanzwesen—von einem ehemaligen Finanzminister* [Stuttgart, 1845], pp. 130–133). Distrust of paper money and of private banks of issue was not confined to Kankrin or to Russia (see Theodor S. Hamerow, *Restoration, Revolution, Reaction; Economics and Politics in Germany, 1815–1871* [Princeton, 1958], p. 6).

[5] For example, TsGIAL, f. 560, op. 22, d. 58, "Zapiska admirala N. Mordvinova i ministra finansov E. F. Kankrina . . . ," p. 13.

The most convenient and readily available source of funds beyond the normal revenues was the deposits in the state banks. The banks were state institutions and nobody outside the government need know if the treasury saw fit to borrow from them. Thus the state's credit remained undamaged, and no threat to the value of the paper assignats was likely to develop. In the 1820's, the primary significance of state banking policy had been in the transfer of funds from the Commercial Bank to the Loan Bank and thence to the gentry via very dubious mortgages on their estates, thereby eliminating a possible source of capital for entrepreneurs interested in manufacturing.

In 1829, state borrowing from the Loan Bank jumped sharply, and it grew steadily thereafter both absolutely and as a percentage of total state debt. After 1829, the amount lent to the state always exceeded that lent to the gentry (see Tables 1 and 5). The initial spurt was the result of a war with Turkey, but transfers from the banks rapidly came to be regarded as a part of normal state "revenues." Kankrin wrote in his "Instruction" of 1840: "Loans from the banks for the state, experience shows, can be made to a significant extent every year; by this means the banks and the state are saved from losses from capital lying idle." [6] The state's borrowing from the banks increased neither their capacity to make other loans nor the supply of money, as it would in a more modern system. Aside from the funds on deposit in the state banks and the other credit institutions that lent to the gentry, there was no capital available that could readily be tapped. Kankrin described the dilemma:

Internal loans, that is special ones not from credit institutions, are not possible here, for almost all free capital is in the credit institutions. Outside loans at the same interest as the banks give could not be floated with success, and at higher rates they would result in an abnormal flow of deposits out of the banks; therefore it would be necessary to support the banks from the identical

[6] "Nastavlenie," pp. 22, 40.

Table 5. Outstanding loans of the Loan Bank, 1822–1856
(at the beginning of the year, in millions of silver rubles)

Year	Lent to the state	Lent to the state, % of total	In private mortgages	In private mortgages, % of total	Total
1822	20.72	65	11.26	35	31.98
1823	20.47	62	12.55	38	33.00
1824	19.50	62	11.71	38	31.21
1825	17.96	52	16.82	48	34.78
1826	19.20	42	26.37	58	45.57
1827	20.39	39	31.58	61	51.92
1828	24.00	41	34.26	59	58.26
1829	31.98	48	34.45	52	66.43
1830	43.85	55	35.49	45	79.34
1831	47.84	57	36.58	43	84.42
1832	50.05	58	36.24	42	86.29
1833	54.86	60	35.94	40	90.81
1834	63.11	63	36.76	37	99.88
1835	67.92	64	38.18	36	106.10
1836	76.25	66	39.09	34	115.34
1837	81.29	67	39.82	33	121.11
1838	85.31	67	41.45	33	126.76
1839	95.03	68	44.45	32	139.49
1840	110.09	70	46.88	30	156.97
1841	115.56	70	50.71	30	166.27
1842	115.11	69	52.60	31	167.71
1843	131.90	71	52.71	29	184.62
1844	143.76	74	50.57	26	194.33
1845	151.97	75	50.39	25	202.36
1846	163.68	77	49.79	23	213.48
1847	178.27	78	50.70	22	228.97
1848	190.55	79	50.94	21	241.49
1849	210.55	81	49.44	19	259.99
1850	234.26	83	49.02	17	283.28
1851	252.53	84	47.34	16	299.57
1852	265.44	85	46.63	15	312.07
1853	279.90	86	46.56	14	326.46
1854	299.03	86	48.00	14	347.03
1855	336.77	87	49.31	13	386.08
1856	346.68	88	49.22	12	395.90

Source: I. I. Kaufman, "Statistika russkikh bankov," pt. 1, *Statisticheskii vremennik rossiiskoi imperii,* ser. 2, no. 9 (1872), p. 3.

loans, the treasury would be left without money, and would have only the burden of high interest payments.[7]

The funds available in the state banking system were always far too limited to meet the demands of a crisis like that of 1830–1831. The only noninflationary alternatives were additional internal loans or foreign borrowing. Internal loans, as Kankrin observed, did not tap new sources of credit, but simply competed with existing institutions for funds. Foreign credit was expensive and hard to get in times of crisis, but in the end both means were used.

In an attempt to mobilize domestic credit to the last ruble, a new form of internal loan called the "state treasury note" was devised. The notes bore 4 per cent interest and matured in four years. They were issued by the treasury to pay large bills if the recipient was willing to accept them in lieu of currency. The state guaranteed to accept them back in payment of taxes or other obligations and paid the interest due to the nearest whole month in such cases. They were not, however, obligatory legal tender for private transactions.[8]

In a memorandum sent to the Minister of Finance in May 1831, Count Speransky pointed out that the then newly projected notes had two independent sources of value—their acceptance as money and the 4 per cent interest they bore. He fittingly described the notes as assignats "in the clothing of bonds."[9] Speransky was quite correct, for insofar as the

[7] *Ibid.*, p. 21. The *sokhrannye kazny* and the *prikazy obshchestvennogo prizreniia* were the only other credit institutions of importance, and they devoted their funds to long-term loans on gentry estates. During the Napoleonic Wars, the *sokhrannye kazny* did lend money to the state. Data for later years is lacking, but the sums lent could not have been sufficient to significantly affect the state's financial position (see S. Ia. Borovoi, *Kredit i banki Rossii [seredina XVII v.–1861 g.]* [Moscow, 1958], pp. 119–123, 193–196).

[8] A. P. Kutukov, "Svedeniia o biletakh gosudarstvennago kaznacheistva (seriiakh)," *Ezhegodnik ministerstva finansov,* IV (1873), 152–153; Russia, Ministerstvo finansov, *Ministerstvo finansov, 1802–1902* (St. Petersburg, 1902), I, 228–229.

[9] M. M. Speransky, "Mysli o novykh biletakh kaznacheistva," *Rus-*

notes' guaranteed acceptance by the state and voluntary acceptance by others gave them value they did not differ from
assignats. On the other hand, to the extent that it was the
4 per cent interest that made them worth holding, they were
simply short-term bonds and as such competed with the banks
for the limited amount of investment funds available. They
were therefore of real use to the government only as long as
its creditors were willing to accept them, in lieu of cash, for
goods and services the government needed. While this condition held, they represented a net addition to the stock of
money.

Although Kankrin's reply to Speransky is unavailable,
there is little doubt that he was aware of the danger that the
notes would fall below their face value if they were too freely
issued. He wrote in 1840, after ten years' experience with
them:

State treasury notes [can be used to cover military expenses] in a
moderate amount. It is impossible to designate that quantity, but
it can be asserted that the amount now circulating and designated for reissue has not hurt circulation; but also in this question much depends on time, for gradually, bit by bit, it is possible to issue a larger quantity than suddenly or in a short time.[10]

The only alternative if internal revenue and all forms of
credit were exhausted was to try to borrow abroad. It was
a course that the Minister of Finance was reluctant to take
but which had already been necessary during the Turkish
war of 1828–1829, when 24 million silver rubles were obtained at a very reasonable rate in Amsterdam. In 1831 and
1832, two large loans were floated in Amsterdam, but at
much greater cost. Investors in western Europe were uncertain about the future, and Russian policy in Poland was
unpopular.[11] Aside from the cost and the need to make pay-

---

skaia starina, VIII (1873), 586–587. Modern economists would call them
"near money."

   10 "Nastavlenie," pp. 38–39.

   11 In 1828 and 1829, the Russian government received 95.09 gulden
for each 100 gulden of face value on the bonds and paid 5.26 per cent

ments to foreign creditors, the great disadvantage of foreign borrowing was that it tended to become very expensive or entirely impossible in periods of war or internal crisis, just when the need was greatest. To avoid this problem, Kankrin, in later years, urged that loans be negotiated as soon as the prospect of war developed. He freely admitted that the "limited internal resources" of the nation were not sufficient for extraordinary demands.[12]

Despite the rapid growth of borrowing from the state banking system, and the increasing share of total state debt that this borrowing represented, foreign debt always exceeded internal borrowing until the 1850's and even then amounted to nearly half of total state debt (see Table 1). There was simply not enough capital available in Russia to meet relatively modest demands for emergency funds, even if virtually all the nation's voluntary savings not tied up in long-term loans was made available through the banks. During the Crimean War, neither internal nor external borrowing was to prove sufficient, and the state was forced to issue additional paper money.[13] Russia was able to weather the fiscal crisis of 1830–1831 because the Polish revolt was relatively short-lived, harvests soon returned to normal levels, internal credit was used to the utmost, and the reputation for thrift that Kankrin had assiduously cultivated helped to maintain Russia's credit rating with foreign banking houses. Had the extent of his internal borrowing been known, Russia's reputation could easily have suffered, even though no inflationary danger was involved.

The official determination to pursue a strict hard-money policy determined the state's attitude toward the budget, the use of bank credit, and the allocation of funds between im-

---

interest. In 1831, it received only 79.32 silver rubles for each 100 of face value with 6.30 per cent interest. In 1832, it received 87.02 per 100 and paid 5.74 per cent (*Ministerstvo finansov*, I, 227; N. Brzheskii, *Gosudarstvennye dolgi Rossii* [St. Petersburg, 1884], p. 279).

[12] "Nastavlenie," pp. 17–18, 23, 40.

[13] Walter M. Pintner, "Inflation in Russia during the Crimean War Period," *American Slavic and East European Review*, XVIII (1959), 85.

mediate needs and long-range projects of economic improvement. It also had a major impact on aspects of monetary policy that had no direct relation to the supply of money. The decision made in 1823 to stop the retirement of the assignats relieved pressure on the budget and left the monetary situation essentially unchanged. This action amounted to a *de facto* devaluation of the assignat, although no fixed value in relation to metal was established. At that time Kankrin still hoped that the restoration of the assignat to its full face value would someday be possible. His position was a realistic one, but it left unsolved the problem of how a stable relationship between paper assignats and silver and gold coins was to be established.[14] Prices were generally set in terms of assignats, and from 1812 on, all payments to the state had to be made in assignats. In private transactions, however, both metal money and assignats were used. According to the law, payment had to be accepted in either currency at the current rate of exchange on the St. Petersburg bourse. The result was constant small fluctuations in the value of the two types of money, from day to day and, because of poor communications, from place to place. The range of fluctuation was not great, but the situation produced great confusion and endless opportunities for the clever speculator to dupe the less sophisticated. Kankrin refused to make significant changes in the monetary system because he felt any change might endanger public confidence in the assignat, although the end result of his policy was exactly the opposite of what

[14] For the sake of simplicity the term "metal money" will be used to refer to silver and gold coins. Copper coins also circulated, but were of lesser significance and are not included in the term "metal money," since there were special problems connected with the copper coinage. Gold rubles circulated with a slight premium over silver rubles, but total sums are generally expressed in terms of silver-ruble units. Kankrin experimented with platinum coins, even though Alexander von Humboldt advised against it. They did not gain widespread acceptance and were of no economic significance (E. F. Kankrin, *Im Ural und Altai: Briefwechsel zwischen Alexander von Humboldt und Graf Georg von Kankrin aus den Jahren 1827–1832* [Leipzig, 1869], p. 17).

he hoped it to be. An illusion of great instability was created in what was actually a very stable monetary situation.[15]

ENOUGH FACTORIES ALREADY?

Fiscal affairs in the early thirties were primarily a struggle to find needed funds, and monetary policy, an attempt to maintain the *status quo* for fear of the possible results of change. The policy toward industry in the early 1830's was one of retreat from the very modest but positive program of the 1820's. The reason for the shift is not clear cut, and the change itself was primarily one of attitude and emphasis, since there were relatively few concrete projects that could be directly affected, given the limited scale of the state's activity in fostering industry in the 1820's.

Outwardly, in fact, the state's position hardly altered. The National Industrial Exhibition of 1829 was followed by others in 1831, 1833, 1836, and 1839, alternating between St. Petersburg and Moscow. In 1833, the Academy of Sciences published a book by an official of the Ministry of Finance that summarized in glowing terms the progress of industry in Russia up to 1832, using language and statistical sleight of hand similar to that used one hundred years later by propagandists for the Soviet five-year plans.[16] The publication of the various technical journals continued. In 1835, exemptions from local taxes were offered to the few manufacturers who already qualified for exemption from the guild tax. These privileges were never of major significance, but their extension proves that the state was not firmly or consistently opposed to industrial enterprise.[17]

[15] A full discussion of monetary policy will be found in Chapter V.

[16] Vikentii Pel'chinskii, *O sostoianii promyshlennykh sil Rossii do 1832 goda* (St. Petersburg, 1833). A slightly earlier example of this type of literature is M. Shchlepnikov, *Mysli o russkoi promyshlennosti* (St. Petersburg, 1830), published by the Department of Manufacturing and Trade of the Ministry of Finance.

[17] *PSZ* II, statutes 1631, 8575.

The only really important new support for industrial development in the early 1830's was the establishment of a substantial tariff wall between Russia and Poland. Prior to 1831,
Polish goods, particularly textiles, had seriously competed
with Russian manufactures, but the position of Congress Poland as a part of the Tsar's realm had prevented the im-
position of higher duties despite the complaints of Russian
manufacturers. The Minister of Finance supported the protection of Russian industry, but he was able to do no more
than block the total abolition of duties on Polish goods. The
revolt of December 1830 changed the situation completely.
On January 2, 1831, all imports from Poland were forbidden.
Kankrin soon reported to the Tsar: "The advantage of the
exclusion of Polish cloth immediately became evident. Especially in Moscow much activity in cloth was noticeable, prices
rose, perhaps even more than corresponded to the interest of
the consumer." [18] In November 1831, a new tariff for trade
with Poland was promulgated, the major provisions of which
were a 15 per cent duty on Polish cloth and the prohibition
of the import of linen and silk from Poland. Even the 15 per
cent duty was sufficient to arouse strong but unsuccessful pro-
test by the Poles. The incentives offered in March 1832 to
Polish manufacturers to move their operations to Russia
probably only added insult to the injury.[19] This change in
policy, though it probably helped some Russian industries,
was obviously the fortuitous result of political events, as was
the "temporary" overall increase of 12.5 per cent in customs
duties introduced in 1830 as an emergency fiscal measure.
Neither of these measures can be considered evidence of increased state interest in industry.

The public posture of the state with respect to industry remained essentially unchanged. Even though, as in the 1820's,
no significant financial aid was provided by the state, industry

[18] *Ministerstvo finansov*, I, 325.
[19] *Ibid.*, p. 326; *Zhurnal manufaktur i torgovli*, no. 3 (1832), pp. 116–
119.

seemed to be regarded officially as a "good thing." A closer look at what was being said within the government and at what the government actually did, however, suggests that the state's attitude was becoming increasingly ambiguous as some of the less attractive aspects of industrial development became known through Russian experience, to some extent, and also through reports of more serious problems abroad.

There was a continuing public discussion in the press about the advantages and disadvantages of industry and agriculture for Russia, both from a strictly economic viewpoint and with respect to the physical and moral well-being of the workers and peasants. Some, like Bulgarin, the prominent exponent of the doctrine of Official Nationality, argued that agriculture was primary, while industry was needed, but secondary. Others, like Mordvinov, took virtually the reverse position.[20] The mere fact that a published discussion was possible under conditions of strict government censorship shows that the state was not committed to any specific policy. The *Journal of Manufacturing and Trade,* an official publication of the Ministry of Finance, published articles on both sides of the question.[21]

Within the government, signs of concern about industrial development began to appear around 1830. Baron Meyendorf, president of the Moscow Council of Manufacturers, reported to the Minister of Finance that industry was developing so rapidly that production was in danger of outstripping demand.[22] A year later Kankrin echoed this fear in commenting on one of Admiral Mordvinov's many memoranda advocating increased attention to industrial development: "In recent years machines have greatly increased here. The gov-

[20] Helma Repczuk, "Nicholas Mordvinov (1754–1845)" (unpublished Ph. D. diss., Columbia University, 1962), pp. 144–145.

[21] For numerous citations and a perceptive discussion of this public debate, see Repczuk, "Mordvinov," pp. 131–145.

[22] M. K. Rozhkova, *Ekonomicheskaia politika tsarskogo pravitel'stva na srednem vostoke vo vtoroi chetverti XIX veka i russkaia burzhuaziia* (Moscow and Leningrad, 1949), p. 230.

ernment promotes this, but a forced and steep increase of factory production is also bad, for production and sales must increase together, and this requires time." [23]

Meyendorf and Kankrin referred to overproduction as at least a potential problem for Russian industry. There is also some evidence that the side effects of successful industrial growth had begun to cause some concern by the mid-thirties. Factories could be dirty and noisy, and they often required the concentration of large numbers of workers in one place. The doubts and second thoughts about industry changed state policy. Interest in technical education waned, some very modest and totally ineffective laws were enacted to regulate the location of factories and the relations of workers and employers, joint-stock companies were put under strict control, and the Ministry of Finance changed its attitude toward the industrial exhibitions.

The Practical Technological Institute in St. Petersburg officially opened its doors in 1831 after more than three years of planning and construction. It was the pet project of the Finance Minister, but this did not protect it from severe financial difficulties. The budget for the purchase of raw materials was inadequate. Kankrin himself vetoed the faculty's request for a small steam engine and ordered them to use a "horse machine" (probably a spinning machine driven by animal power), and he favored the construction of models rather than actual machinery by the students. Later he prevented the faculty from printing their lectures and translations of foreign texts.[24] Taken individually, any of these decisions could, presumably, be argued on pedagogical or technical grounds, but all together they suggest a regime of the strictest economy and the most modest goals for the new institute.

[23] TsGIAL, f. 560, op. 22, d. 58, "Po doneseniiu Mordvinova o rospisi na 1831 god," p. 16.

[24] Russia, Tekhnologicheskii Institut imeni Leningradskogo Soveta rabochikh, krest'ianskikh, i krasnoarmeiskikh deputatov, *Sto let (1828–1928)* (Leningrad, 1928), pp. 26–36.

The institute, which was really what would now be called a secondary trade school, faced severe difficulties in recruiting students with even the barest minimum of preparation. The lower merchant guilds and the burgher classes never provided enough applicants. The state sent boys from orphanages and, with very little success, peasant children from the military colonies. But nothing in the history of the first ten years of the institute suggests that the matter was considered very important or that a real effort was made to do the best possible job with the students who were available.[25] In all, the institute produced 129 graduates between its opening and 1843. They apparently had little difficulty in finding employment, although Count Stroganov complained that even the seven best graduates, hand picked by Kankrin, were not fully qualified "masters." [26]

In the more advanced institutions, the Mining Institute and the Institute of Transport Engineers, there was no significant change in enrollment. Militarization of school life increased in accordance with the Tsar's personal inclination. In the Institute of Transport Engineers, the student body became increasingly aristocratic in origin, and under the authority of Kleinmichael, discipline was tightened to an absurd degree.[27] The entire focus of interest seemed to shift away from the intrinsic importance of technology as a subject for study to one that emphasized discipline, outward order, and military application. There was no real decline in the total effort applied to technical education—the needs of the times were too clear to permit that—but the drive and enthusiasm of the twenties were gone. The existing institutions

[25] TsGIAL, f. 560, op. 38, d. 297, "Otchet Departamenta manufaktur . . . za 1831 god," p. 24; Tekhnologicheskii Institut, *Sto let,* pp. 44–46.

[26] *Ibid.,* pp. 40, 46.

[27] Russia, Institut inzhenerov putei soobshcheniia, *Spisok lits okonchivshikh kurs nauk v Institute inzhenerov putei soobshcheniia Imperatora Aleksandra I, s 1811 po 1822 g.* (St. Petersburg, 1883), pp. 70–76; Russia, Gornyi Institut, *Nauchno-istoricheskii sbornik* (St. Petersburg, 1873), pp. 86–107.

continued to operate, but there was no expansion and no new industrially oriented establishments were created.[28]

In 1836, the Minister of Finance made a proposal that might have had a major impact on Russian education. His suggestion was to expand the curriculum of local classical schools to include technical subjects, or to establish a separate *Realschule,* and to institute a broad program of public lectures on applied science in university cities. For the considerable number of students attending seminaries who did not wish to become priests, Kankrin urged a more practical educational program and legal provision for their social class status after graduation. Graduates of science programs in local schools were to be automatically exempted from corporal punishment and, on payment of five hundred rubles, from military service as well. The Procurator of the Holy Synod promptly rejected any changes in the seminary curriculum and the remaining educational proposals were referred to the Ministry of Education.[29]

Three years later, in 1839, provisions were actually made for setting up practical classes, including elementary science, in the secondary schools in Tula, Kursk, Vilna, Riga, and Kerch, to be paid for by the Ministry of Finance, and practical sections in one *Gymnasium* in Moscow and probably in one in St. Petersburg to be financed from local revenues.[30] This was a much more limited program than that proposed

[28] The only possible exception to this statement was the establishment of a merchant-marine school in Kherson in 1834, following the opening of a similar one in St. Petersburg in 1829 (N. I. Barbashev, *K istorii morekhodnogo obrazovaniia v Rossii* [Moscow, 1959], pp. 135–136).

[29] TsGIAL, f. 560, op. 38, d. 378, "Otchet departamenta manufaktur . . . za 1836 god," pp. 15–18.

[30] *PSZ* II, statutes 12186, 12187. Statute 12276 provided for the training of six teachers for practical classes in the St. Petersburg University (at the expense of the Ministry of Finance). I have been unable to find a statute establishing "practical classes" in St. Petersburg, but it may very well have been done. See also E. N. Medynskii, *Istoriia russkoi pedagogiki do velikoi oktiabr'skoi sotsialisticheskoi revoliutsii* (Moscow, 1938), p. 146.

by Kankrin. The minister of education, Uvarov, like the Procurator of the Holy Synod, was not interested in practical
education. In areas where there was a demand for additional
educational facilities because of the growth of industry, said
Uvarov, the state would permit the establishment of church
schools, but the primary responsibility for specialized education lay not with his ministry, but with other bodies. The
costs of the practical classes established in 1839 were not
borne by the Ministry of Education. The most that Uvarov
was willing to concede was the addition of faculties of agriculture to the universities and public lectures on technical
subjects.[31]

The position taken by the Minister of Education effectively limited practical education to the minimum needed to
meet the needs of various government agencies; no department was likely to spend much more than was really necessary for its own needs simply to provide trained staff for
private enterprises. The only agency with responsibility and
interest in the economy as a whole was the Ministry of Finance, and it was Kankrin who suggested a broader program
of practical education in 1836. But the concerns of the Finance Ministry were primarily fiscal and Kankrin, however
much he favored technical education in principle, was not
one to be free with funds, even for projects of such special
personal interest such as the technological institute. Had the
Ministry of Education pressed for funds for more general
technical education, or shifted them from other projects
under its control, there might well have been significant
progress. In the face of government indifference and the hostility of Uvarov, Kankrin's personal interest was insufficient.

The static policy of the state during the 1830's in the field
of technical education implied, at most, a lack of enthusiasm
for industrial and commercial development. The first concrete step of a possibly anti-industrial character came in September 1833, when a law was issued governing the location

[31] [Sergei Uvarov], *Desiatiletie Ministerstva narodnago prosveshcheniia, 1833–1843* (St. Petersburg, 1864), pp. 10, 20–21.

of factories in St. Petersburg. It was simply a zoning regulation that specified the locations in which various objectionable or dangerous types of industrial activity could be undertaken. The original proposal, made in 1832, was for a general regulation covering the whole empire. The St. Petersburg statute was issued instead, presumably in an attempt to evaluate the problems likely to arise from such legislation.[32] Substantively the new regulation was nothing more than a step toward rational urban planning, but it also was one of the earliest measures taken by the Russian state to limit industry in any way. The official attitude had always been at least passively permissive, if not actively encouraging. From the early 1830's on, the state came to think more and more about controlling the negative aspects as well as about achieving the obvious benefits of a more productive economy.

Exactly what came to be considered the significant negative aspects of industry is most intriguing. The smoke, noise, and smells of some manufacturing activities obviously influenced the law of 1833. Of much broader significance is the attitude of the state toward the industrial worker and his problems. The tendency, especially among Soviet historians, is to suggest, without justification, that a distrust or fear of the urban proletariat appeared very early and rapidly became the primary factor that governed the state's attitude toward industry.[33]

[32] *PSZ* II, statute 6431; *Ministerstvo finansov*, I, 344; *Zhurnal manufaktur i torgovli*, no. 12 (1833), pp. 57–69; I can find no evidence whatever to confirm M. K. Rozhkova's unsupported statement that this law was designed to limit the growth of the urban proletariat in St. Petersburg ("Ekonomicheskaia politika pravitel'stva," *Ocherki ekonomicheskoi istorii Rossii pervoi poloviny XIX veka: Sbornik statei*, ed. M. K. Rozhkova [Moscow, 1959], p. 378).

[33] Rozhkova, "Ekonomicheskaia politika pravitel'stva," pp. 377–379; N. S. Kiniapina, "Promyshlennaia politika russkogo samoderzhaviia v gody krizisa feodal'noi sistemy," *Voprosy istorii*, no. 6 (1965), pp. 61–75; S. B. Okun', *Ocherki istorii SSSR, vtoraia chetvert' XIX veka* (Leningrad, 1957), pp. 35–37; and M. K. Rozhkova, "Razlozhenie feodal'no-krepostnicheskogo khoziaistva i razvitie kapitalisticheskikh otnoshenii

The first Russian law dealing with labor-management relations was enacted in May 1835. It had no real effect on either workers or employers, but it is indicative of the state's attitude to both groups. The initiative for legislation came from the military governor of Moscow, Prince Golytzin, who frequently received petitions regarding disputes between workers and employers, but who had no clear basis for disposing of them, since there were no regulations governing relationships between the two groups. Golytzin submitted a draft statute to the Moscow branch of the Manufacturing Council and later to the St. Petersburg body as well. The draft provided: (1) that the owner of a serf working in a factory could not recall him before the serf's passport expired, (2) that the employer must maintain written records of the conditions under which the worker was hired and of transactions with him, and (3) that the obligations of the worker must be posted in the factory. Except for the first point, the Manufacturing Councils were not pleased by these suggestions, and the legislation eventually adopted was more favorable to the employer. To the first point, that the worker could not be recalled by his owner before the expiration of his passport, was added the provision that the worker could neither leave nor change his terms of employment. The employer could dismiss a worker for misconduct on two weeks' notice, but was obliged to keep full accounts of wages paid and was urged to make written agreements with his employees. The rules of the factory were to be hung in public view and the worker was given the right to consult them and the accounts in case of dispute. Employers whose workers were illegally hired by other employers were entitled to police aid in recovering the workers and the offending employer was to pay damages. There were, however, no penalties provided in the case of employers who ignored their obligations

v pervoi polovine XIX v.," *Istoriia SSSR, I (S drevneishikh vremen do 1861 goda)*, ed. M. V. Nechkina (Moscow, 1956), 843. See also below, Chapter VI, pp. 235–237.

to the workers.[34] The Ministry of Finance regarded the law as a purely administrative measure. The report of the Department of Manufacturing and Internal Trade for 1833 notes only that the proposal of the military governor of Moscow was designed to save the police trouble.[35]

A few days before the law was promulgated, Tsar Nicholas himself spoke to a meeting of manufacturers at the industrial exhibition in Moscow and said, according to Benkendorf's report:

Now that industry has gotten off to a good start, and cannot fail to develop further, both the state and manufacturers must turn their attention to a subject, without which the very factories would become an evil rather than a blessing; this is the care of the workers who increase in number annually. They need energetic and paternal supervision of their morals; without it this mass of people will gradually be corrupted and eventually turn into a class (*soslovie*) as miserable as they are dangerous for their masters.[36]

Later in the same year, at the Tsar's request, Kankrin submitted a memorandum stressing the importance of the moral education of the workers and the need to protect them from the sometimes selfish attitude of employers, "not weakening, in the meantime, their [the employers'] power, which is necessary for the order and well-being of the enterprise." [37] Kankrin proposed that the members of the Moscow Manu-

---

[34] M. Tugan-Baranovskii, *Russkaia fabrika v proshlom i nastoiashchem,* I (3rd ed.; St. Petersburg, 1907), 137–140; *Zhurnal manufaktur i torgovli,* no. 7 (1835), sec. 1, pp. 26–34.

[35] TsGIAL, f. 560, op. 38, d. 327, "Otchet departamenta manufaktur . . . za 1833," pp. 4–5. In actual practice the factory law of 1835 had little effect, although its application was quickly extended from the two capital cities to include Riga, all the Baltic provinces, Tula, Vladimir, Kaluga, Tver, and all Moscow province (*PSZ* II, statutes 8401 [1835], 8821 and 9675 [1836], 10037 and 10734 [1837], 12975 [1838], and 17330 [1843]; Tugan-Baranovskii, *Russkaia fabrika,* p. 172).

[36] A. Kh. Benkendorf, "Iz zapisok Grafa A. Kh. Benkendorfa," *Istoricheskii vestnik,* XCI (1903), 38.

[37] Quoted in Tugan-Baranovskii, *Russkaia fabrika,* pp. 173–174.

facturing Council urge their fellow industrialists to improve sanitary conditions, not require workers to sleep at their machines, provide separate sleeping quarters for men and women, and so forth. The Tsar approved, and the council named four members to review the matter, but no further action was taken.[38]

Kankrin never shared the Tsar's concern about labor unrest in Russia, although he did deplore the condition of factory workers elsewhere. In November 1835, he assured the Tsar that although the urban proletariat was a problem in western Europe there was no similar danger in Russia—the workers were attached to the existing order because they were peasants who had only temporarily left their villages and would return to them when factory work was unavailable.[39] It was a conviction he held firmly to the end of his life.[40]

In the 1820's, the growth of the towns had been considered to be a very good thing, even though not much had been done to bring it about. In the thirties, it did not become a bad thing, although there were hints in this direction with respect to the two capitals. The question almost ceased to be a matter of discussion within the government because nobody proposed to do anything at all about it. There were just a few hints of uneasiness. A law of December 22, 1832, made it easier for state peasants to move legally into towns and be registered as members of the burgher class. Kankrin successfully urged the inclusion of provisions for the allotment of small pieces of land to the new "city dwellers." It was a recognition of the widespread practice of appropriating common pasture land, but it was also a shift from his view in 1826, which had stressed the need to separate urban and rural activity.[41] Another very minor statute issued in Decem-

[38] *Ibid.*, pp. 174–175; TsGIAL, f. 560, op. 38, d. 362, "Otchet departamenta manufaktur . . . za 1835," p. 8.

[39] Quoted in M. Tugan-Baranovskii, *Russkaia fabrika*, p. 178.

[40] TsGIAL, f. 560, op. 22, d. 79, 1834–1837, "Dokladnye zapiski Ministra finansov . . . ," pp. 95–96; Kankrin, *Die Oekonomie*, p. 243.

[41] *PSZ* II, statute 5842; Pavel G. Ryndziunskii, *Gorodskoe grazhdan-*

ber 1836 gave longer tax exemptions to the founders of new
factories if they were in the provinces rather than St. Petersburg or Moscow. The exemptions did not amount to much,
so whether they were for three or six years made little difference. Clearly, new industry was still desired, but it was
now thought to be preferable to avoid concentrated development in the two largest cities.[42]

Neither the Tsar, nor Kankrin, nor Golytsin said that the
growth of industry and the city population was a potential
danger to the state because of the growth of the working
class, but such a possibility is certainly implied in Nicholas'
remarks in 1835. If, as he said, the workers were to become
so miserable that they would constitute a danger to their
masters, then the state could not fail to be involved. There
was a mixture of paternalistic concern for the welfare and
morals of the peasant turned worker and some awareness of
the potential threat to public order, but no hint in the discussions of the thirties of concern about the urban worker
as a political or revolutionary danger. Nor was there any
suggestion that industrial growth should be reduced or eliminated because of problems connected with the labor force.

The capitalists as well as the workers attracted the attention of the state in the 1830's. Joint-stock companies with
limited liability were becoming popular, and there was even
a small speculative boom that involved prominent figures in
the government including the foreign minister, Count Nesselrode.[43] The Minister of Finance, however, took a very dim
view of the development. Risky ventures, he said, drew capital
away from productive investment. He probably thought, but
did not add, that the lure of high returns could also reduce
the deposits in the banks and the amount of credit easily

stvo doreformennoi Rossii (Moscow, 1958), pp. 174-182; also see Chapter
II, pp. 58–59.

[42] *PSZ* II, statute 9760.

[43] V. K. Iatsunskii, "Krupnaia promyshlennost' Rossii v 1790–1860
gg.," *Ocherki ekonomicheskoi istorii,* ed. Rozhkova, pp. 175–176; Schiemann, *Geschichte Russlands,* III, 260. I am indebted to Repczuk,
"Mordvinov," p. 165, for these references.

available to the state. According to Kankrin, it was "better to refuse ten not absolutely positive companies, than to allow one to the injury of the public and business itself." Despite a more liberal position taken by the Minister of the Interior, the statute enacted was highly restrictive and gave the minister of finance, or in appropriate cases, the director of the Transport and Buildings Administration,[44] wide discretion in issuing company charters and supervising company operations.[45] As long as these offices were held by Kankrin in Finance and the like-minded Tol' in Transport there was little danger that Russia would see a repetition of the speculative excesses and fraud that characterized the late thirties and the forties in France. The strong distrust of joint-stock companies was by no means confined to Russia; in Germany they were unusual in most of the states until almost the middle of the century.[46]

Of all the evidence of a change in the official view toward industry, the most striking is the reversal of the Minister of Finance's attitude toward the periodic industrial exhibitions in St. Petersburg and Moscow, the most spectacular of the measures taken by the state in the twenties to encourage development. By sponsoring them, the state had formally endorsed the efforts of Russian entrepreneurs to emulate the achievements of western Europe. The exhibitions were continued in the thirties, but Kankrin, who had originally supported the exhibitions with great enthusiasm, changed his mind about them. In 1835, he proposed to the Committee of Ministers that exhibitions be held, not every two years, but only every four, because the frequent awarding of prizes at the exhibitions "to some degree tends to increase manufacturing enterprises, not completely commensurate with the

[44] A rather free translation of the awkward *Glavnoe upravlenie putei soobshcheniia i publichykh zdanii*, literally "Chief Administration of Routes of Communication and Public Buildings."

[45] *Ministerstvo finansov*, I, 345–346; *PSZ* II, statute 9764, esp. pars. 14–16, 53.

[46] J. H. Clapham, *The Economic Development of France and Germany, 1815–1914* (Cambridge, Eng., 1936), pp. 131–132.

gradual growth of demand, for the increase of production resulting from the introduction of machines only stimulates demand when it takes place along with a decrease in price." [47]

As he clearly states in the quotation above, fear of overproduction prompted Kankrin to urge a modification in the state's attitude toward industry.[48] In the annual report for 1835 he stated flatly that "the state of affairs is now such that we have almost to fear an excess of factories." [49] Kankrin obviously rejected "Say's Law," the notion advanced early in the nineteenth century by J. B. Say that increased production will automatically produce a proportional increase in demand, but he never systematically explained what he felt the consequences of overproduction for the state would be. For Kankrin, unemployment was not a major concern; the worker-peasant could simply go back to his village until needed again.[50] Nor did he ever express any concern for the fate of the capitalist who goes bankrupt. His view was national, increased industrial production inevitably led to a dependence on foreign markets (since internal demand was fixed). Kankrin wrote in 1840: "I would not think, however, that it would be useful for Russia to become a factory land for foreign parts, except for the Asian trade, . . . because work for foreigners involves dependence, at times very injurious." [51] This warning merely rephrased, from the Russian point of view, his comments on England made nearly twenty years earlier, before becoming minister of finance.[52]

Nicholas and his chief economic adviser, Kankrin, saw different problems arising from industrial development, but their conclusions were in agreement: there was certainly no reason to stimulate development further; conceivably it

[47] Quoted in Rozhkova, *Ekonomicheskaia politika Tsarskogo pravitel'stva na srednem vostoke,* pp. 231–232.

[48] See his comments on Mordvinov's 1831 proposal, above, pp. 93–94.

[49] TsGIAL, f. 560, op. 38, d. 354, "Obshchii otchet . . . za 1835," p. 32.

[50] See above, p. 101.

[51] "Nastavlenie," p. 90.

[52] Kankrin, *Weltreichthum,* p. 112.

should be discouraged a little, or at least more carefully regulated. In fact, however, no action was taken to slow down growth or to regulate industry.[53]

Were there any real grounds for the concern expressed by the Tsar and his minister or, for that matter, for the glowing claims made by Pel'chinskii and other industrial enthusiasts? That there was some industrial growth in the twenties and thirties is unquestioned. But economic policy was determined not just by the impact on the economy of the growth that did take place, but by what state officials thought was happening. It has been seriously argued that an industrial revolution began in Russia in 1830, or even earlier.[54] To a large extent the debate is simply over the definition of "industrial revolution." In the sense that the term signifies the rapid and widespread introduction of major technological innovations, especially power-driven machinery, and a substantial increase in the percentage of the population engaged in industrial activity, Roger Portal has convincingly argued that there was no revolution in the first half of the century.[55]

The available statistical material is limited in both quantity and quality.[56] The government tended to classify as "fac-

[53] The regulation of joint-stock companies did not affect the bulk of Russian enterprises.

[54] S. G. Strumilin, *Ocherki ekonomicheskoi istorii Rossii* (Moscow, 1960), pp. 445 ff.; Strumilin's thesis was first published in the pamphlet, *Promyshlennyi perevorot v Rossii* (Moscow, 1944). B. Iakovlev contends that the industrial revolution in Russia began with the first introduction to Russia of certain types of machinery, regardless of the extent of its use, "Vozniknovenie i etapy razvitiia kapitalisticheskogo uklada v Rossii," *Voprosy istorii*, no. 9 (1950), pp. 102–103.

[55] "Das Problem einer industriellen Revolution in Russland im 19. Jh.," *Forschungen zur Osteuropäischen Geschichte*, I (1954), 205–216.

[56] There has been extensive discussion of the real state of industrial development in the first half of the nineteenth century. For general comments and references, see Portal, "Das Problem"; Blum, *Lord and Peasant*, ch. 15; and especially M. Zlotnikov, "Ot manufaktury k fabrike," *Voprosy istorii*, nos. 11–12 (1946), for critical discussion of the data used by the major writers, Tugan-Baranovskii, Liashchenko, and others.

tories" tiny craft shops with only one or possibly no hired workers, thereby making the data on the number of factories and the number of employees very difficult to evaluate. The most satisfactory data covering a long period of years are for the cotton-weaving and spinning industries, since they were totally dependent on foreign raw materials. Import statistics for cotton thread and raw cotton provide a reasonably good index of the physical output of the two branches of the industry. The growing importance of spinning as compared to weaving is demonstrated by the increase of raw-cotton imports in the late thirties and in the forties in contrast to constant or declining levels of thread imports in the same period.[57]

Fortunately, for the years 1825–1837, output as well as employment data are available for a number of specific industries (see Table 6). These data are taken from the annual reports of the Department of Manufacturing and Trade. They therefore provide an excellent indication of what the government believed the situation to be, regardless of the actual accuracy of the statistics.

The textile industries, wool, cotton, linen, and silk, accounted for about 65 to 70 per cent of the total employment in industries reporting.[58] Of these four, both wool and linen remained at approximately the same level of output and employment from 1825 to 1834 (see Table 6). Only cotton textiles and the much smaller silk industry made rapid, although far from uninterrupted, progress. In 1825, cotton output was

---

[57] K. A. Pazhitnov, *Ocherki istorii tekstil'noi promyshlennosti dorevoliutsionnoi Rossii—khlopchatobumazhnaia, l'no-pen'kovaia i shelkovaia promyshlennost'* (Moscow, 1958), p. 22.

[58] These figures include some metal-fabricating industries, which were little developed, but do not include mining and crude-metal producing, of which the large Ural pig-iron industry was the most important by far. This major industry, however, was in a state of almost total stagnation in the first half of the nineteenth century. Production was about 10 million poods in 1801, did not reach 12 million until 1846, and was at a peak, for the reign of Nicholas I, of 16 million in 1855 (S. G. Strumilin, *Istoriia chernoi metallurgii v SSSR*, I [Moscow, 1954], 367).

about 36.6 million arshins and forty-seven thousand workers were employed in the industry; in 1834, output was about 76.0 million arshins, with eighty thousand workers. Nearly half the total increase in all industrial employment reported between 1825 and 1834 was accounted for by the cotton-textile industry, the remainder being scattered among many other branches of production so that there was no spectacular increase in employment in any other important activity. The obvious conclusion is that the government's concern about industry, if it came from internal developments at all, was the result of the growth of the cotton-textile industry. Russia was following in the path of western Europe, where cotton textiles led in the early industrial development. The data seem to suggest that those, like Kankrin, who saw England as the worst possible model for the national economy had firm grounds for their fears.

Such an interpretation, however, cannot, in fact, be supported, either by the actual nature of the Russian textile industry or by the reported production data. The Russian cotton-textile industry of the 1820's and 1830's was in no way comparable to the British. It was, in fact, primarily devoted to weaving English thread. The spinning of raw cotton made little progress in Russia until after 1842, when England removed its restrictions on the export of the necessary machinery. Nor were horse- or water-powered looms widely used in this early stage of development. The cotton-weaving industry of the twenties and thirties was based on hand weaving, much of it done by peasants in their homes.[59] The rapid rise in output was not the result of the experiments with up-to-date machinery at the state-owned Alexandrovskii factory in the 1820's, but of the existence of a protective tariff on cotton cloth, combined with the steady fall in price of imported English thread. The average price per pood was 111 assignat rubles in 1821–1825, 82 in 1826–1830, and 59 in 1830–1835.[60] Cotton textiles were not truly industrial in the modern sense.

[59] Pazhitnov, *Ocherki istorii,* pp. 14–15, 40–42.
[60] Calculated from data in Pazhitnov, *Ocherki istorii,* p. 22.

Table 6. Physical output and employment

Year	Cotton cloth (arshins)*	Woolens (arshins)*	Linen (arshins)*	Silks (arshins)*	Iron products
1825 output	36,588,278	7,534,238	16,512,499	2,216,927	‡
employment	47,021	63,603	26,832	10,204	22,440
1826 output	57,238,713	8,829,177	16,001,443	2,944,773	‡
employment	45,415	56,955	24,566	11,671	25,059
1827 output	75,017,820	9,821,517	16,446,121	5,265,326	‡
employment	45,415	59,935	24,566	11,202	25,059
1828 output	79,074,898	9,504,751	17,929,543	4,948,334	‡
employment	55,966	60,502	27,565	10,280	22,352
1829 output	84,000,000§	‡	‡	‡	‡
employment	58,203§	‡	‡	‡	‡
1830 output	51,872,844	8,265,889	19,167,437	4,764,094	‡
employment	76,228	67,241	26,845	19,452	19,989
1831 output	63,281,218	10,521,528	19,271,671	4,808,424	‡
employment	‡	‡	‡	‡	‡
1832 output	60,395,795	8,498,943	17,739,962	4,934,470	‡
employment	80,848	68,340	30,768	12,475	19,386
1833 output	60,829,713	9,210,130	22,876,656	5,024,760	‡
employment	79,360	69,236	27,398	12,465	25,552
1834 output	76,020,297	8,898,636	19,359,206	6,464,681	‡
employment	79,925	68,121	28,842	12,670	27,267
1835 output	‡	‡	‡	‡	‡
employment	80,928	69,425	26,801	12,841	33,272
1836 output	‡	‡	‡	‡	‡
employment	94,751	73,403	25,581	13,835	43,573
1837 output	95,784,288	13,223,938	18,839,243	1,508,891	‡
employment	‡	‡	‡	‡	‡

* Physical output data for all types of products expressed in comparable units. In some cases, minor items are not included because they were reported in an incompatible unit of measure.
† The figures include small industries not listed here, but exclude the mining industry.
‡ Not available.
§ Figures are from P. A. Khromov, *Ekonomicheskoe razvitie Rossii v XIX–XX vekakh, 1800–1917* (Moscow, 1950), pp. 49 and 437.

They did not concentrate large numbers of workers in one place, and therefore the growth of textile output should have been less alarming from the social standpoint than the figures would otherwise suggest. There was at least some basis for Kankrin's complacency about the social aspects of industrialization.

The output data reported to the Ministry of Finance suggest another explanation for the Minister's growing uneasi-

in eleven Russian industries, 1825–1837

Leather (hides)	Paper (reams)	Glass and crystal (pieces)	Tallow (poods)	Rope (poods)	Refined sugar (poods)	Total employment in all industry†
2,525,626	743,467	19,748,022	1,553,254	639,892	1,090,243	
8,001	8,272	5,765	3,481	2,503	1,374	210,568
2,553,507	646,005	16,951,112	1,460,674	472,298	986,646	
7,743	8,781	5,864	3,770	2,357	1,149	206,408
2,726,093	652,910	20,591,222	1,438,264	469,592	961,391	
7,743	8,781	5,864	3,770	2,357	1,149	209,547
2,972,469	660,475	18,638,463	1,768,583	549,173	1,067,945	
9,755	9,031	5,888	3,859	2,437	1,340	225,414
‡	‡	‡	‡	‡	‡	
‡	‡	‡	‡	‡	‡	231,600§
2,929,783	807,566	20,388,082	5,000,300	591,530	1,372,563	
10,547	10,180	6,616	4,398	2,780	1,687	253,893
3,001,208	1,124,871	20,522,370	3,871,926	710,239	1,379,469	
‡	‡	‡	‡	‡	‡	264.358
2,842,200	1,095,280	20,828,700	3,878,640	640,910	1,407,250	
9,875	11,993	7,322	4,884	3,158	2,754	272,490
2,851,114	1,140,440	20,793,200	3,781,350	646,970	1,406,250	
10,240	11,894	7,765	4,931	2,809	2,418	273,969
3,389,374	1,350,548	32,768,208	3,112,900	752,811	1,435,965	
10,012	11,950	8,494	4,363	3,010	2,809	279,673
‡	‡	‡	‡	‡	‡	
10,425	13,278	8,592	4,486	2,942	2,840	288,058
‡	‡	‡	‡	‡	‡	
10,512	13,472	8,849	6,021	2,992	4,633	324,203
2,274,247	900,324	21,096,387	1,877,403	485,083	1,194,224	
‡	‡	‡	‡	‡	‡	376,838

Source (except as noted above): TsGIAL, f. 560, op. 42, d. 1, 1825; f. 560, op. 38, d. 234, 1826; f. 560, op. 42, d. 3, 1827; f. 560, op. 42, d. 4, 1828; f. 560, op. 38, 1830–1837, with the following *dela* numbers: 297, 312, 327, 344, 362, 378, 494, 410. The title of the document varies. It is an annual report of the Department of Manufacturing and Trade.

ness about the problem of marketing increased output. The progress of the cotton industry was rapid in the years 1825–1834, but it was not smooth. The years 1830–1833 show a sharp decline in reported output compared to the peak years 1827–1829.[61] The concern about excessive expansion ex-

[61] Data on the import of British thread also indicate sharp fluctuation in the early thirties, although the pattern is not exactly parallel to that of reported output (Grigorii Nebolsin, *Statisticheskoe obozrenie vneshnei torgovli Rossii* [St. Petersburg, 1850], II, 92).

pressed by Meyendorf and Kankrin in the early thirties was probably the result of the failure of output to maintain its previous high levels. The problem was not the social side effects of too much industry, but the instability created by fluctuating production. The sharp fluctuation in output was confined to the cotton-textile industry. Other products do not show a similar sharp fall in production in the early 1830's.[62] The only indicator of the general condition of trade is the annual volume of sales at the Nizhni-Novgorod market fair, where the volume rose without setbacks from 1824 through 1833.[63] In view of the very rapid growth in cotton-textile production in the late twenties, a temporary decline in output is hardly surprising, nor is it remarkable that it was during a period when the fastest growing industry suffered reverses that misgivings about it first appeared. As long as expansion proceeded without interruption, there was little to draw the attention of the state to the development underway. Once the growth halted, the pessimists, notably Kankrin, could view with alarm the difficulties that lay ahead, the immediate problem of markets for increased output, and the remote danger of being dependent on the world market for exported manufactures. This happened at the same time that other people, including the Tsar, looked around them, read reports from abroad, and discovered that factories were ugly and displaced peasant workers a potential problem.

The Tsar and his chief economic adviser both saw growing problems connected with industrial development, but for different reasons. The reaction of both, and especially Kankrin, was to withdraw positive state support for development, not to attack the difficulties themselves. Kankrin saw no hope

[62] The surprising increase in the number of workers reported for 1830 and subsequent years at the time that output fell must reflect some change in statistical practices, perhaps involving the role of the newly established Manufacturing Council (1828). The phenomenon cannot be explained by a shift to more labor-consuming types of cloth. Virtually every major type of cotton cloth declined in output in 1830.

[63] See the table in P. A. Khromov, *Ekonomicheskoe razvitie Rossii v XIX–XX vekakh, 1800–1917* (Moscow, 1950), p. 482.

of finding new markets for Russian cotton goods; he spoke only of adjusting expansion to existing demand.[64] Nicholas I actually took a slightly more positive approach toward worker distress, the problem that concerned him, and encouraged Kankrin to turn his attention to the problem that the Minister refused to recognize.

AGRICULTURE TO THE FORE

A somewhat similar divergence between the Tsar and the Minister of Finance began to develop in the early thirties over the problems of agriculture. Here too Nicholas took the more positive approach, while Kankrin showed no inclination to make serious efforts to improve the existing situation. During the late 1820's, the economic problems of agriculture had received little attention, except for the provision of credit for gentry landowners and the state recognized that this aid was more likely to serve the ends of good living than good husbandry. Concern over low agricultural prices expressed itself in discussion of how to increase demand by developing the cities. Only in a few specialized areas had the state taken any direct action to improve agricultural practice. As already mentioned, sheep breeding, which was making progress at private initiative in southern Russia, was encouraged by articles in the *Journal of Manufacturing and Trade,* the visit of a foreign expert, and a subsidized wool-grading plant. Forestry also had received considerable atten-

[64] There was some contemporary interest in Asia as a market for Russian goods, but difficulties of transport and competition from England prevented successful development. See "Nastavlenie," p. 81; Michael Herman Freiherr von Nolcken, *Der russische Finanzminister Graf Georg Kankrin und seine Handelspolitik* (Riga, 1909), pp. 61–73; *Ministerstvo finansov,* I, 331–336; and Vikentii Pel'chinskii, "O rasprostranenii sbyta rossiskikh manufakturnykh izdelii v Zakavkaze i Persii," *Zhurnal manufaktur i torgovli,* no. 1 (1831), pp. 94–98. The entire issue of the *Zhurnal manufaktur i torgovli,* no. 1 (1836), was devoted to trade with China.

tion for a few years. A scientific commission on forestry was established in 1826, followed by the Forestry Society in 1832, both at state expense. Kankrin, however, soon became discouraged by the difficulty of putting improved practices into actual use.[65]

The Committee of the 26th December 1826 had, of course, considered at great length the question of improving the legal position of the privately owned serfs and had worked out a draft law embodying several significant measures, especially a prohibition of the sale of serfs without land. These measures were submitted to Nicholas in early July 1830 but were never promulgated, presumably because of the Tsar's concern over the European revolution.[66] The social and legal problems of the privately owned serfs temporarily ceased to be a matter of active governmental concern, and attention shifted first to the state peasants and then to the general question of the improvement of agricultural productivity. In both instances Kankrin advocated a highly conservative approach and was eventually overruled by Nicholas.

The Minister of Finance naturally viewed both these questions primarily from the fiscal standpoint. The state peasants, who were administered by a department of his ministry, were a major source of revenue. Agricultural improvement, on the other hand, meant large expenditure with no immediate likelihood of return. Agriculture was the occupation of most Russians, and therefore any program that could possibly produce results would have to be large and costly, both in money and administrative effort. In contrast, industry, or even an agricultural specialty like sheep raising, could be significantly helped by modest expenditures. Kankrin was highly skeptical of programs of broad agricultural reform. In 1828, he sar-

[65] TsGIAL, f. 560, op. 42, d. 4, "Otchet . . . Departamenta manufaktur . . . za 1829," p. 131; *AGS*, IV, pt. 1, 1413–1416; Lesnoi departament, *Stoletie uchrezhdeniia Lesnago departamenta, 1798–1898* (St. Petersburg, 1898), pp. 69, 79, 89–94; *Zhurnal manufaktur i torgovli*, no. 3 (1832), pp. 120–128; and Kankrin, *Im Ural und Altai*, p. 80.

[66] V. I. Semevskii, *Krest'ianskii vopros v Rossii v XVIII pervoi polovine XIX veka*, II (St. Petersburg, 1888), 14–17.

castically questioned criticism of the system of strip cultivation by observing that it was used widely in the most progressive parts of Europe.[67]

Immediately after the suppression of the Polish revolt, the
attention of the state was drawn to the state peasants, not
because of their needs, but as a result of the severe fiscal difficulties that were facing the government. In preparing the
budget estimates for 1832, Kankrin again put forward the
plan for increasing revenues that he had first suggested in
1829. The plan was simply to classify the districts of each
province, rather than just whole provinces, into four categories according to the productivity of the land, the prevailing regional prices for agricultural products, the extent of
local industry, and value of nonagricultural resources—forests, fisheries, and so forth. State peasants in the more prosperous districts were then to be subject to higher rent (*obrok*)
payments. As an attempt to adjust the tax burden to the ability to pay and thereby decrease the amount of uncollectable
arrears, the measure was obviously crude, since there were
certain to be differences within districts. From the standpoint
of the Ministry of Finance, however, it had the great advantage of eliminating the costly and slow process of surveying
and evaluating the land of individual villages.

After this initial step had been taken, further progress was
envisaged, in the direction advocated by Speransky and
Kochubei, to transform the *obrok* into a true land rent and
establish heredity tenure. As a first step in implementing the
program, a school of surveying was set up in the Institute of
Forestry, but nothing else was accomplished, not even Kankrin's grouping of districts into four classes.[68] The plan did
receive the approval of the State Council in July 1832, but
the Emperor failed to implement it by approving the table of
rates established for the various categories of districts. His

[67] *Arkhiv grafov Mordvinovykh,* ed. V. A. Bilbasov, IV (St. Petersburg, 1902), xlviii. I owe this citation to Repczuk, "Mordvinov."

[68] M. N. Druzhinin, *Gosudarstvennye krest'iane i reforma P. D. Kiseleva,* I (Moscow and Leningrad, 1946), 186–189; *Ministerstvo finansov,*
I, 266–268; "Nastavlenie," p. 33.

attention instead was drawn to the success that Perovskii was having in extracting additional revenue from the estates assigned to the imperial family: "There are no arrears, and revenues from the land tax have increased." It would be better, continued the Tsar, to go all the way at once rather than upsetting the state peasants repeatedly through a gradual series of changes.[69]

Kankrin insisted that a system based on widespread land surveys could not be quickly introduced. He repeatedly diverted the attention of the various committees considering reform by proposing to give the local administration of the state peasantry to bodies directly subordinate to the Ministry of Finance instead of to the local fiscal board (*kazennaia palata*), which was primarily the tool of the provincial governor and the local gentry. These proposals of Kankrin's drew caustic criticism from Speransky as calling for nothing but an empty administrative structure with no indication of what goal it was to work for or what means were to be employed.[70]

After five years of delay, Nicholas finally acted decisively and removed the state peasants entirely from Ministry of Finance jurisdiction. From May 3, 1836, Count Kiselev was in effective control of the administration of state lands. Kankrin's refusal to act, which had been successful for so long, ended in his total defeat and the loss of a major department of his ministry. What had begun in 1831 as a primarily fiscal question of how to maximize revenues from the state peasants became, in the hands of Kiselev, a reform program of far-reaching significance.[71]

The story of the developing difference in outlook between Nicholas and Kankrin about improving agricultural technology in the early 1830's is equally clear, but the results were less dramatic than in the larger issue of the state peasants.

[69] *Ministerstvo finansov,* I, 266–268; Druzhinin, *Gosudarstvennye krest'iane,* I, 190.

[70] Druzhinin, *Gosudarstvennye krest'iane,* I, pp. 190–193, 200–203, 280–295, esp. p. 293.

[71] A. P. Zablotskii-Desiatovskii, *Graf P. D. Kiselev i ego vremia* (St. Petersburg, 1882), II, 11.

Here there was no question of major administrative change, but simply of how much could be spent, and for what. On such questions the Finance Minister's position was strong, money was short, and needs were great. Nicholas was not willing to contemplate reducing the military budget or resorting to inflationary fiscal measures to provide funds for agriculture. These principles were so firmly established that they were not even mentioned as possibilities. In 1833, the state first gave serious attention to measures designed to improve the general level of agricultural productivity. In September, Admiral Mordvinov, as president of the Free Economic Society, requested a grant of 78,000 rubles to enable the society to greatly expand its activities. He proposed, among other projects, to invite foreign experts to Russia, train serfs in modern methods, subsidize the sale of books, and establish an experimental farm.[72] Mordvinov had been making similar suggestions, in one form or another, for years, but in 1833 they received serious consideration and action was actually taken despite Kankrin's energetic opposition to spending money.

The cautious Kankrin, who had long been the target for much criticism from the optimistic and imaginative Mordvinov, could hardly be expected to take kindly to anything coming from the old Admiral. Of Mordvinov's eight major suggestions, Kankrin accepted one, the sending of young Russians overseas for study. The Finance Minister's comments were, as usual, intelligent and to the point. He was by no means a stupid obstructionist, but rather a man who knew all too well the problems of getting anything done under Russian conditions. The training of serfs at state expense was not justified, he felt, because wealthy landlords could do it themselves and poor ones could not afford to improve their agricultural practices in any case. The same argument held against subsidizing the sale of books. Poor men could not afford to engage in modern agriculture, so why help them learn about it? The manufacture of the best agricultural

[72] *Arkhiv grafov Mordvinovykh,* VII (1903), 148–153.

equipment was certainly useful, but expensive, and there were not enough trained men to do it. Foreign equipment was not suited to Russian conditions, particularly to the limited strength of Russian draft animals.[73]

The Committee of Ministers recognized the general validity of Mordvinov's contention that agriculture sorely needed attention, but accepted Kankrin's specific objections and took the course of least resistance. It recommended the appropriation of 20,000 rubles for the purposes that Kankrin approved and the establishment of a special committee on agriculture to consider further measures. Mordvinov was to be chairman, but Kankrin one of the members. Early in 1834, this special committee made a report advocating the establishment of an agricultural journal, schools, and other measures that differed in detail but not in spirit from those originally proposed by Mordvinov. The Committee of Ministers again supported the position of the Ministry of Finance and rejected the proposals as excessively expensive. There the matter would have ended but for the direct intervention of the Tsar himself, who ordered the Minister of Finance to consider the problem further and come forward with new proposals. Thus, two years before the decision on the state peasantry, Nicholas acted to overrule Kankrin and force his reluctant but obedient minister to take positive action.[74]

The actual results of the Tsar's intervention were small. Kankrin successfully blocked the establishment of a separate agricultural administration, a serious threat to his power to control the allocation of funds and the formation of policy.[75] The *Agricultural Journal* was established in 1834, and in 1836 two agricultural schools were established; both these projects were consistent with Kankrin's previous policies in

[73] *Ibid.,* pp. 416–418.

[74] *Ibid.,* pp. 416–422.

[75] Of course two years later he lost the state peasants to the new Ministry of State Domains under Kiselev, but at least that body had limited jurisdiction, although it did eventually become the Russian Ministry of Agriculture in 1894.

the industrial field, although he had opposed them when Mordvinov suggested them for agriculture. A much more radical departure from his past practice was Kankrin's willingness to make an interest-free loan of 70,000 assignat rubles to the Butenop brothers to expand their Moscow agricultural-machinery plant and to establish distribution depots in Kharkov, Kiev, and Simbirsk.[76] The loan to the Butenops was undoubtedly the result of the Tsar's personal interest in agricultural machinery, expressed publicly in 1835, when he stated that the time had come "to turn special attention" to agriculture and specifically mentioned his wish that an agricultural-machinery factory be established in Moscow.[77]

The reasons for the Emperor's increased interest in general agricultural improvement are not clear. Crop failures like that of 1833 were nothing new, nor were elaborate and imaginative proposals by Admiral Mordvinov. He was a sort of eccentric but loyal one-man opposition, tolerated and even respected, but not to be seriously regarded as a voice likely to influence the Tsar.[78] The Emperor's concern about the peasant problem in general and his exasperation at Kankrin's dilatory tactics on the question of the state peasants may have made him increasingly amenable to the positive suggestions of others; the most likely source of inspiration, however, as in the case of state peasant reform, was the program underway on the lands of the appanage peasants under the direction of Perovskii. The Tsar himself had cited it in connection with the discussion of changes in collecting rent from the state peasants.[79] The changes in the land-rent system begun in the late twenties were designed primarily to increase revenue collections. Their success, easily measured by counting

[76] V. Veshniakov, "Komitet 1833 goda ob usovershenstvovanii zem-ledeliia," *Russkii vestnik*, LXXXII (1869), 290–304; TsGIAL, f. 560, op. 38, d. 378, "Otchet departamenta manufaktur . . . za 1836 god," p. 42.

[77] Stepan Maslov, *Istoricheskoe obozrenie deistvii i trudov impera-torskago moskovskago obshchestva sel'skogo khoziaistva so vremeni ego osnovaniia do 1846 goda* (2nd ed.; Moscow, 1850), p. 48.

[78] See Repczuk, "Mordvinov," pp. 39–41, 86–87.

[79] See above, pp. 113–114.

receipts, strengthened Perovskii's reputation in the eyes of the Tsar and enabled him to attempt a series of improvements that would otherwise have appeared reckless and financially unsound. To some degree Perovskii tried to do, on a limited scale, what Mordvinov freely advised on a nation-wide basis.

In 1832, imperial approval was obtained for the construction of an agricultural school designed to train appanage peasant youths in practical techniques of good husbandry. Only a year later, the school opened and the first students began the six-year course. Total enrollment was 250 and in 1839–1840 the first graduating class was assigned to 37 individual farms (*usadba*). Perovskii was careful not to create a new elite that would scorn agricultural life after finishing their studies, and the food, the students' dress, and the general atmosphere of the boarding school was kept as close to the conditions of peasant life as possible. Unfortunately the graduates of the school tended to move into handicraft operations because they did not have enough labor under their personal control to use the new techniques of cultivation they had learned.[80] At the time, however, the project gave every indication of great promise and it made an excellent impression on Baron Haxthausen in the early 1840's.[81] Throughout the thirties, Perovskii's appanage department continued to make constructive efforts in the field of agricultural progress and peasant welfare. A serious attempt was made to develop primary education. Banks and fire insurance for peasants were established for the first time, and potatoes and other new or improved crops and implements were introduced.[82] The significance of these measures lies not in

[80] Russia, Glavnoe upravlenie udelov, *Istoriia udelov za stoletie ikh sushchestvovaniia, 1797–1897* (St. Petersburg, 1902), I, 86–88, and II, 402–408.

[81] Baron von Haxthausen, *The Russian Empire, Its People, Institutions and Resources,* trans. Robert Farie (London, 1856), I, 187–191; Blum, *Lord and Peasant,* pp. 497–498.

[82] Glavnoe upravlenie udelov, *Istoriia udelov,* I, 88–93, and II, 156–158, 186–191, 222–227, 247–254, 283–289, 318–328.

their success, or their much more frequent failure, but in the fact that they represent the first serious and sustained attempt by a state agency to develop the agricultural economy and provided an example for the much broader program of Kiselev for the state peasantry that was ultimately to produce a real ministry of agriculture.[83] Perovskii had no more success than did Peter the Great in trying to convince Russian peasants that scythes were better than sickles, but unlike the years of the mid-eighteenth century the middle and later nineteenth century saw increasing state involvement in agricultural development, although never on a scale sufficient to meet the great needs or even keep up with the growing problems and demands of the population.

The economic policy of the early thirties can be viewed in two ways. Outwardly, in terms of accomplishments and in terms even of plans and discussions, it was largely barren except for the beginnings of activity in the field of agricultural development. These were the years in which Kankrin seemed to make all significant decisions, and he had become discouraged and ceased to emphasize the modest but constructive programs that characterized the 1820's. For different reasons the Tsar and his finance minister agreed that industrial growth was adequate and possibly too rapid, but in other areas Kankrin's reluctance to experiment or admit the need for change exceeded that of his master, a man never noted for progressive outlook. The gradual divergence in views can be explained in part by Kankrin's weariness and frustration over the impossible tasks assigned to him and the difficulty of implementing any positive program. There was also an increasing divergence between the Finance Minister's relative satisfaction with the *status quo* and the nation's

[83] The military colonies of Alexander I did involve schools and agricultural improvements, but they can hardly be regarded as institutions concerned chiefly with agriculture. They certainly did not provide a useful example for those primarily interested in the economic position of the peasantry.

need to maintain its position in the world. Western Europe and England were developing economically far more rapidly than Russia. The consequences of industrial development were known to many Russians, admired by some and rejected by others. The Tsar was not one to ape western-European patterns, particularly after the appalling political events of 1830, but unlike his minister of finance, he was unable to convince himself that everything necessary was already being done to strengthen the nation economically. That imperial initiative should first become evident in the field of agricultural improvement is not surprising. Perhaps Nicholas' instruction during his youth by Heinrich Storch that Russia was an agricultural country had made some impression on him; in any case, his concern with the peasant problem was clear from the earliest days of his reign. The change in emphasis in the early thirties was from legal and social aspects of the peasant question to economic and technical problems, and from the privately owned serfs to the appanage and state peasants.

Kankrin was always ready to admit that problems existed, but he was increasingly unwilling to make any attempt to correct or improve the situation. Nicholas was less pessimistic. He knew all was not well with Russia, but the example of early western-European industrialism was by no means attractive, and he was therefore willing to support attempts to improve Russian agriculture in the early thirties despite the opposition of his trusted minister of finance, whose advice he had hitherto almost invariably accepted.

CHAPTER IV

The End of the Kankrin Era

Two men, Kankrin and Nicholas I, had determined the economic policy of the Russian state in the twenties and thirties. The Tsar's role had been essentially the passive one of accepting the advice of his minister. The state's program in the twenties was restrained, but despite the primacy of fiscal considerations, it contained elements that indicated an interest in economic progress and in laying the basis for future development, particularly through various educational measures. The early and mid-thirties showed a pattern of withdrawal and doubt about the value of attempts to encourage industry because of growing fiscal problems, fear of overproduction, and the realization that industries brought problems as well as benefits. At the same time there was some increased interest in agriculture. Kankrin's influence continued to predominate, but the Emperor showed signs of a growing awareness of economic affairs, and it was he, not Kankrin, who directed the increased attention to agricultural matters.

In the last years of Kankrin's ministry, from the later thirties into the early forties, there were major departures from the *status quo* policy he advocated in three important areas—monetary reform, agriculture, and transport. All three of these new undertakings were the result of the Tsar's intervention. Taken in isolation, the period roughly from 1836 to 1843 could easily be described as the beginning of a new and vigorous era of state-sponsored economic change. The persistent problems of the currency system were solved by a reform that gave Russia a sound paper currency convertible into silver on demand.[1] An ambitious program was begun to improve the social and economic position of the state peasants, nearly half the rural population. Finally, a key feature of the modern industrial world, the railroad, was introduced into Russia.

Each development was essentially independent of the others. There was no total reappraisal of policy, and a new era of progress and dynamic state activity did not begin. Nobody seems to have said to himself, "We need peasant reform, monetary reform, and railroads in order to achieve such and such a general goal." Monetary reform was stimulated by growing difficulties with the existing currency system that produced widespread complaints. The state-peasant program was the product of Nicholas' growing interest in agriculture and the peasants for their own sake and the example of the seemingly successful program carried out on the appanage estates by Perovskii. Railroad construction began because, once they became established in western Europe, England, and the United States, the advantages of railroads were too great for a country as large as Russia to continue to overlook, despite strong opposition within the government.

---

[1] Monetary problems and the reform of 1839–1843 are discussed in full in Chapter V. The program is sometimes called "Kankrin's monetary reform," although he had little to do with developing its basic features and he opposed its implementation. Nevertheless the reform is sometimes grouped with the protective tariff or Kiselev's state-peasant reforms in an attempt to show the "progressive" side of Nicholas I's reign. See, for example, Alexander Kornilov, *Modern Russian History,* trans. Alexander S. Kaun (New York, 1943), pp. 266–278; and Herbert J. Ellison, *History of Russia* (New York, 1964), pp. 172–177. In contrast to the interpretation in many general histories, Kankrin's role in the monetary reform has been long established in the specialized literature (Ilarion I. Kaufman, *Iz istorii bumazhnykh deneg v Rossii* [St. Petersburg, 1909], pp. 98 ff.).

In a very real sense then, despite these major projects, the overall economic policy of the state remained what it had been in the early thirties. Industrial development was looked on with suspicion, no effort was made to revive the interest in technical education that was prominent in the twenties, and credit policy was as restrictive as ever, serving only the state and the gentry. The new projects only began to correct some of the glaring deficiencies of the preceding decades. Monetary reform had been discussed since the end of the Napoleonic Wars and even before. The question of the peasantry had been increasingly on the minds of educated Russians, including the rulers themselves, since the end of the eighteenth century. Railroads, like many other devices and techniques, were introduced to Russia at a relatively early date, but did not become well developed for many decades after their introduction. It was almost as if, once some construction began, the feeling of urgency disappeared because Russia had shown that she was equal to the rest of Europe. A growing duality, or inconsistency, characterized state policy. On one hand, the tradition of fiscal restraint and the maintenance of the *status quo* and outright distrust of change remained the dominant theme. On the other hand, the growing problems of the day, the tensions engendered by the independent growth of the Russian economy, and particularly the economic development of other nations made the need for specific changes increasingly evident.

The decline of Kankrin's influence might have had far more important consequences had some other figure with a strong commitment to a definite policy replaced him as the Tsar's chief economic adviser. Nicholas, however, was not inclined to add new faces to the small group of men who were his chief aids. Except for the responsibilities given to Kiselev for the state peasants, he gradually took into his own hands matters no longer entrusted to Kankrin. In 1840, when the financial situation looked especially gloomy, Kankrin became seriously ill and asked to resign, but Nicholas replied, "You know that there are two of us who cannot leave our posts alive, you and I." [2] But other members of the government, and not only his perpetual opponent, Mordvinov, were less satisfied with Kankrin's administration. Prince Vasil'chikov, president of the State Council, submitted a memorandum to the Tsar accusing Kankrin of failing to develop new sources of state revenue and of relying on the easy expedients of foreign and domestic borrowing to the long-run detriment of the economy. To remedy the situation, Vasil'chikov proposed that some functions might be delegated to other ministries and that an independent advisory council be established to assist in overall financial planning. The Tsar hesitated for some time, but finally named a special secret committee to consider the problem. The committee of six prominent officials met at Vasil'chikov's home under virtually conspiratorial circumstances, leaving their coaches out of sight and stationing a servant at the door to inform visitors that the Prince was not at home. [3]

The discussions were prolonged, but when the time came to prepare a written report for the Tsar, the members of the committee found it difficult to put their harsh words down in an official document. Kankrin's health had improved and there was no longer any immediate prospect of his leaving office. The embarrassment was avoided by submitting general recommendations in the official report and leaving the harsher comments to be transmitted to the Tsar in a personal letter from Prince Vasil'chikov. The only concrete result of the entire incident was that Nicholas forced Kankrin to designate a deputy minister to act in his absence. The post was filled by Vronchenko, an elderly official of the Finance Ministry, who was most reluctant to accept increased responsibilities. [4] The designation of Vronchenko, presumably at Kankrin's suggestion, made his eventual succession to the post of finance

[2] M. A. Korf, "Iz zapisok barona (vposledstvii grafa) M. A. Korfa," *Russkaia starina*, XCIX (1899), 282.

[3] The members of the committee were Chernyshev, Nesselrode, Menshikov, Levashov, Kiselev, and Korf (*ibid.*, pp. 283–284).

[4] *Ibid.*, pp. 284–286.

minister a virtual certainty and made any radical change in economic policy unlikely. A man trained in the Kankrin tradition but without the personal prestige and the self-confidence of his mentor could hardly do more than follow the traditional policies, but with less vigor, deviating only with direct orders from the Emperor.

Despite what Nicholas said to Kankrin about their mutual indispensability, there was at least one major figure, Prince Drutskii-Liubetskii, who was regarded by some as a possible minister of finance and who advocated a more active and imaginative economic role for the state.[5] The Prince came from an old Polish noble family and was educated in the Imperial Corps of Pages in St. Petersburg, where one of his teachers was the famous German mathematician Euler. Always completely loyal to the Russian empire and the Tsar, he served under Suvorov in Italy and in various administrative positions during the Napoleonic era. In 1819 and 1820, he helped to settle financial claims of Prussia and Austria arising from the war. Liubetskii's experience as finance minister of the independent Kingdom of Poland from 1821 to 1830 made him a potential rival to Kankrin in later years. The program that he undertook in Poland involved vigorous efforts to stimulate industrial development not only by technical education, advice, and tariff protection, but also by supplying capital borrowed abroad, guaranteed by the state and largely invested in state-owned enterprises. In his efforts to mobilize available domestic capital he established the Polish state bank and rural credit societies. The expansionist aspects of Liubetskii's program did not make him an inflationist. He strove to achieve a balanced budget just as Kankrin did in Russia.[6]

Liubetskii remained true to the empire during the Polish

[5] *Arkhiv grafov Mordvinovykh,* ed. V. A. Bilbasov, VII (St. Petersburg, 1903), 265. The Polish spelling is Druckii-Lubeckii.

[6] Ezhi Edlitskii, "Gosudarstvennaia promyshlennost' v tsarstve pol'skom v XIX v.," in Akademiia Nauk, Institut istorii, *Genezis kapitalizma v promyshlennosti* (Moscow, 1963), pp. 284–286.

uprising of 1830 and spent the rest of his career outside Poland in Russian service. In 1832, he was named to the State Council, but was soon sent to Paris in a hopeless attempt to negotiate a settlement of claims still outstanding from the Napoleonic Wars and did not return to St. Petersburg until 1837. Thus it was not until the late thirties that an outspoken and technically competent opponent of Kankrin's policies (other than the elderly Mordvinov) became firmly established within the government. Liubetskii had a low opinion of Kankrin and described him as "a cashier, not a minister." [7] The Polish statesman's entire approach to economic policy was active and ambitious, and in Poland he had demonstrated the ability to put his policies into practice. In Russia he had the disadvantage of being a foreigner who never fully mastered the Russian language, but so, of course, had Kankrin. Liubetskii was given to interminable and overly complex presentations of his ideas, but probably more injurious to his position was the long-standing personal enmity of the influential Count Novosil'tsev, and of Kankrin himself. Liubetskii's opposition to Kankrin does not make him a "liberal." He too was firmly committed to the financial support of the gentry and opposed the sale of heavily mortgaged estates. The difference between the two men was that between active optimism and cynical pessimism. Liubetskii wanted to give the gentry debtors "the means to repay," while Kankrin, with greater realism, simply lent them the money and gave no evidence of any hope that it would be repaid. [8]

There were undoubtedly other men in Russia who would have made capable finance ministers, but contemporary accounts provide no evidence that any others were ever mentioned as possibilities. The two other prominent officials with

[7] V. V. Novodvorskii, "Drutskii-Liubetskii, Kniaz' Frantsisk-Ksaverii (1779–1846)," *Russkii biograficheskii slovar'*, Vol. Dabelov-Diad'kovskii (St. Petersburg, 1905), p. 701.

[8] K. Drutskii-Liubetskii, "Mnenie ob otsenke i prodazhe imenii pomeshchikov," *Chteniia*, III (1863), 143–145. For Kankrin's views on this subject, see Chapter II, pp. 39–42.

appropriate experience, Kiselev and Perovskii, took over other ministries: State Domains and Interior, respectively.

THE FISCAL CRISIS OF 1839–1842:
CREDIT AND THE CURRENCY

No foreign war or revolution occurred during the decade from the mid-1830's to the mid-1840's to place a heavy strain on the Russian economy and government finance. Warfare in the Caucasus continued and regular military expenditures rose steadily after 1830, to Kankrin's great distress. Steady fiscal pressure, however, was nothing new. It was, perhaps, more severe than it had been in the twenties, but the difference was not drastic. The series of poor harvests of 1839–1841 had a more serious effect on the economy and on state finance than any external event of Nicholas' reign before the Crimean War. For a short time the situation was so bad that military expenditures were cut and even the size of the army reduced. The crisis delayed the completion of monetary reform that had been begun in 1839, and it stimulated a thorough but inconclusive reconsideration of the entire money and credit system.[9]

The Tsar took an active part in this discussion and chaired a special committee that dealt with the financial crisis. Prince Drutskii-Liubetskii proposed that the State Commercial Bank be reorganized and made into an active institution independent of the Ministry of Finance. To give the Bank the needed capital, a new type of state treasury note should be issued that would not only bear interest as did the existing ones, but would also be compulsory legal tender. From Kankrin's standpoint the plan was not only a threat to his ministry's control over the Commercial Bank, but a step in the direction of a currency that could be readily expanded and

[9] Theodor Schiemann, *Geschichte Russlands unter Kaiser Nikolaus I*, IV (Berlin, 1913), 2; TsGIAL, f. 560, op. 38, d. 433, "Obshchii otchet za . . . 1840," p. 2.

a banking system not totally subordinate to the state, and notably not subject to the Minister of Finance. He had always opposed anything that conceivably threatened the value of the existing paper currency (the assignats) and the authority of the ministry. During the Kankrin administration, virtually every proposal for the establishment of independent banks was blocked and even the State Commercial Bank was allowed to have branches in only a few of the largest cities.[10]

With some difficulty Kankrin was able to prevent the adoption of Prince Drutskii-Liubetskii's ambitious plan. His first maneuver was to find, at the last minute, that the funds needed to cover the anticipated budget deficit for 1841 were, after all, available from the proceeds of a loan floated in Amsterdam in anticipation of increased military expenditures in the Caucasus.[11] When it became evident in 1841, however, that both the State Loan Bank and the *sokhrannye kazny* were in serious difficulty, with increasing defaults produced by poor harvests, Kankrin was faced by a far more formidable adversary, the Tsar himself. In a memorandum written in his own hand, Nicholas proposed the adoption of what was essentially a part of Drutskii-Liubetskii's plan: that these credit institutions be permitted to issue "safekeeping-notes" which would both bear interest and circulate freely as legal tender and which would be secured only by the

[10] S. Ia. Borovoi, *Kredit i banki Rossii (seredina XVII v.–1861 g.)* (Moscow, 1958), pp. 218–220, 232–234, 241–243. In 1823, there were seven offices; by 1843, three more had been opened (in Kiev, Rybinsk, and Kharkov), but one (Astrakhan) had closed, leaving a net gain of two under Kankrin. On Kankrin's opposition to Commercial Bank branches see TsGIAL, f. 1152, op. T. II, d. 85, 1842–1843, "Ob uchrezhdenii v Khar'kove kontory Kommercheskago banka," pp. 8–9, 15–16; and *Rtb.*, I, Supp. II, 63.

[11] Ia. I. Pecherin, *Istoricheskii obzor rospisei gosudarstvennykh dokhodov i raskhodov s 1803 po 1843 god vkliuchitel'no* (St. Petersburg, 1896), pp. 200–202; M. A. Korf, "Imperator Nikolai v soveshchatel'nykh sobraniiakh: (Iz sovremennykh zapisok staats-sekretaria barona Korfa)," *Sbornik IRIO*, XCVIII (1896), 135–159, esp. 155 and 158; and Russia, Ministerstvo finansov, *Ministerstvo finansov, 1802–1902* (St. Petersburg, 1902), I, 231.

issuing institution's mortgages on the estate of the borrower.[12] The implications of this plan were certainly inflationary because the security of the mortgaged estates meant little. It would have been impossible to sell any large number at a reasonable price to prevent a fall in the value of the notes.[13] Of course inflation was not a necessary result of such an operation. The consequences depended on the number of notes issued, the growth of the economy, and other factors. Nicholas expected opposition and wrote with some irony to Prince Vasil'chikov: "Probably one must expect to endure a severe struggle with the Minister of Finance in this instance; but I hope to emerge from it the victor." [14] Kankrin's opposition was based on his conviction that notes bearing interest lower than that given by banks and recognized as legal tender would fall in value just as did the assignats. Instead he urged that the credit institutions be aided through issues of the conventional type of state treasury note and with cash from the military reserve fund.

At a meeting of the special committee, the Tsar read his proposal and Kankrin's written comments. Nicholas then asked the members of the committee to criticize his project without mercy because, he said, he considered himself a "dilettante" in the subject. The interest feature aroused some criticism, and Nicholas then proposed to issue the notes without interest, maintaining that they would not be assignats since they were secured by land. Kiselev argued that they be made redeemable in metal on demand and Kankrin agreed to the plan on this basis. Metal backing would provide a fixed limit to the total number that could be issued and would eliminate the essentially open-ended nature of a system based on land, which was available in vast quantities and of uncertain value. After some discussion, the Tsar decided that initially the backing fund of silver and gold should equal

---

[12] Korf, "Imperator Nikolai," pp. 160–161.

[13] The original assignat of France had been "secured" by land confiscated by the revolutionary government.

[14] Korf, "Imperator Nikolai," p. 161.

the notes issued, but that after they became generally accepted one-sixth backing would be sufficient.

The details were worked out swiftly. The public was not
to be told of the 100 per cent initial backing, but only of
the one-sixth permanent backing fund. The notes were to be
called credit notes and an issue of thirty million silver rubles
was decided upon, fifteen million for the Moscow *sokhran-
naia kazna,* eight million for the St. Petersburg office, and
seven million for the State Loan Bank. The manifesto was
issued July 2, 1841.[15] By 1843, only about eleven million
rubles' worth were issued.

The creation of state credit notes introduced an element
of flexibility into the Russian monetary system. Since 1823,
the number of assignats had been fixed and the amount of
metal money circulating depended on domestic gold and
silver production and the net gain or loss from transactions
with foreign countries and could not be controlled by the
state. The creation of the credit notes was a step in the direction that Mordvinov and Drutskii-Liubetskii had been advocating for years, and it violated Kankrin's long-standing
policy of opposing any mechanism that permitted discretion
in additions to the money supply. Nevertheless, he supported
the introduction of the credit note as an alternative to Drutskii-Liubetskii's more far-reaching proposal for a new type of
state treasury note and the reorganization of the state commercial bank as an active institution, independent of the
Ministry of Finance.[16]

Perhaps even more important than the substantive changes
implied in the creation of the state credit notes was the Tsar's
active participation in the policy-making process, not merely
in ordering action but by presenting his own proposals and
insisting that decisions be reached at once. That the content
of Nicholas' proposal may be attributed to Drutskii-Liubetskii is less significant than the Tsar's personal sponsorship
of one particular plan. In the past he had selected among al-

[15] *Ibid.,* pp. 162–169. The text of the law is on pp. 271–273.
[16] TsGIAL, f. 560, op. 38, d. 449, "Obshchii otchet . . , za 1841," p. 2.

ternatives presented by advisers, or simply confirmed the position adopted by Kankrin.

WHY RAILROADS?

Monetary reform, Kiselev's program for the state peasants, and the beginning of railroad construction were the three major projects initiated by the state in the area of economic affairs during Nicholas' reign. Each has its own special importance. Monetary reform solved a troublesome problem that had hampered commerce for many years. The reform did not, however, fundamentally change the existing situation. Changes in the status of the state peasants, if put into practice, were important simply because they involved so many people, and they had implications for the future of privately owned peasants as well. But the task was an enormous one and real momentum was hard to generate. The railroad was different; it was a new technological development that could be brought in almost whole. There was no need for slow and difficult local experimentation. You did not need to educate a peasantry or alter the village commune before you built one, nor did railroads seem to threaten public confidence in the currency. All that was required was some money for foreign equipment and advice and a lot of peasants with shovels. Yet the potential for change, rapid change, was immense, particularly in Russia, where great distances and poor transport had always been a more serious problem than in western Europe. As a prerequisite for a modern industrial society, the railroad can be considered as revolutionary in its own way as the emancipation of the serfs.

Russians in the thirties and forties could hardly be expected to have realized all this. Railroads were new, to some extent still unproven, and their total impact on the economy and society largely unknown. The state could experiment with a new device that offered certain specific immediate advantages. A decision by the state to build or not to build railroads did not have to imply a broader decision for or against industrialization, modernization, or social change. Some officials saw great and injurious consequences from railroad building, others saw the immense potentials for development, but it was quite possible to view the whole question narrowly and to say: Yes, a line from St. Petersburg to Moscow did seem to have some advantages over existing water and overland systems, and since it would probably pay for itself, it might as well be built.

Like many other technological innovations, the railroad was actually introduced to Russia at a very early date, but did not become important until long after its widespread acceptance in western Europe. In the late eighteenth century, at least two short rail lines using horses were in operation, one at a mine in the Altai, another in the Alexandrovsk factory in Petrozavodsk. Early in the nineteenth century a third line was built in the Altai. Perhaps even more surprising was the construction of a locomotive in 1833 by two serfs attached to a factory in the Urals, belonging to the Demidov family. Although these accomplishments were reported in the capitals, neither had any connection with later railroad building.[17] The mere presence of an innovation in Russia was not sufficient to ensure its introduction on a wide scale. A railroad requires substantial capital and at least governmental approval, if not actual support. The Demidovs were interested in the success of their mining ventures and not in risky projects that their talented serfs developed for the extensive

[17] V. S. Virginskii, "Zheleznodorozhnyi vopros v Rossii do 1835 goda," *Istoricheskie zapiski*, no. 25 (1948), pp. 137 and 145; V. S. Virginskii, *Tvortsy novoi tekhniki v krepostnoi Rossii* (Moscow, 1947), chs. 8 and 10. The story of the two Demidov serfs. the Cherepanovs, father and son, is an interesting example both of how high serfs, under certain circumstances, were able to rise (they both visited England and Sweden as agents of their master) and of the ultimately frustrating position such men were likely to find themselves in, as when they were forced to turn their attention to the everyday management of the factory and neglect their interest in locomotives.

use of steam engines. Without his owner's support, of course, a serf could do nothing.

The two clever but unfortunate mechanics in the Urals were the only men in Russia who had built locomotives and run a steam-powered railroad, but there were other, more favorably placed individuals in the 1830's who knew about railroads and were excited by them. Interest was evident not only in published discussions but increasingly in formal proposals submitted to the state.[18] Some of these were requests for concessions, like that of K. Iankevich, submitted in September 1830, for a ten-year monopoly of the right to introduce into Russia, tax free, railless steam cars of his own design. Nicholas referred the proposal to the Transport and Buildings Administration, which rejected it.[19] One of the earliest proposals for an actual railroad was that of Andrei Bestuzhev, submitted in April 1834, for a line linking the Volga and Don rivers. Bestuzhev proposed to supply 6,500 assignat rubles himself and requested two million from the state. A year later, the energetic civil governor of Tambov, N. M. Gamaleia, proposed to form a joint-stock company with one million rubles' capital to build a short line in his province to supplement existing water routes. Neither proposal received official approval, although Gamaleia had not asked for financial support.[20]

Although these projects may well have been poorly conceived or entirely impractical, they received far less consideration than was their due because the major government officials directly concerned were fundamentally opposed to railroad construction. Kankrin, as minister of finance, was opposed on both financial and social grounds, but at this early stage his position was not particularly important be-

---

[18] Such as N. Shcheglov, "O zheleznykh dorogakh i preimushchestvakh ikh nad obykhnovennymi dorogami i kanalami," *Severnyi Muravei*, no. 1 (1830), p. 5, cited by V. S. Virginskii, *Vozniknovenie zheleznykh dorog v Rossii do nachala 40-kh godov, XIX* (Moscow, 1949), p. 79.

[19] Virginskii, *Vozniknovenie*, p. 85.

[20] *Ibid.*, pp. 126–129.

cause the agency directly concerned, the Transport and Buildings Administration, was independent and reported directly to the Tsar. Its primary interest had traditionally been water transport and roads. The weight of tried and tested tradition lay on their side, and so did the voice of Moris Destrem, the most respected engineer of the day.

Destrem was one of four French engineers invited to Russia in 1810 by Alexander I to establish the Institute of Transport Engineers. He served as editor of the *Transport Journal* from its establishment in 1826 to 1834, and he later became director of the projects division of the Transport and Buildings Administration. In 1831, he delivered at the institute a strongly antirailroad lecture, which was also published in the *Journal* and later reprinted separately. According to Destrem, railroads were technologically impractical in Russia because of the severe climate, which would block them with snow in winter and floods in spring. From the economic standpoint he argued that the lack of skilled workers in Russia would raise costs and make their rates too expensive for Russia's bulky exports. The alleged advantage of year-round and rapid service offered by railroads over the seasonal and slow service possible with water or winter roads was, he claimed, of no importance for the agricultural products that Russia shipped abroad. The details of the argument are not nearly as important as the fact that the opposition of a man with Destrem's reputation led many to believe that railroads were a matter that did not concern Russia.[21] The directors of the Transport and Buildings Administration, Duke Alexander of Würtemberg up to 1833 and General Karl Tol' from 1833 to 1842, were military men with no special training in engineering or finance. It is hardly surprising that they were inclined to follow the counsel of the nation's senior engineer

[21] P. P. Mel'nikov, "Svedeniia o russkikh zheleznykh dorogakh," *Krasnyi arkhiv*, XCIX (1940), 140–142. These are Mel'nikov's memoirs, written in 1871. See also Virginskii, *Vozniknovenie*, pp. 82–83. Destrem's article appeared in the *Zhurnal putei soobshcheniia*, no. 21 (1831).

that the traditional ways were best for Russia, especially when the advice came at a time marked by modest but worthwhile progress in the construction of roads and canals.

The improved highroad between Moscow and St. Petersburg was opened in 1834, and a new statute on road construction was issued in 1833 that resulted in the construction of 780 more kilometers by 1840.[22] In 1820, a private joint-stock company had established regular passenger service by coach between the two capitals, and by the early thirties the coach routes reached the major cities of European Russia and even to Tiflis in the Caucasus.[23] Water transport depended primarily on the natural river system of Russia. In the late 1820's, the Duke Alexander of Würtemberg Canal was opened, connecting the northern Dvina and the Volga. It had only limited practical success, but its construction demonstrated the state's active interest in water transport.[24]

The pigeonholing of railroad projects in the Transport and Buildings Administration, however, could not continue indefinitely. Railroads were being built, not only in England and the United States, but on the continent as well. The advantages of the new form of transport for Russia were becoming increasingly clear to some observers, both Russian and foreign. The Institute of Transport Engineers in the twenties and early thirties had devoted little or no attention to railroad construction.[25] By the mid-thirties, however, it was possible for one of the institute's outstanding graduates, P. P. Mel'nikov, who had returned to it as a faculty member, to introduce problems relating to railroads in his course on applied mechanics and to publish the first technical work in

[22] *PSZ* II, statute 6076.

[23] Virginskii, *Vozniknovenie,* pp. 32–37.

[24] "Istoricheskoe obozrenie putei soobshcheniia i publichnykh zdanii s 1825 po 1850 god," *Sbornik IRIO,* XCVII (1896), 538–539.

[25] Virginskii, *Vozhiknovenie,* pp. 96–97, citing the manuscript version of the memoirs of A. Del'vig, a student at the institute at that time. See also Sergei M. Zhitkov, *Institut inzhenerov putei soobshcheniia, Imperatora Aleksandra I* (St. Petersburg, 1899), p. 48.

Russia dealing with railroads.[26] At the Mining Institute, the other major training ground for Russian engineers, under the sympathetic direction of K. V. Chevkin, interest in railroads was also growing in the mid-thirties.[27]

The interest and approval of a number of young engineers, valuable though it would be when railroads actually came to be built, could have little direct influence on the decision to build them. They had neither the capital nor the influence at court that was necessary for such an undertaking. They could, of course, encourage those who did. In 1834, Chevkin, in his capacity as director of the Mining Institute, invited the Austrian engineer and promoter, Franz Anton Ritter von Gerstner, to visit Russia to inspect mines and factories in the Urals. It seems probable that Chevkin hoped Gerstner would take an interest in Russia's transportation problems, for Gerstner was known primarily as a builder of one of the first railroads on the continent, connecting the Danube and the Moldau rivers in Austria. In any case, after extensive travels the Austrian became seriously interested in developing railroads in Russia, if indeed he had not been from the beginning of his visit. He prepared a proposal for the construction of railroads that was submitted to the Tsar on February 6, 1835. Although the Austrian's qualifications were questioned by some, Gerstner enjoyed widespread respect at this early stage. The Austrian ambassador helped him to obtain an audience with the Tsar. High officials such as Baron Korf spoke well of him and even General Tol', chief of the Transport and Buildings Administration, accepted him as an expert on railroads.[28]

---

[26] Mel'nikov, "Svedeniia," p. 135. According to Virginskii, similar but less successful attempts were made somewhat earlier by M. S. Volkov (*Vozniknovenie*, pp. 97–105).

[27] Virginskii, *Vozniknovenie*, pp. 111–113.

[28] Korf, "Imperator Nikolai," pp. 124–125; M. Krutikov, ed., "Pervye zheleznye dorogi v Rossii" (Report by Tol', Feb. 17, 1835), *Krasnyi arkhiv*, LXXVI (1936), 97 (this important collection of documents will hereafter be cited as Krutikov, with a summary title of the document, in English).

Gerstner's memorandum was a general one on the advantages of railroads for Russia from an economic and particularly a military standpoint, stressing English experience during an Irish rebellion to prove their value for troop transport. In a letter Gerstner elaborated:

Imagine that at the time of the last three wars, with Persia, Turkey, and Poland, there had existed a line from Petersburg via Moscow to Kazan, from Moscow to Odessa and from Petersburg to Grodno or Warsaw. Who could calculate the advantages these railroads would have afforded in that epoch? Grodno is 989 versts from Petersburg, which means that it would have been possible to send an army corps there in five days! . . . If Petersburg, Moscow, and Grodno or Warsaw had been connected by rail, it would have been possible to subdue the Polish insurgents in four weeks.[29]

Specifically, Gerstner proposed that lines be built from St. Petersburg to Moscow and possibly to Kazan, Nizhni-Novgorod, and other points under a concession granted to a company he would form. The concession would grant the company a complete monopoly on all railroad construction throughout the Russian empire for twenty years. Construction would be financed by the public sale of shares and no funds were requested from the state. At the end of the twenty-year period the lines built would remain the permanent property of the company. The state would receive a 50 per cent discount on all shipments and the company would stand ready to transport, on twenty-four hours' notice, at least 5,000 infantry and 500 cavalry with all artillery and horses for a distance of 200 versts per day. The concession was to be canceled if after four years 100 versts had not been built, using English rails. If the use of Russian-made rails were to be required, six years would be granted for the initial 100 versts.[30]

[29] Quoted in Virginskii, *Vozniknovenie*, p. 131. Virginskii translates from the unpublished French original of April 20, 1835. The general substance of his account is supported by the paraphrase given by Tol' in his report of February 17, 1835 (Krutikov, pp. 90–91).

[30] Krutikov, Report by Tol', Feb. 17, 1835, p. 93.

Since the minimum distance from St. Petersburg to Moscow is nearly 600 versts, Gerstner was not obliging himself to fulfill his vast design very rapidly, and the strategic advantages that he described in such glowing detail would have been slow to materialize.

In sharp contrast to the earlier railroad projects, Gerstner's plan received extensive consideration at the highest levels and eventually led to the actual construction of the first Russian railroad of any importance, although under conditions very different from those first requested. Gerstner owed his success to the fact that he was a foreigner with a substantial reputation who had already participated in building a railroad, and also to his ability to arouse the Tsar's interest, in all likelihood by his stress on the military advantages. Nicholas turned the proposal over to his chief assistant, Count Benkendorf, who in turn sent it to Tol' of the Transport and Buildings Administration. There it was considered by a commission of four engineers, including Major P. P. Mel'nikov, an enthusiastic but as yet uninfluential advocate of railroad construction. The commission reported to Tol' that there were two separate aspects of the problem, those relating to technology and those relating to the state. On the technical side their report favored Gerstner. His Austrian experience had shown, they felt, that snow would not be a major problem and steep grades would present no obstacle in level Russia. Steam engines would be used for freight service, but horses for passenger trains, because of the high cost of making a roadbed capable of safely carrying a heavy steam engine at high speed.

From the standpoint of the state's interests the commission had major reservations. A monopoly could only be granted between two specific points, free import of rails could not be allowed, no monopoly should be granted on hotels built along the line, and limits should be placed on the extent to which state land could be used without charge. Tol' 's own comments were noncommittal, although in subsequent discussion he was to take a strongly antirailroad position. He had perhaps not made up his own mind, or possibly was waiting to see if it

was advisable to express strong disapproval in the light of
the Tsar's favorable attitude. To Tol' the question of the
railroad company's right to condemn privately owned land
seemed to present serious problems because of the possible
infringement of property rights, a reflection perhaps of the
gentry's sensitivity to any measure that might threaten their
monopoly on rural landownership.

Despite the reservations of Tol' and the commission,
Nicholas' interest in the project continued. After some discussions with Gerstner, a new version of the proposal was
submitted to a distinguished committee, chaired by the Tsar
himself, and consisting of President of the State Council
Novosil'tsev, Minister of the Imperial Court Volkonskii, Tol',
War Minister Chernyshev, Kankrin, Benkendorf, Speransky,
and Minister of the Interior Bludov.[31]

Nicholas made his position clear at the beginning of the
meeting by summarizing the advantages to be gained by
large-scale railroad construction, especially for the transport
of troops in emergencies, and concluded with a joke about
the glorious day when one could "ride from here to Moscow
to dine with Prince Dimitri Vladimirovich [Golitzyn] and
then return again by nightfall." [32] There was therefore no
serious consideration of the economic and military value or
of the technical feasibility of railroads, although the stubborn
and outspoken Kankrin argued they would injure the peasants engaged in transporting goods and the steam engines
would destroy the forests for lack of coal.[33] Discussion, instead, was concerned with fiscal problems and the desirability
of accepting Gerstner's proposal. Volkonskii and Kankrin
were fearful that the use of foreign capital, which they felt
was inevitable, would mean that all the returns would go to
foreigners and the state would not benefit until the fifty-year
tax exemption had expired. The other members, led by Spe-

[31] *Ibid.*, pp. 93–97.
[32] Korf, "Imperator Nikolai," pp. 125–126.
[33] *Ibid.*, p. 126; Mel'nikov, "Svedeniia," pp. 145–146; Virginskii,
Vozniknovenie, pp. 135–138.

ransky and ultimately supported by Nicholas, saw considerable value in an influx of capital. According to their argument, most of this capital would be spent in Russia, and it would help the domestic economy in the same way that the receipts from Russian foreign trade did, even though the business was largely carried out by foreign merchants in Russia.

The most important decision was made during the discussion of the financial viability of the proposed railroads. Tol' took the position that this need concern only the private investors. The Tsar, however, asserted that in the case of an enterprise of such magnitude and so closely connected with the general prosperity, the state must not allow it to proceed without full assurance of success, because if it failed, "all the burden of maintaining such an enormous undertaking would lie on the state, and the investors themselves would have grounds to complain that they were drawn into error by my word and the concession given at my order." Further discussions with Gerstner were ordered to check on the accuracy of his calculations and to revise the conditions of the proposed concessions. The only specific point that Nicholas insisted on was a political one. If foreign specialists were brought in to help in the construction, they were to be approved in advance by Benkendorf, and none were to be French. Austrian civil servants, however, would be acceptable and would receive equivalent rank in Russian service.[34]

The discussions of this committee of February 28, 1835, is important, but not because of the concrete results that followed. Gerstner's grandiose plans soon were reduced to a short experimental line in the suburbs of St. Petersburg. But the vital question of the Tsar's attitude toward railroads now seemed to be resolved. He was convinced that railroads were worthwhile and practical, and paid no heed to the fears of those, like Kankrin, who saw them as producing all sorts of evils; but Nicholas was not determined to have them at any cost. They did not seem to be essential. Only if railroads

[34] Korf, "Imperator Nikolai," pp. 124–128. This section is also reprinted in Krutikov, pp. 98–101.

could pay their own way was he willing to give state backing, even indirect moral support, for their construction. If he was thinking primarily in terms of military advantages, as Virginskii argues, he was not in a hurry or willing to pay a very high price for the strategic gains.[35]

The further negotiations with Gerstner were carried on by a small committee consisting of Novosil'tsev, Speransky, Tol', and Korf. Colonel Kraft of the Corps of Transport Engineers was sent to Austria to investigate Gerstner and his railroad there. The report he submitted on returning was most unfavorable. The Danube-Moldau line was badly built and a financial failure. Nevertheless, discussions continued, and although the committee received Gerstner's estimates of the costs and revenues of a St. Petersburg–Moscow line with considerable skepticism, it was willing to grant an exclusive concession for a railroad from St. Petersburg to Moscow and Nizhni-Novgorod if he could give evidence of adequate financial support. This Gerstner was unable to do, and at a very early stage in the discussions he suggested that a start be made with the construction of an experimental line to Tsarskoe Selo. It would be built by a company with three million rubles' capital that could later expand to assume the task of building the St. Petersburg–Moscow line, then estimated to cost between 75 (Gerstner's estimates) and 140 (the committee's estimates) million rubles. Thus his scheme had shrunk from a vast empire-wide monopoly to a line of twenty-five versts to the Tsar's summer palace.[36]

The special committee was doubtful that investors could be found for even this limited project, but the group was willing to approve it if the funds could be raised, and Nicholas gave his formal endorsement in June 1835. With the support of the wealthy Count Bobrinskii, already known

[35] Virginskii, *Vozniknovenie,* pp. 130–131, 137–138. Virginskii may have felt obliged to take this position in the light of a vague statement of Lenin's, which he cites.

[36] Mel'nikov, "Svedeniia," pp. 146–150, 154; Virginskii, *Vozniknovenie,* pp. 140–143.

for his extensive and successful investment in the sugar-beet industry, the company's shares were sold. The charter of the line, which said nothing of other routes, was finally issued on March 21, 1836.[37] The Tsar took an active interest in the project, even to details such as how to be sure that passengers would not get off until they had paid their fares.[38] Construction began in May 1836 and the official opening was in October 1837, a year later than planned. At first steam engines were used only on holidays when traffic was heavy, and horses at other times; but from the spring of 1838 steam power was used exclusively.[39]

The Tsar's conviction that the company would fall back on the state proved to be correct when the three-million-ruble capital raised proved to be insufficient. In July 1837, the company requested a loan of 1.5 million to enable it to complete its project. Kankrin, of course, opposed the loan on the grounds that railroads were a doubtful business. He argued that the only security offered was the track already laid, and in Russia there was certainly no market for second-hand rails. Nevertheless, the company received the money and, doubtless to Kankrin's great surprise, the line proved to be a financial success.[40]

The history of the railroad question, from the opening of the Tsarskoe Selo line in the fall of 1837 to the final decision in January 1842 to build a railroad from St. Petersburg to Moscow, is a curious one. If there were any lingering doubts about the technical feasibility of steam power and rail transport under Russian climatic conditions, the successful operation of Gerstner's company should have dispelled them. Published opposition to railroads, however, became more widespread. After the death of Speransky, railroads had no enthusiastic supporters among the Tsar's major advisers and

[37] *PSZ* II, statute 9009, Virginskii, *Vozniknovenie,* pp. 162–163.

[38] Mel'nikov, "Svedeniia," p. 159.

[39] Virginskii, *Vozniknovenie,* pp. 165, 172.

[40] Krutikov, Kankrin's presentation in the Committee of Ministers, July 29, 1837, pp. 105–107; Virginskii, *Vozniknovenie,* p. 173.

there were several bitter opponents. Nicholas continued to be favorably inclined, but did not pursue the question with energy or enthusiasm. Projects for new lines were submitted and referred to the Transport Administration, which would produce a negative report. Only when the sponsors were particularly influential was any further progress made. Gradually, however, almost imperceptibly, the state came closer and closer to a firm commitment to further construction.

In 1838, three important proposals were made, two for a St. Petersburg–Moscow line and one for a connection between Warsaw and Vienna. The Polish project was approved and supported by the state. It became the second railroad to be built in the Russian empire, but neither plan for a link between the two capitals of the empire came to anything. One of these, that of N. N. Murav'ev, a former governor of Novgorod province, was little more than an argument in favor of railroads and the advantages they would bring to Russia. Murav'ev asserted that it would be reasonable to issue 300 million rubles in new assignats to pay for construction, but he presented no specific proposals for carrying out the enterprise.[41] The Moscow gentryman and entrepreneur A. V. Abaza was far more specific and suggested the formation of a joint-stock company with a capital of 120 million rubles. It would be possible, he thought, to sell them in Russia, if the state would make one small concession—gentrymen were to be permitted to add fifty rubles per soul to the existing mortgage debt on each of their serfs if they bought fifty rubles' worth of stock in the St. Petersburg–Moscow railroad company.[42] The security of the heavily mortgaged estates meant little. The proposal was simply a request for an indirect government loan. In their comments on the projects of Murav'ev and Abaza, Tol' and Kankrin questioned the possibility of raising the capital required and of obtaining

[41] Krutikov, Memorandum of N. Murav'ev to Nicholas I, pp. 123–124; Mel'nikov, "Svedeniia," p. 162.

[42] Krutikov, Project of A. V. Abaza for a joint-stock company to build a railroad from St. Petersburg to Moscow, March 12, 1839, pp. 113–114.

adequate revenues once the line was completed, and Tol'
especially stressed the lower costs of existing water transport
and belittled the advantages of the greater speed afforded by
railroads.[43]

Nicholas was undoubtedly reluctant to commit the state to
the support of a venture that was difficult to finance and
severely criticized by two of his most trusted advisers. The
example of the Warsaw-Vienna railroad suggests, however,
that the lack of really influential sponsors was the primary
reason why no progress was made toward the construction of
a St. Petersburg–Moscow line. In 1838, a Warsaw banker and
the governor of the Bank of Poland obtained the support of
Field Marshal Paskevich-Erivanskii, the Tsar's viceroy in Poland, for the formation of a joint-stock company. The goal of
the enterprise was to build a railroad from Warsaw to the
Austrian border, where it would connect with another line
to Vienna. With the influential support of Paskevich, the
company received, in January 1839, not only a concession but,
more important, a government guarantee of a 4 per cent return on its capital of 6.2 million silver rubles, with only the
added condition that steam rather than horse power be used.[44]

That the Tsar would grant a concession to a well-financed
private company is not surprising; he had done so for Gerstner's group despite the doubts raised by some of his closest
advisers. What is interesting is the government guarantee,
probably the first given to a railroad by a European government. It is true that Nicholas had said earlier that the granting of a concession was a moral guarantee, but now it was put
down in black and white for a railroad on the edge of the

---

[43] These advantages were substantial. It normally took two navigation seasons to deliver grain from the lower Volga region to St. Petersburg (P. P. Mel'nikov, "Poezdka na Volgu," *Krasnyi arkhiv,* LXXXIX–
XC [1938], pp. 315–319).

[44] N. A. Kislinskii, *Nasha zheleznodorozhnaia politika po dokumentam arkhiva Komiteta ministrov* (St. Petersburg, 1902), I, 18–19;
Julius Salomon, "Die Warschau-Wiener Eisenbahn und ihre Verstattli-
chung," *Archiv für Eisenbahnwesen,* XXXVII (1914), 1257–1281; Virginskii, *Vozniknovenie,* pp. 189–190.

empire. The exceptional feature of the Warsaw-Vienna project is the role of Paskevich-Erivanskii. Abaza and others who proposed a St. Petersburg–Moscow line as yet had no such prestigious supporters. The relatively small amount of capital required for the Polish line may have been an added attraction, but it should have provided a warning, for the projected cost per verst was less than half that of the Tsarskoe Selo line; in fact, the Warsaw-Vienna company was bankrupt by 1842. The state had to make good on its guarantees and eventually finished the project at its own expense.[45]

There is further evidence that by 1839 Nicholas was ready to approve well-supported proposals for railroad construction. In January 1839, he noted in the margin of the Committee of Ministers' report supporting Tol' 's negative evaluation of the Murav'ev plan:

It would not be superfluous, however, to order Count Tol' to busy himself now with all the necessary considerations regarding the construction of a railroad from Rybinsk to St. Petersburg, for the advantages of such a line, it seems, would be undeniable.

And two months later, he wrote on another report from Tol', "I am more inclined to admit the railroad as a thing very useful, significantly facilitating internal trade." Tol' replied with his usual arguments that railroads were good for passenger travel but not freight, which was the main potential source of business between St. Petersburg and Rybinsk. He introduced a new consideration when he quoted a French writer who claimed that railroads were the most democratic of institutions and would certainly transform society. The argument was one that Kankrin later included in his private diary, but there is no evidence that it made any particular impression on Nicholas, who simply maintained his attitude of relatively passive interest.[46] The Tsar took no more deci-

[45] Private construction stopped in May 1842, the state took over in October 1843, and the entire line was finally opened in April 1848, just in time to help transport troops to crush the Hungarian revolution.

[46] Both quotations are in Kislinskii, *Nasha zheleznodorozhnaia politika*, I, 18–19. The first quotation and Tol' 's remarks are also quoted

sive action than the despatch of two engineers, Mel'nikov and Kraft, to the United States to inspect railroads there.

It is sometimes suggested that the report subsequently made by Mel'nikov and Kraft, both enthusiastic supporters of railroad building, stimulated Nicholas to decisive action.[47] Mel'nikov's own account, however, gives an entirely different picture. Their six-volume report remained unread and they could accomplish nothing themselves because:

Count Tol' would never see any of us, access to him was only possible through Deviatin, who managed all the affairs of the Corps [of Transport Engineers] and stubbornly expressed his opposition to railroads. Access to other ministers was even more impossible. Published articles by men in service were not permitted except with strict censorship by their supervisors. One hope remained, the Tsar himself, who, it seemed, was inclined to favor railroads, or at least wanted one between the two capitals, but here too, of course, it was possible to act only through an intermediary.[48]

The intermediary was found in the person of the same Count Bobrinskii who had financed Gerstner's project. In 1841, he contacted the Leipzig bankers' house with whom he dealt and persuaded them to renew an earlier interest in the construction of a line from St. Petersburg to Moscow.[49] A formal proposal was submitted early in 1841 that included a request for a state guarantee of a 4 per cent return on capital and other privileges. The Tsar's response was to establish a "Committee for the preliminary preparation and consideration of a project for a railroad from St. Petersburg to Moscow" on March 7, 1841.[50] The members were Benkendorf,

by Krutikov, pp. 152–153, n. 20. Kankrin's private comments on railroads are in *Rtb.*, I, 23, 141, 216, and II, 15, 31.

[47] Kislinskii, *Nasha zheleznodorozhnaia politika,* I, 23; J. N. Westwood, *A History of Russian Railways* (London, 1964), p. 27.

[48] Mel'nikov, "Svedeniia," p. 166.

[49] *Ibid.,* pp. 166–167.

[50] By the time it made its report in September 1841, it was known as a "Commission on the construction of a railroad between St. Petersburg and Moscow."

Chevkin, Kraft, Mel'nikov, Bobrinskii, and later Abaza; all these men, except possibly Benkendorf, were favorably inclined toward the project, a fact that the Tsar must have known. The major opponents of the past, Tol' and Kankrin, were conspicuously absent. The technical work was done by Chevkin, Kraft, and Mel'nikov, and, if one believes his account, mostly by Mel'nikov, despite the fact that Tol' sent him off on a two-and-a-half-month trip to study the possibility of steam navigation on the Volga, presumably to eliminate an energetic partisan of railroads from the committee. The local commercial aspects were assigned to Abaza, and Bobrinskii dealt with the foreign financiers.[51]

Before this group completed its detailed report another, somewhat overlapping committee was formed at the Tsar's order on July 11, consisting of Stroganov (minister of interior), Deviatin (Tol' 's deputy), Vronchenko (Kankrin's deputy), plus Chevkin and Bobrinskii from the first group. The purpose of the new committee was to negotiate terms with the foreign capitalists. In view of the antirailroad position of at least two of the members, Deviatin and Stroganov (Vronchenko's position is uncertain, although there is no doubt of Kankrin's opposition), it is not surprising that they refused to make all the concessions demanded by the Leipzig bankers.

The state was willing to provide the guaranteed return, but agreement could not be reached on when it would take effect—with the opening of the railroad or, as the bankers demanded, with the establishment of the capital fund. It is important that Nicholas was entirely willing to have construction of the St. Petersburg–Moscow line undertaken by foreigners with foreign capital, under conditions essentially the same as those granted to the Warsaw-Vienna company. Interest in railroads was so strong by this time that the state continued its investigation of the project even after the private sponsors dropped out in August 1841.[52]

[51] Mel'nikov, "Svedeniia," pp. 167–171.
[52] Virginskii, *Vozniknovenie,* pp. 213–214.

The original committee, now called a commission, delivered its report on September 15, 1841. It was a detailed and thoughtful document, obviously prepared by men anxious to anticipate all possible objections, and it contained estimates of construction costs and operating expenses, designed, they said, to produce the most pessimistic picture possible. Nevertheless, the conclusion was that the line would yield a 6 per cent profit on the invested capital. A critical review committee of the Transport and Public Buildings Administration reduced this revenue estimate to 2.11 per cent, well below prevailing rates of interest, but not even this hostile group was able to claim that the project was financially impossible.[53]

Aside from the predicted return, the commission supporting railroad construction stressed the extensive building of railroads in Europe and North America, where, it said, more than 2,000,000,000 rubles had been invested in less than fifteen years to build 10,000,000 versts. Networks there were still rapidly expanding "because they satisfy one of the chief demands of the present century—speed, accuracy, and ease of contact, so important for saving valuable time, for easing turn-over, and for increasing capital." The commission emphasized that recent experience abroad had shown, in contrast to the pattern on some early lines, that freight, not

---

[53] Krutikov, Report to Nicholas of the commission on the construction of a railroad between St. Petersburg and Moscow, Sept. 15, 1841, pp. 130–133. It is noteworthy that Destrem, the long-time champion of water transport, dissented from the review committee report and predicted a 10 per cent return. He had either "seen the light" from the technical standpoint or, as Mel'nikov suggests, he realized which way the wind was blowing and decided to go along (Mel'nikov, "Svedeniia," pp. 172–173). In fact, the railroad cost twice what even the review committee estimated, but revenues were also much greater, so for the early years of operation their profit estimates were very close to the mark. Profits did not exceed 5 per cent until after 1862, a decade after the line opened (Arnuf Manfred Steinwald, "Der Staatsbahngedanke in der russischen Eisenbahnpolitik," *Archiv für Eisenbahnwesen,* XLVIII [1925], 872; Krutikov, Findings of the committee of the Transport and Buildings Administration, Oct. 10, 1841, pp. 146–147).

passenger traffic, would be the most important source of revenue, even in the face of competition from canals. The chief benefit to be gained from the St. Petersburg-Moscow line was in the transport of grain to St. Petersburg and thence to northern European markets via the Baltic Sea. The state would save money because of lowered grain prices, and less timber would be used in building river barges.

Perhaps the most interesting comment was about the relation of railroads to industry. The projected line would, according to the commission, prevent the excessive concentration of the "factory population" in the two capitals by permitting manufacturers to avoid the high costs of urban locations while still enjoying easy access to the cities from factories located along the main line. The report did not suggest that the building of a railroad would encourage the development of industries in general. The omission may have been a tactical one; those opposed to railroads were likely to regard more factories as a highly questionable benefit. Finally, the commission closed its argument by stressing the psychological importance of tying St. Petersburg closer to the rest of Russia: "In the present circumstances St. Petersburg can only be the head of Russia; when a railroad line unites it with Moscow it will also be the Russian heart." [54]

In addition to the technical review committee of the Transport and Public Buildings Administration already mentioned, Nicholas requested the opinion of Minister of the Interior Count Stroganov, and of Count Perovskii, who was about to replace Stroganov. Both opinions were negative. Stroganov argued on economic and technical grounds that the railroad would not pay and that it would not work in Russia because of the low level of skills among the population. Perovskii agreed and added:

One more important consideration cannot be ignored, the first consequence of this new and very close tie of the focal point of

[54] Krutikov, Report to Nicholas of the commission on the construction of a railroad between St. Petersburg and Moscow, Sept. 15, 1841, pp. 140–144.

Russia, via St. Petersburg, with foreign countries would be an excessive influence of a foreign spirit on our heartland. Such a circumstance cannot be considered in any way advantageous for Russia.[55]

The final decision was not made until early in the following year. At a meeting of the Committee of Ministers on January 13, 1842, Kankrin and Tol' repeated their previous objections and were supported by Volkonskii. More significant was the uncertain attitude of Kiselev, Minister of War Chernyshev, and the president of the State Council, Vasil'chikov. Kiselev was favorably inclined in general, but wanted further study, and the other two men wanted shorter lines starting in Moscow. Of those present at the meeting, only Chevkin and Bobrinskii were committed supporters of railroads.[56] Neither of these men were leading figures in Nicholas' administration. Nevertheless, the decision was made to build the St. Petersburg–Moscow railroad, and at state expense.[57] Doubtless, as Virginskii argues, the military factor was important for Nicholas; but it should not be overlooked that he waited for years, until railroads seemed to be a reasonably safe bet financially. It is something of a tribute to Nicholas' independence of mind that he finally overruled many of his chief advisers and proceeded with this great undertaking. It is also indicative of the relatively free atmosphere in which decisions were made that these men could and did oppose the project long after it must have been clear that the Tsar was in favor of it. The unquestioning obedience that Nicholas expected is obvious in the composition of the committee established on January 27 to direct the building of the railroad. It included Tol', Kankrin, and Perovskii, ardent opponents of the whole affair.[58]

[55] Mel'nikov, "Svedeniia," pp. 173–174.

[56] Benkendorf's precise role is unclear. He participated in many committees dealing with railroads, but if he expressed a clear position, it does not seem to have been recorded.

[57] Virginskii, *Vozniknovenie,* pp. 222–223.

[58] The familiar anecdote about the construction of Russian railroads is that Nicholas I determined the route of the St. Petersburg–Moscow

The decision to build the railroad at direct state expense is not nearly as significant as it might seem at first glance. There was never any firm ideological commitment to state or private enterprise under Nicholas I; each case was determined on practical and specific grounds. As early as the first discussion of Gerstner's original project, it was clear that the Tsar regarded a major railroad as an essentially national undertaking, whether or not it was formally in the hands of a private entrepreneur, with or without a guarantee from the state. Once a guarantee became necessary, as was demanded by the Leipzig bankers, the practical difference between state and private operation became even less. Nicholas was willing to have private enterprise build the line and operate it if the terms were satisfactory. If they were not, the logical thing to do would be to have the state build it, once the basic decision was made that the railroad was needed and could be financed. In either case, most of the money had to come from abroad, either by direct state borrowing or by private financing guaranteed by the state. The total cost of 43 million silver rubles as estimated by the commission was over 25 per cent of total state revenues for 1841. No responsible statesman of the time suggested that there was any other possible source for the large sums required.

The development of steam navigation on the Volga River provides an interesting contrast to the story of state versus private operation of railroads in Russia. In 1817 and 1823, long-term exclusive concessions had been granted to private

---

railroad by putting a ruler on a map and drawing a line connecting the two points. He may have done this; but if he did, it was simply to confirm the recommendations of the various advisory committees and of Mel'nikov. It was not an arbitrary expression of preference for orderly straight lines that nobody dared oppose. The direct route was shorter and cheaper to build than the alternative route following the highway through Novgorod. Kiselev and a few others supported this latter route, protesting that, by bypassing Novgorod, the direct route would injure the town; Nicholas took the trouble to argue at some length that this was not the case, because Novgorod's water and road transport would not be affected (Kislinskii, *Nasha zheleznodorozhnaia politika*, I, 26–29).

companies for the operation of steamboats, but as Mel'nikov discovered during his trip in 1841 and vividly described in his report, the use of the Volga remained confined almost entirely to vessels drawn by men or horses. In 1843, the policy was reversed, all concessions were canceled, and the alternative of direct state operation was rejected on the reasonable ground that private capitalists were as capable as the state of building a steamboat. Within a few years, at least one company had extensive and successful operations underway.[59] The state was flexible, not dogmatic. Monopoly concession had not worked, state support was not needed, so let the capitalists have a chance to try their luck. If they failed, the state would not be committed to support their enterprise. The only misgivings were that large operators might squeeze out the small ones, and rate regulation was considered, but not adopted.[60]

In summary it can be said that the beginning of large-scale railroad building in Russia was less significant than it should have been. It was the result of prolonged discussion and consideration and began in 1842, when Nicholas finally was sure that a railroad from St. Petersburg to Moscow would be useful and financially feasible. There was no larger plan to construct a railroad network, and the first line was justified, from an economic standpoint, largely on the grounds that it would facilitate the existing trade in grain. There was hardly a suggestion of the possible implications that railroads might have for economic growth in general, and the only impact on industry mentioned by the supporters of the project was the dispersal of factories outside the two capitals. The building of the St. Petersburg–Moscow line was revolutionary only in a symbolic sense, as an indicator of what was to come much later; the undertaking itself was approached in a conservative way with limited and specific goals, just as was the monetary reform that was underway during precisely the same period.

[59] Mel'nikov, "Poezdka na Volgu," pp. 309–312, 326–330; I. A. Shubin, *Volga i volzhskoe sudokhodstvo* (Moscow, 1927), pp. 396–404.
[60] Mel'nikov, "Poezdka na Volgu," pp. 320–329.

THE PEASANTRY: ACTION AT LAST

The construction of Russia's first railroad was a symbol of future economic change, but was not a real departure from traditional policy. The enthusiasts and visionaries might see great possibilities for change in the line from St. Petersburg to Moscow. The archconservatives might fear it. But the state could and did treat it as a limited technical and fiscal problem. Agriculture and the peasantry, as already noted, were another matter entirely. What affected them affected almost all Russia and virtually every aspect of Russian life. From at least the late eighteenth century to the great reforms of the 1860's, and in a somewhat different form almost to the present day, the peasant question has been the central issue facing Russian society and has been widely recognized as such.

During the reign of Nicholas I the status of the peasantry could not be openly discussed in the press, but was debated in the famous "circles" of the liberal intellectuals and in the pages of Herzen's radical newspaper, *Kolokol*, published abroad. It was also considered at great length within the government by the series of "secret committees" appointed by Nicholas I to determine what could and should be done. Most of this discussion, official and unofficial, is necessarily beyond the scope of this study of state economic policy. The state failed to take meaningful action affecting any aspect of the status of the privately owned serfs largely because it was unable to resolve the conflict between two basic principles that were accepted by virtually all of the participants in the secret committee discussions: (1) the land used by the peasants belonged to the gentry, but (2) a landless emancipation was impossible because it would create a rootless and dangerous class of rural laborers. Any solution had to involve some compromise of one or both of these principles. There was lengthy discussion, and Nicholas apparently had a real interest in reform. In the end, however, he was unwilling to force the acceptance of any change in the *status quo*.

A few gentrymen were interested in the possibilities of a "Baltic type" of emancipation, one that made the peasant a landless laborer dependent on the landlord, but the state would not accept such a program and the only substantive measure taken was a law that permitted serfs and masters to negotiate voluntarily a contract establishing their mutual obligations. In addressing the State Council in March 1842, Nicholas emphasized his belief that the new law neither endangered the property rights of the gentry nor cut the peasant off from the land.[61] In practice the law was ignored by the landlords and had no significant effect on the status of the peasantry.

Throughout the early 1830's, Kankrin had fended off proposals for major changes in the management of the state lands and of the peasants on them. He had rejected positive programs as too expensive and diverted attention by suggesting empty administrative changes.[62] In 1835, a new secret committee was established, officially called "A Committee for the Finding of Means for the Improvement of the Condition of Peasants of Various Categories." Like the earlier committees, its discussions were not formally confined to any single group of peasants. It produced a general statement of goals that embraced all the peasantry and envisaged the ultimate transformation of them into free men, not tied to the land.[63] The two substantive proposals that were presented to the committee concerned only state land and state peasants, areas in which the government had a much freer hand than it did, or thought it did, with respect to the gentry-owned land and

[61] Semevskii, *Krest'ianskii vopros v Rossii v XVIII i pervoi polovine XIX veka* (St. Petersburg, 1888), II, 60–64. A report of the secret committee of 1835, after affirming the gentry's title to the land, went so far as to admit a free, landless peasantry as a desirable ultimate goal, but quickly qualified this statement by pointing out the dangers of any rapid move in that direction ("Zapiska, predstavlennaia Gosudariu . . ." in A. P. Zablotskii-Desiatovskii, *Graf P. D. Kiselev i ego vremia* [St. Petersburg, 1882], IV, 148–151).

[62] See above, Chapter III, p. 114.

[63] See note 61 above.

serfs. Neither of the two measures, the one proposed by Kiselev dealing with the confiscated estates of rebellious Polish gentrymen nor the other, proposed by Kankrin on the administrative organization of his own ministry's Department of State Domains, are of particular importance in themselves. But from the discussion of these two proposals came the important decision to embark on a major program of reform for the state peasantry that took control away from Kankrin and gave it to Kiselev.

The committee's discussions centered on the perpetual question of the land surveys needed to provide a more equitable basis for taxation and to prevent appropriation of state land by the gentry. Kankrin, as always, argued that this was a slow and expensive process which could not be done on a large scale. He repeated his earlier idea of using province-wide norms for tax collection, instead of individual surveys and appraisals.[64] Kiselev's proposals for the utilization of the confiscated Polish estates provided that there the obligations of each peasant would be carefully defined—all of them would be granted land, the right to personal property, and the right to engage in another occupation after meeting their tax obligations. These principles were adopted and put into practice. The decrees, however, remained unpublished and applied to these particular properties only. There was some fear of arousing the false expectation that similar measures would be enacted for the entire empire.[65]

When the committee of 1835 failed to produce any overall program for the state peasantry, Nicholas lost patience with Kankrin, removed the state peasants from the jurisdiction of the Ministry of Finance, and put Count Kiselev in charge of their administration. A few months after the decisive action, the Tsar described his feelings to Kiselev:

I long ago became convinced of the need to reform their [the state peasants'] position; but the Minister of Finance, from stub-

[64] M. N. Druzhinin, *Gosudarstvennye krest'iane i reforma P. D. Kiseleva,* I (Moscow and Leningrad, 1946), 292–295.

[65] *Ibid.,* pp. 290–292.

bornness or inability, finds it impossible. I know him, and therefore I insisted on the necessity of taking up the matter instantly.
Seeing that it got nowhere under him I decided to proceed with
it myself and to lay the basis under my own direction.[66]

A careful student of the problem, N. M. Druzhinin, believes
that reports of disturbances among state peasants in 1835
stimulated Nicholas to take decisive action, but there is no
positive evidence that this is true, only the approximate
chronological coincidence of the two developments. It is
equally reasonable to imagine that the Tsar was convinced
that nothing at all would be done unless an energetic administrator was appointed. Kiselev was on the scene and had
several qualifications that made him a natural choice. He
combined the military background that had always appealed
to Nicholas with experience in administering the Danubian
Principalities, and he had ideas about the peasant question
that were stimulating but not excessively radical. Any explanation of the appointment must assume that Nicholas did
want to make some changes in the status of the peasantry;
there was certainly no pressure from inside his government,
much less from without, that was strong enough to make him
take action against his will.

Although Kiselev was given charge of a major segment of
the population, and of the economy, he never influenced the
shaping of overall economic policy as Kankrin had. Kiselev
showed no inclination to become seriously concerned with
economic problems outside the area of his immediate responsibilities, nor did Nicholas lean upon him in other matters such as monetary reform, railroad construction, or tariff
policy. The new director of peasant affairs may have read the
English political economists Smith and Bentham in his youth
and certainly was more or less familiar, if only at second hand,
with the theories they espoused, but he never tried to develop
a general theory of state economic policy. In managing his
own estates he made no significant economic innovations.[67]

[66] Zablotskii-Desiatovskii, *Kiselev*, II, 11.
[67] What little is known about Kiselev's reading is discussed in Dru-

Kiselev came from an old, well-connected, and reasonably prosperous Russian gentry family. He received the usual home education from tutors followed by military service starting at the age of seventeen. Later he served as an aide to Alexander I in Paris and in 1816 submitted to him a proposal for the gradual abolition of serfdom. As the superior officer of Pestel', he knew and admired this energetic leader of the southern branch of the Decembrists and even shared some of their ideas. By 1825, however, he had cut himself off from them and took an energetic part in the suppression of the movement.[68]

There was nothing unusual in this biography; it was typical for a man of his class. Kiselev came to play an important role not because of special knowledge of economics, or the originality of his ideas, but because he was an energetic and effective administrator who won the personal confidence of the Tsar. He was committed to the existing political system and firmly believed that reforms could and should be made from the top down, through the will of an enlightened monarch and the action of a capable bureaucracy, working in accordance with established legal procedures.[69]

To start the reform program, the Tsar created the Fifth Section of His Majesty's Own Chancellory, headed by Kiselev, and assigned to it the reorganization of the state peasant administration of St. Petersburg province. The committee of 1835 ended its active existence in May 1836 by requesting Kiselev to report to it on certain topics in the light of his investigation and experience in St. Petersburg province. The list had been prepared by Kiselev himself, with the aid of Speransky, so he was, in effect, writing his own instructions. The major problems he selected were:

(1) the most convenient way of shifting from a per capita charge (*obrok*) to one based on land;

---

zhinin, *Gosudavstvennye krest'iane,* I, 262–263. For estate management, see pp. 248–256.

[68] Zablotskii-Desiatovskii, *Kiselev,* I, chs. 1–10; Druzhinin, *Gosudarstvennye krest'iane,* I, 256–272.

[69] Zablotskii-Desiatovskii, *Kiselev,* II, 175, 189.

(2) the best way to impose a levy on handicrafts;

(3) the introduction of hereditary family plots;

(4) the distribution of land to those without enough;

(5) the distribution of forest land to the peasants, and its protection;

(6) the improvement of village and county (*volost*) administration and its protection from extortion and oppression;

(7) a general consideration of levies and the possibilities of raising receipts from them;

(8) a comparison of the administration of state and appanage peasants in St. Petersburg province.[70]

The emphasis in the program is clearly on a more equitable system of taxation, provision of adequate land to the peasants, and changes in the system of land tenure. Administration and increased revenue are mentioned but not stressed. The possibility of increasing productivity through the use of better agricultural techniques, and the various ways that this goal might be achieved, is not mentioned at all.[71] Kiselev's own views differed somewhat from the formal statement that he prepared for the committee's use. In a memorandum to Speransky in February 1836, he emphasized that the great accumulation of arrears was not solely the result of the poor distribution of land and inequitable tax system that followed from lack of surveys:

The cause of it [impoverishment] is the lack of: first, protection, and second, supervision. Because of the lack of protection the peasants are burdened with illegal requisitions and personal taxes. Because of the lack of supervision debauchery and drunkenness destroy the basis of rural well-being at the very source.[72]

---

[70] *Ibid.*, pp. 15–16. I follow the quoted text given with respect to grouping of topics, but have shorted the substance. Druzhinin (*Gosudarstvennye krest'iane*, I, 297) gives essentially the same list, somewhat rearranged and more severely shortened.

[71] Druzhinin (*Gosudarstvennye krest'iane*, I, 297–298) gives a similar interpretation with more emphasis on both the state's fiscal interests and the pressure of peasant discontent. He does not note the omission of technological and educational questions.

[72] Zablotskii-Desiatovskii, *Kiselev*, II, 18.

A lengthy inspection trip to the provinces in the summer of 1836 convinced Kiselev more than ever that the immorality and corruption both of the local administrators and of the unfortunate peasants themselves was the major barrier to economic progress. Often, arrears were collected from peasants who had already paid in full. Education of an appropriate kind was needed and had been sorely neglected by both government and church. He attributed the success of the schismatic sects to their own internal organization, which provided order and mutual assistance. In Kiselev's view, the introduction of good administrative practices was the essential first step that must precede changes in the system of taxation and, presumably, other reforms as well. To prove his point, Kiselev cited the situation on the appanage estates, where no real reforms had been carried out, according to Kiselev, but an independent and effective administration kept good order and there were few arrears.[73] The extent of Kiselev's authority had not yet been defined. It was in his interest to stress the importance of strong and independent administration. Yet there is no doubt that he was quite sincere in this evaluation of the situation. In the same period he commented privately that land redistribution must be carried out with caution, loans to the peasantry must come from capital funds they themselves have accumulated, most of the land must remain under the control of the village communal organization and be subject to repartition where this was the practice, tax collection should be put into good order, and ways found to tax handicraft production. Finally, he said that education was more a question of moral and political instruction than of practical or technical training, although he did mention the great value of model farms.[74]

The Kiselev program emphasized the crucial role of administration, the need to guide the peasant in improving all aspects of his life. The term he used to describe the idea was

[73] *Ibid.,* pp. 19–22, 52.

[74] Druzhinin, *Gosudarstvennye krest'iane,* I, 478–483; also Druzhinin's summary on pp. 491–500.

"guardianship" over the state peasantry. Kiselev did not pro-
pose to achieve his ends by freeing the peasant from the traditional restraints of the village commune to give scope to
individual initiative.[75] Even direct economic assistance
through loans and agricultural training did not have a prominent place in his plan. By emphasizing the crucial role of administration, Kiselev made the whole program depend primarily on his ability to create a bureaucratic apparatus far
more effective than any known theretofore in Russian experience. With a vast area and millions of people soon to be
committed to his authority, it was a truly formidable undertaking.

On January 6, 1837, all state lands and peasants, not just
those in St. Petersburg province, were assigned to the new
Fifth Section headed by Kiselev. During the following year,
detailed plans were made that culminated in the establishment of the Ministry of State Domains on December 26,
1837.[76] The reason for the establishment of the new ministry,
as stated formally in the statute, was: "For the administration
of state domains, for the guardianship of the free rural residents, and for the management of agriculture." The first of
these three functions was by no means new. Administration
of the state's holdings for the most part meant simply the
collection of revenue. Guardianship (*popechitel'stvo*) over the
"free rural residents" (the new and awkward term for state
peasants) embraced both the traditional task of maintaining
order and a greatly expanded, if not entirely new, concern
for health, education, and morals. The inclusion of the "management [*zavedyvaniia*] of agriculture," was an important departure from earlier practice. Never before, except for small
groups like the appanage peasants, or in the military colonies,
had the state assumed any responsibility for the primary eco-

---

[75] Kiselev also rejected the extreme "free enterprise" view of those,
including Mordvinov, who proposed in earlier years that state lands and
peasants be turned over to the gentry for proper economic management. See Druzhinin, *Gosudarstvennye krest'iane*, I, 125–130.

[76] *PSZ* II, statute 10834, ch. 1.

nomic activity of the peasantry. The state had always depended on the fruits of the peasants' labor for its revenue, but even the process of collection had not been one that normally put the peasant in direct contact with the state. The system of gentry landholding, the village communal organization, and even repartitional tenure, the basic institution of rural Russian life, were all developed largely as means to enable the wealth produced by the peasant to be mobilized with an absolute minimum of administrative effort. Kiselev's program represented the first large-scale plan for the central political authority to operate more directly and on a much lower level—not simply in the village after the crop was in the barn, but in the muddy field at planting time, in the hope that by fall there would be a larger crop for both the peasant and the state.

The new and the long-established functions were not unrelated. The size of the tax burden and the way it was levied could affect productivity, so too could the maintenance of order in the villages. A great deal of the activity of the new ministry was necessarily concerned with the more traditional activities. Revenues had to be collected, disputes settled, and so forth. But there was a shift in emphasis from maximizing immediate fiscal gains with minimal administrative effort, the policy of Kankrin, to one that strove to create an effective bureaucratic apparatus that would enable the ministry to introduce changes in old administrative practices and move into new areas of direct agricultural improvement.

The traditional fiscal-administrative functions and the new goal of bettering peasant welfare and agricultural productivity were assigned to different parts of the new ministry's central apparatus. Under the heading of "guardianship," which soon came to encompass agricultural management as well as welfare, virtually all the newer functions were assigned to the Third Department of the new ministry. Its responsibilities included the whole problem of land surveying, plus relief, education, and technological innovation. The First and Second Departments had responsibility for the traditional revenue-collection activity in different regions, with the division of responsibility based on differences in the existing system of fiscal administration. In practice, the Second Department had jurisdiction in west Russia and the Baltic provinces and the First Department covered the rest of the empire.[77]

On the local level, all the various functions of the three departments were carried out by a four-layer administrative system established by a decree of April 30, 1830.[78] The statute setting up the new administrative system was long and detailed, taking up 249 pages in the Complete Code of Laws. Kiselev took great pains to point out that in the main it represented a systematization and collection of existing statutes on the administration of state peasant affairs.[79] Inevitably, most of the text was devoted to the structure of the new administration, establishing who was responsible to whom, how the various officials were to be appointed, and so forth. The new functions of direct economic intervention, perhaps because they were new, were confined to brief hortatory statements. The county (*okrug*) inspector, for example, was given an incredible number of tasks, covered in some 397 separate paragraphs of the statute. One of these paragraphs described what could easily have been a full-time job by itself, for it implied extensive supervision of peasant activity:

The *okrug* inspector shall see to it (a) that the land of the peasants shall not be neglected, but will be carefully cultivated and that all agricultural work will be carried out on schedule and (b) that the poorest land shall be gradually cleared and improved.

[77] *PSZ* II, statute 10834, chs. 2–4. Druzhinin's discussion of the general organization of the new ministry is on pp. 521–526 of *Gosudarstvennye krest'iane,* Vol. I. See also Zablotskii-Desiatovskii, *Kiselev,* II, 54–58.

[78] *PSZ* II, statute 11189. The administrative apparatus is described at length in Druzhinin, *Gosudarstvennye krest'iane,* I, 526–570.

[79] *Ibid.,* pp. 570–571, contains a table that Kiselev prepared to prove his contention, showing that only 10 per cent of the 2,077 articles of the statute were new.

Economic activities were not spelled out in detail nor were they assigned to specific officials freed of other tasks.[80] It was clearly up to the new administration to chart its own course.

LAND AND TAXES

The major economic programs of the newly created ministry involved land distribution, taxation, and direct attempts to improve peasant welfare and agricultural productivity. In each instance there were significant opportunities for improvement, but also effective restrictions on what could in fact be done. The distribution of additional land to the peasantry was limited not only by the actual amount of usable acreage accessible in the prerailroad era, but also by the continuing ability of the gentry to assert its claims to specific pieces of land and block any steps that seemed to infringe on their dominant position in the countryside. On the land already used by peasants, it was possible to encourage individual initiative by establishing hereditary tenure, but the state hesitated to move decisively in this direction for fear of creating an unstable social situation in the villages.

The problem was much the same in the area of taxation. The methods of imposing taxes might be improved, but the state could not afford to reduce the total tax burden. The weakness of the administrative system and particularly its inability to carry out the surveys and assessments sharply reduced the effectiveness of tax reforms. The scope for direct assistance to the peasantry was virtually unlimited, but the funds available for education or for loans were not. Here too the capability of the administrative apparatus was a severe limiting factor.

Before Kiselev could turn to tax reform or the improvement of peasant welfare, it was necessary to devote an immense effort to the relatively simple matter of land surveys.

[80] *PSZ* II, statute 1189, pt. 4, par. 281.

The government had only the vaguest notion of how much land its peasants were living on, and hardly any idea at all of the nature and quality of the land in any given area. Was it forest, arable field, pasture, or swamp? A visual inspection would reveal the general character of a district, but only a vague guess could be made of the actual acreage of each type of land in each village. About the total numbers of state peasants the government had a somewhat better idea, because for more than a century taxes had been levied on a per capita basis, requiring periodic "revisions" of the tax lists. As long as land was very plentiful and the population thin, the lack of accurate land surveys could easily be ignored. The peasant simply used all the land he could till. What really mattered on both sides was the relationship of the peasant to either an individual gentryman or a state official. By the mid-nineteenth century, land had ceased to be unlimited in supply throughout European Russia, and in some areas a real shortage was developing. Surveys to fix boundaries were necessary to determine which peasants needed more land and how much and to prevent the local gentry from illegally appropriating state land, a practice long established. If taxation was to be based on the land's productive capacity rather than on population, surveys were the first step in assessing its value.

When the Ministry of State Domains was established in 1838, the total area of state lands in European Russia was thought to be about 90 million desiatins (1 desiatin = 2.7 acres). Of this only 736,000, less than 1 per cent, were surveyed.[81] Surveying proceeded throughout the entire reign of Nicholas, but despite substantial progress the job was not finished. In 1857, the ministry claimed a total of 65,793,269 desiatins completed, a figure that was exaggerated and ignored the poor quality of much of the surveying.[82]

---

[81] Druzhinin, *Gosudarstvennye krest'iane*, II (1958), 171; Ministerstvo gosudarstvennykh imushchestv, *Istoricheskoe obozrenie piatidesiatiletnei deiatel'nosti Ministerstva gosudarstvennykh imushchestv, 1837–1887* (St. Petersburg, 1888), II, pt. 2, 3–4.

[82] Druzhinin, *Gosudarstvennye krest'iane*, II, 171–172; Ministerstvo

Even more difficult than simple surveying was the task of assessing the value of peasant holdings so that the charge (*obrok*) paid to the state could be based on its productive potential. The evaluation of land proved to be difficult and slow. In areas where craft production was an important source of peasant income, it was particularly complex. The land in such areas was often poor, but the peasant income high. As experience was accumulated, an increasing effort was made to convert the old per capita charge (*obrok*) into what amounted to a crude income tax rather than a land tax, a task that was much more complicated than land evaluation. The officials in charge later admitted that the work turned out to be far more difficult than it had ever been expected and that possibly it was entirely beyond their capabilities.[83] Nevertheless, between 1842, when work commenced, and Kiselev's retirement in 1856, assessments were completed for twenty-five provinces and the new tax system was actually introduced in nineteen of them, affecting 3,843,285 adult male peasants on 15,984,378 desiatins of land. In eleven provinces, with 2,328,515 souls and 11,895,425 desiatins of state land no progress had been made.[84] It is absolutely clear that both in general surveying and in the more complex task of assessment there was real progress, and a continuing and even increasing effort was made to further these projects during Kiselev's administration of the state lands (1837–1856).

---

gosudarstvennykh imushchestv, "Obozrenie upravleniia gosudarstvennykh imushchestv za posledniia 25 let s 20 noiabria 1825 po 20 noiabria 1850 g.," *Sbornik IRIO,* XCVIII (1896), 477.

[83] K. S. Veselovskii, "Vospominaniia K. S. Veselovskago," *Russkaia starina,* CXVI (1903), 20; E. F. Fon-Bradke, "Avtobiograficheskie zapiski Egora Fedorovicha Fon-Bradke," *Russkii arkhiv,* nos. 1–3 (1875), 289.

[84] The six provinces where assessments were complete, but the new tax system not yet started, accounted for 1,179,440 souls and 8,726,228 desiatins (Ministerstvo gosudarstvennykh imushchestv, *Istoricheskoe obozrenie,* II, pt. 2, 58. Druzhinin lumps these provinces together with the eleven where no work had been done (*Gosudarstvennye krest'iane,* II, 145). For a general discussion of assessment see *Istoricheskoe obozrenie,* II, pt. 2, 44–63, and Druzhinin, II, 142–149.

Surveying and assessment received so much attention because of the belief that surveys would enable the state to
assist peasants with insufficient land and that charges based
on rational assessment would make the burden of taxation
less onerous and easier to collect. Illegal use of state land by
private owners did become far more difficult after surveys
were completed. Some improperly appropriated land was
even restored to state control. The practice of officially granting state land to high officials as a sign of unusual favor did
not stop, despite Kiselev's efforts and the promulgation of
several laws on the subject, but it was kept within bounds
and did not greatly change the total extent of state lands.[85]
But if the amount of land that gentrymen received from the
state was limited, so too was the acreage transferred to state
peasants in need of it. During the Kiselev administration the
gentry acquired some 1.5 million desiatins and the peasants
about 2.8 million desiatins of cropland from the state. Despite
efforts to make more forest land available, the total amount
under peasant control fell slightly during Kiselev's administration. Wood was needed for fuel and construction, and the
peasants cleared land of trees faster than new forest tracts
could be assigned to them.[86]

The effects of the shift from the soul tax to one based on
the estimated income-producing capacity of land and income
from handicraft production are not easy to assess. Druzhinin
points out that total tax arrears in provinces that underwent
the reform increased in almost all instances between 1838
and 1856, while in some of those where no change was made
arrears fell. In all but two of the "reformed" provinces, however, the annual average amount of taxes unpaid, taken as a
percentage of the annual tax burden, fell after the reform
was carried out, even though the absolute amount of these

[85] Druzhinin estimates that the amount of state land, excluding forests, fell 6 per cent between 1841 and 1856 (*Gosudarstvennye krest'iane*,
II, 173–174).

[86] *Ibid.*, pp. 13–16, 172–188.

unpaid taxes rose during the same period (see Table 7).[87] The influence of major factors, independent of the system of taxation, such as the different weather conditions from year to year and from area to area, the growth of the population, or the efficiency of provincial authorities, cannot be effectively

Table 7. Average annual arrears as a percentage of
total annual tax levied*

Province	% in years prior to reform	% in years after reform
St. Petersburg (1843–1844, 1845–1855)	0.0	2.6†
Voronezh (1843–1844, 1845–1855)	14.5	8.5
Tambov (1843–1845, 1847–1855)	21.3	11.4
Penza (1843–1845, 1847–1855)	31.0	30.8
Riazan' (1843–1847, 1848–1855)	13.5	9.1
Tula (1843–1847, 1848–1855)	19.2	5.4
Orlov (1843–1847, 1848–1855)	6.5	2.0
Kursk (1843–1848, 1849–1855)	12.4	4.3
Pskov (1843–1850, 1851–1855)	26.0	9.6
Moscow (1843–1851, 1852–1855)	1.0	1.9
Ekaterinoslav (1843–1851, 1852–1855)	46.9	10.1
Smolensk (1843–1852, 1853–1855)	21.2	16.3
Kharkov (1843–1852, 1853–1855)	8.9	1.6

* The years covered by the average for each province are indicated in parentheses, the first pair for the years prior to reform, the second pair indicating the years after the reform for the given province. No data for 1846 are included in the table.
† This average reflects one year with high arrears (1845); in all other years there were virtually none.
Source: Calculated from data in M. N. Druzhinin, *Gosudarstvennye krest'iane i reforma P. D. Kiseleva,* II (Moscow and Leningrad, 1958), 148, table 5.

isolated with the available data. In theory the new tax system should have been better adjusted to the ability of peasant villages to pay, but the advantages could have easily been wiped out by poor administration or inaccurate evaluation, and such was undoubtedly the case in many instances. Even if it is assumed that the shift to the new system of taxation was as successful as Kiselev and his aides hoped, it was clearly

[87] *Ibid.,* pp. 147–149.

not a measure designed to change the nature of the Russian agricultural economy. Tax reform could distribute burdens more equitably, but it could not be expected to influence the technological level of peasant agriculture.

Resettlement was another important and fundamentally conservative aspect of the Kiselev land program. There was much untilled land in Russia to the east and south, and the obvious answer to a land shortage was to move the peasants there. The numbers who wished to resettle, especially in years of poor harvests, were very large, far more than the Ministry of State Domains could handle with available funds. As usual in Russia's history, there was a substantial spontaneous movement that was discouraged, but could not be stopped. Once the unofficial migrants arrived in the areas where land was available, they were sooner or later accepted as legal residents; it was too hard and too foolish to send them back. Kiselev's limited program added a group of sponsored settlers from crowded provinces to this natural flow. Between 1838 and 1856, a total of 166,267 male souls migrated with official support, enough to make a real impact on the areas of settlement, but hardly enough to relieve the crowded areas from which they came.[88] Like surveying and assessment, migration did not directly affect the quality of the peasant's economic activity. Even if these programs had been extensive enough, and fully successful, the peasant would still have been tilling the land as he always had, and the real wealth of the nation would have increased very little.

One of the factors that kept the level of productivity low in peasant agriculture was the periodic redistribution of land and the general influence of the village communal organization, which destroyed much of the incentive for individual effort. The creation of peasant land allotments with hereditary rather than repartitional tenure had been one of the

[88] *Ibid.*, pp. 189–195; Ministerstvo gosudarstvennykh imushchestv, *Istoricheskoe obozrenie,* II, pt. 2, 34–35; Donald W. Treadgold, *The Great Siberian Migration* (Princeton, 1957), pp. 28–31.

major objectives of earlier proposals for state-peasant reform, particularly those of Gurev and Speransky.[89] In the early formulation of Kiselev's program, the principle was retained but not emphasized.[90] Once the Ministry of State Domains was established, however, Kiselev took the highly conservative position that although hereditary tenure might stimulate the economic initiative of the individual peasant, the maintenance of the village commune was necessary because it discouraged the development of a rural proletariat.[91] The only positive step taken toward encouraging the spread of hereditary tenure was a law of December 9, 1846. The introductory paragraph of the statute described the disadvantages of repartitional tenure and stressed the argument that the lack of incentive for improvements caused poverty. The new legislation was described as an experiment in the assignment of hereditary plots to change this situation, but with the major qualification that the change cannot be made everywhere, or all at once, and that it would, in fact, actually be dangerous to try to change the "centuries-old custom of millions." The experiment was therefore to be confined to newly settled areas, with purely voluntary participation.[92]

The law of 1846 was implemented in only one place, a section of Simbirsk province. The land was fertile, but the material aid extended to the colonists was limited, despite pressure from some enthusiastic supporters of the project. According to Kiselev, the Russian peasant was neither sufficiently mature nor sufficiently well off to establish successful independent farming operations. The colony of about 750 families became reasonably prosperous after overcoming the normal initial difficulties of any settlement on new land, but no further experiments were made with hereditary tenure,

[89] Druzhinin, *Gosudarstvennye krest'iane*, I, 122, 157–159, 183.

[90] Zablotskii-Desiatovskii, *Kiselev*, II, 16, 56; Druzhinin, *Gosudarstvennye krest'iane*, I, 498.

[91] Druzhinin, *Gosudarstvennye krest'iane*, II, 21.

[92] *PSZ* II, statute 20684.

despite requests from groups of peasants in several provinces.[93]

Kiselev's various projects involving land and taxes were the most extensive that the ministry undertook, yet they were limited in their potential effect because they did not attack the central economic problem, low productivity. Only the small experiment with individual tenure looked in that direction. In preserving the existing form of village organization and repartitional tenure, Kiselev rejected what seemed to some contemporary as well as modern observers to be the most practical method of fostering economic improvement among the peasantry. He did this because of his concern for the maintenance of order in the countryside. Repartitional tenure stifled individual initiative, but it did assure every peasant a certain share of the available land.

"GUARDIANSHIP"

The various measures that Kiselev and his ministry used to improve the productivity of agriculture were all grouped under the broad concept that he called "guardianship" (*pope-chitel'stvo*) over the peasantry. The term embraced a wide range of projects, including education, both technical and religious, public health measures, fire insurance, emergency food reserves, credit facilities, and temperance campaigns. They were all attempts to provide new facilities or to persuade the peasantry to do things in a new and better way. The success of these varied projects depended on the resources made available and competence of the personnel who administered the programs. Tax reform and resettlement demanded a major initial effort, but once the new system was introduced or the colonies established, it was reasonable to expect benefits to be forthcoming without continued large-scale expenditures. The policy of "guardianship" necessarily involved a much more long-term commitment. Certainly an adequately

[93] Druzhinin, *Gosudarstvennye krest'iane*, II, 195–203; Ministerstvo gosudarstvennykh imushchestv, *Istoricheskoe obozrenie*, II, pt. 2, 13–15.

educated, sober, healthy peasant would produce more wealth both for himself and the state, but large numbers of such men clearly could not be created overnight. "Guardianship" committed the state to far greater direct involvement with matters of popular welfare than had hitherto been known in Russia.

The fundamental problem for any program of economic assistance was to find the funds needed to finance it. Kiselev was determined not to start out with the unpopular step of increasing the financial levies on the peasantry. The Ministry of Finance, under Kiselev's old opponent Kankrin, was equally determined that the state peasantry's contribution to general state revenues should not be reduced. The result was a compromise. Certain specific sources of revenue were assigned to special accounts to be used for "guardianship" activities.[94] The total capital in these accounts approached twenty million silver rubles by the mid-1850's, but the really significant figure is the annual amount spent. The data are somewhat uncertain and are not available for all years. Expenditures from the special accounts were usually between one and two million rubles (see Table 8). Direct expenditures by the Third Department of the ministry were less than half a million more. The other departments of the ministry spent somewhat over three million silver rubles a year on the traditional activities of administration and revenue collection. Total revenues from state lands between 1840 and 1856 were between thirty and thirty-four million silver rubles per year.[95] The sums spent on "guardianship" were thus not large, either in comparison to the amounts spent on other activities or in terms of the total revenues collected by the ministry. It could hardly have been otherwise, given the severe pressures on the overall finances and the policy, firmly established by Kankrin, of coming as close as possible to a balanced budget.

[94] Druzhinin, *Gosudarstvennye krest'iane,* II, 42–45; Zablotskii-Desiatovskii, *Kiselev,* II, 80–81.

[95] Ministerstvo gosudarstvennykh imushchestv, *Istoricheskoe obozrenie,* I, Supp. I, 96–97, 100–101.

Table 8. Funds spent for "guardianship" activity, 1842–1856
(in silver rubles)

Year	By the state directly	From the "economic account"	From all accounts
1842	394,864	245,237	*
1843	399,874	433,637	*
1844	400,297	253,989	*
1845	326,327	219,736	2,738,795
1846	397,254	*	1,996,940
1847	403,520	*	1,089,209
1848	395,173	*	2,388,919
1849	367,128	*	1,630,778
1850	393,880	*	1,479,019
1851	403,428	*	1,830,609
1852	391,239	*	2,048,194
1853	344,195	*	3,081,213
1854	340,168	*	1,474,171
1855	257,514	*	*
1856	257,511	*	*

Source: Column 1—Russia, Ministerstvo gosudarstvennykh imushchestv, *Istoricheskoe obozrenie piatidesiatiletnei deiatel'nosti Ministerstva gosudarstvennykh imushchestv, 1837–1887* (St. Petersburg, 1888), I, supp. 1, 100–101; columns 2 and 3—Russia, Ministerstvo gosudarstvennykh imushchestv, *Izvlechenie iz otcheta ministra gosudarstvennykh imushchestv za 18— god*, annual vols. for 1842–1854 (St. Petersburg, 1843–1855).
*Not available.

Even more significant than the total involved is the breakdown of expenditures (see Table 9). A large part of the one to two million silver rubles spent was for what might best be called relief projects: aid to victims of fire and famine and constructing storehouses for emergency grain reserves. The building of churches was another major item that cannot be considered economic development.

Support of primary education had long-run implications for the economy, and the Ministry of State Domains was aware of them. In 1842, its official journal noted, "A man, burdened by ignorance, follows the routine of his fathers with a blind and dumb attachment. . . . In contrast, education, communicating new ideas, inclines one to confidence and

Table 9. Uses of funds in "guardianship" accounts, 1848–1854 (in silver rubles)

Year	Church building	Emergency food storehouses	Primary-school support	Aid to victims of fires	Peasant resettlement	Vocational education	Famine relief	Other*
1848	158,075	220,945	364,450	1,189,103	227,575	27,012	0	201,759
1849	164,023	163,520	313,005	561,226	156,308	20,289	113,233	139,174
1850	150,520	155,556	324,182	543,054	71,026	54,994	44,317	135,370
1851	§	§	§	§	§	§	§	§
1852	148,774	170,526	343,063	383,055	344,847	71,011	304,321	282,597†
1853	76,921	294,068	321,545	418,837	394,507	86,563	132,079‡	1,356,693†
1854	73,586	278,952	244,921	479,241	151,051	82,176	0	164,244

* Largely medical and veterinary.

† Includes surveying (166,403 in 1852; 136,406 in 1853) and, in 1853, a 1,000,000 repayment of an earlier loan from the state treasury.

‡ For transport of food to central warehouses.

§ Not available.

Source: Russia, Ministerstvo gosudarstvennykh imushchestv, *Izvlechenie iz otcheta minstra gosudarstvennykh imushchestv za 18 — god*, annual vols. for 1848–1854, (St. Petersburg, 1849–1855).

therefore to the perfection and imitation of better things." [96] The question of raising moral standards, which from the official standpoint certainly included public order and respect for authority, however, was as much or more a reason for peasant education as was encouraging peasant enterprise. "Education of the peasantry, within the limits of their particular way of life, would be an important step toward the improvement of their morals," wrote Kiselev at the start of his work with the state peasants.[97] Despite his criticism of the church for failing to undertake the task in the past, the entire program of ordinary primary education was carried on through the church, and the curriculum was under church control with instruction primarily by priests. To describe it as "religious education" would, however, be misleading. The three year course was too short to admit of any specialization. It was a start at basic education, reading and arithmetic plus religious instruction. There was no attempt to relate this educational program directly to the vocational needs of peasant children. The only impressive aspect of the effort in primary education was quantitative. In 1842, there were 226 schools with 11,386 pupils. In 1856, 2,536 schools and 112,460 pupils.[98] Whatever the quality of instruction offered, and it was certainly very bad in many places, such extensive development cannot be dismissed, but it was not viewed primarily as a matter of economic policy and it can have affected the economic position of the peasantry only gradually and indirectly.

The only substantial "guardianship" expenditure that was directly aimed at raising the productive capacity of the peasant economy was the support of technical education (see Table 9). On a relatively advanced level the ministry's efforts were limited to the Gorygoretskii Agricultural School (Insti-

[96] Quoted in Druzhinin, *Gosudarstvennye krest'iane*, II, 248, from the *Zhurnal Ministerstva gosudarstvennykh imushchestv*.

[97] Zablotskii-Desiatovskii, *Kiselev*, II, 20, 94.

[98] Druzhinin, *Gosudarstvennye krest'iane*, II, 248–256, statistics on 250.

tute after 1848), which graduated 241 students between 1848 and 1856. On a somewhat lower level, some sixty or seventy students completed their studies at an agricultural school in Kharkov, and larger numbers learned basic horticulture in five provincial schools.[99]

The most extensive effort in technical education, however, was the establishment of school farms that were to teach young peasants good agricultural techniques, which they were then expected to spread, upon returning to their villages. Seven new farms were established in addition to the one that had been opened in 1825. The eight farms had a total of 8,130 students between 1844 and 1856. Of the total, only 1,373 completed the full course of training. Eight of the most promising graduates were given individual allotments and other assistance in setting up model farms in their own villages. The experiment was promising, but the needed buildings and livestock were expensive. Furthermore, the widespread success of such farms would certainly have undermined the village communal organization that Kiselev was so anxious to maintain.

The former students of the school farms who returned to their villages without special support had a very difficult time. Because most of them either were orphans or came from impoverished families, they frequently had no land and no support from the rest of the community. It was extremely difficult for an individual, especially a young person, to operate independently in a village that practiced periodic repartition and where the elders traditionally enjoyed great influence and were suspicious of anything new. After 1850, the ministry tried to recruit students for the school farms from the families of prosperous and influential peasants, but the fathers proved unwilling to give up their sons' labor for an extended period. According to official reports, only the handful of school-farm graduates who were the peasants of pro-

[99] *Ibid.*, pp. 236–237; Ministerstvo gosudarstvennykh imushchestv, *Istoricheskoe obozrenie*, IV, 84–88, 104–108.

gressive gentrymen, rather than state peasants, were able to utilize the training that they had received.[100]

The most determined effort to encourage innovation in agriculture was the promotion of potato growing. Already very important in western Europe, the potato was known, but little used, in Russia. It seemed to offer great promise as an alternative source of food in periods of crop failure. Laws issued in 1840 and 1842 introduced the obligatory planting of potatoes on a large scale. The peasants did not like it, called the potatoes "devil's apples," and in some places they rioted. The new crop was not only unfamiliar but took up land they thought was better devoted to grain, or working time better spent in craft production. The disturbances usually occurred in areas where there was already dissatisfaction with existing conditions and with the state's administration. Potatoes were simply the trigger that set things off. Only the most careful and understanding approach by administrators could prevent the spread of unfounded fears among the peasantry. In practice, of course, administration was crude and often more attention was paid to exploitation than to education.[101] Kiselev eventually admitted that compulsion was not effective:

Improvements introduced by force can be neither successful nor lasting. On the other hand, with the dissemination among the peasantry of useful information and the belief in the advantages of improved agriculture, the peasant will get a clearer understanding of things, a better sensitivity to the new demands, and the wish and the effort will be born in him for the improvement of his economic activity.[102]

In 1843, the extent of compulsory sowing was reduced, and in 1844 it was abandoned.[103] There is little doubt that the

[100] Ministerstvo gosudarstvennykh imushchestv, *Istoricheskoe obozrenie*, IV, 125–133; Druzhinin, *Gosudarstvennye krest'iane*, II, 237–242.

[101] Druzhinin, *Gosudarstvennye krest'iane*, II, 470–476, 490–497.

[102] *Ibid.*, pp. 235–236; "Geschichte des Kartoffelbaues in Russland," *Archiv für Wissenschaftliche Kunde von Russland*, VII (1849), 578–588.

[103] Druzhinin, *Gosudarstvennye krest'iane*, II, 53–55; *PSZ* II, statutes 16538, 17900.

ministry's efforts produced a substantial increase in the cultivation of potatoes, but it is impossible to say by how much.
The available data, reported by the ministry itself, indicate
only that sowing potatoes remained nearly constant during
the later years of Kiselev's administration, as did the share
of the total crop planted by state peasants, despite continued
official encouragement (see Table 10). The level of produc-

Table 10. Potatoes planted, 1842–1854 (in chetverts)

Year	By state peasants	By privately owned peasants	Total*	Amount planted by state peasants as % of total
before 1840	328,117	‡	1,000,000 †	‡
1842	1,199,802	‡	‡	‡
1843	1,344,659	3,978,969	5,323,628	25.3
1844	‡	‡	6,009,785	‡
1845	‡	‡	5,535,674	‡
1846	‡	‡	5,735,000	‡
1847	‡	‡	5,954,301	‡
1848	1,795,727	4,286,900	6,082,630	29.5
1849	1,578,414	4,257,216	5,835,630	27.0
1850	1,555,879	3,843,447	5,399,326	28.8
1851	1,618,087	3,807,481	5,425,568	29.8
1852	1,649,568	3,677,337	5,326,905	31.0
1853	1,648,519	3,616,333	5,264,852	31.3
1854	1,592,991	3,683,714	5,276,705	30.2

* The figures for harvested potatoes are, of course, larger, but fluctuate
more sharply from year to year because of weather conditions.
† The figure is for 1837 and is obviously an approximation (Ministerstvo
gosudarstvennykh imushchestv, "Obozrenie upravlenie gosudarstvennykh
imushchestv za posledniia 25 let s 20 noiabria 1825 po noiabria 1850 g.,"
Sbornik IRIO, **XCVIII** [1896], 492).
‡ Not available.
Source: Russia, Ministerstvo gosudarstvennykh imushchestv, *Izvlechenie iz
otcheta ministra gosudarstvennykh imushchestv za 18— god*, annual vols. for 1842–
1854 (St. Petersburg, 1843–1855).

tion reached was never very high, and even much later, in
the 1880's, after substantial growth in output, potatoes occupied only 2 per cent of total sown land. Only in Estonia did
they become a major crop, occupying more than 10 per cent

of cultivated land.[104] The spread of potato growing was the most important technical innovation made in Russian agriculture by the Ministry of State Domains, but even it amounted to little.

The Ministry of State Domains undertook a number of other less expensive projects designed to help the peasant to improve his economic position. Over five hundred savings offices and over one thousand auxiliary offices were opened to make credit more readily available to the peasants. By 1855, the savings offices had deposits of nearly a million rubles and the aid offices had outstanding loans of over 1.6 million.[105] To encourage better farming, agricultural exhibitions were held in many provinces, and the *Agricultural Gazette* and the *Journal of the Ministry of State Domains* were published by the ministry in the hope of enlightening the few literate peasants, and state officials themselves.

Taken together, the programs of reform and improvement launched by Kiselev, with the firm and continuing support of Nicholas I, were far more ambitious than either of the other important positive steps in economic policy, the monetary reforms and the inauguration of railroad construction. Yet the programs' ambitiousness was a reflection of the size of the problem dealt with rather than the kind of thing Kiselev wanted to do. He wanted to make the existing agricultural society produce more through providing more land to peasants who needed it and by instructing or even forcing them to grow better crops and use more advanced methods. He hoped to reduce injustice and make the peasant's life a little more secure by improving the system of collecting *obrok* and by protecting him better from fire, famine, and disease. To some extent he succeeded in these aims, but the limited funds available and the poor quality of the administrative person-

[104] Russia, Ministry of Crown Domains, Department of Agriculture, *The Industries of Russia* (St. Petersburg, 1893), III, 96, 102.

[105] Savings offices accepted deposits from peasants and made loans. Auxiliary offices (*vspomogatel'nye kassy*) used capital supplied by the state from one of the special funds.

nel severely reduced the effectiveness of the various projects. Kiselev was reluctant to increase the state's demands on the peasants for fear of creating opposition to his program as a whole. The result was a lack of money for new projects and the restrictive emphasis on self-financing for the entire "guardianship" program.

The problem of effective administrative implementation was crucial, because the Kiselev program was largely positive rather than simply permissive. At the highest level, the quality of personnel was very good. Kiselev had as his immediate aids men like A. P. Zablotskii-Desiatovskii, K. I. Arsenev, whom even the usually critical Druzhinin considers both talented and liberal.[106] There was some bureaucratic foolishness at the top, such as discussion by the Scientific Advisory Committee of whether or not a particular cow should be sold by an experimental farm,[107] but it was at the middle and lower administrative levels that the real problems developed.

Some officials were merely lazy and incompetent, like retired Lieutenant Colonel Krukovskii, for eight years director of the Board of State Domains in Nizhni-Novgorod and for three years director in Viatka. For this service he was awarded the order of St. Stanislav second class, the order of St. Anne second class, and the order of St. Anne (with the imperial crown). Nevertheless an inspector reported that this veteran civil servant "could not . . . write two lines without grammatical and logical errors," needed constant supervision, and knew nothing of law or administrative affairs. His subordinates simply bound together piles of papers, which he usually approved without reading. He was also accused of dishonesty, but apparently was not intelligent enough to steal large sums. Others were more talented. Colonel Frederiks, director of the Board of State Domains in Tver' province, did not appear on the job for months at a stretch, but he contracted with the board he headed to construct ten grain-storage buildings and a number of other structures, all at inflated prices. Some

---

[106] *Gosudarstvennye krest'iane*, II, 88–89.
[107] Veselovskii, "Vospominaniia," p. 32.

were entirely unneeded, they lacked foundations, cracks allowed rain and snow to get in, and the peasants refused to put grain in them.[108] Such examples could be multiplied almost without end, but they prove little by themselves. Similar cases could be found in almost any large organization in any country and in any century. The important thing is how widespread the problem was. On the basis of extensive archival work, Druzhinin concludes that corruption and incompetence were typical rather than exceptional in the middle- and lower-level administration.[109] Druzhinin is not sympathetic to the Tsarist bureaucracy, and he might be suspected of painting an overly dark picture were it not for the strong confirmation provided by Kiselev's own statements. He was always aware of the problem, but he assumed that it could be solved, and virtually the entire reform program was based on that assumption. In 1850, however, he reported to the Tsar:

For success, even the most well-planned administration needs educated, honest, and energetic administrators. They exist in Russia, but not to the extent needed by the ministry, and therefore one often finds incompetence or even self-interest, not only in the lower level of officials, but sometimes among people on whom depends the proper administration and welfare of thousands.[110]

It was this same problem that had led Kankrin to abandon the state vodka monopoly in 1827, reject an excise tax, and return to the farming-out system. It was much more a disagreement about what *could* be done than about what *ought* to be done that separated Kiselev from Kankrin; neither

[108] Druzhinin, *Gosudarstvennye krest'iane,* II, 94–96.

[109] *Ibid.,* pp. 91–100. Similar accounts of corruption can be found in John S. Curtiss, *The Russian Army under Nicholas I, 1825–1855* (Durham, 1965), ch. 11, and there are innumerable examples in literary works, such as Gogol's *Inspector General.*

[110] Ministerstvo gosudarstvennykh imushchestv, "Obozrenie upravleniia," pp. 494–495; Druzhinin, *Gosudarstvennye krest'iane,* II, 86–101.

thought seriously of leaving important matters to private initiative or the free-market mechanism. They both thought in terms of positive state action, but Kankrin was far more pessimistic about its efficacy.

The very term that Kiselev used for the most dynamic and ambitious part of his entire program, "guardianship," shows that, correctly or not, he was convinced that the peasant had to be shown, even directed, how to do things better. The new ministry was thus almost totally dependent on the effectiveness of his subordinates, down to the thousands of villages. Change without close control and supervision was not felt to be safe. Kiselev clearly stated his position in the report quoted above:

Summoned by the most high trust of your Imperial Majesty to the fulfillment of your lofty intentions, I followed your instructions exactly, acting with insistence in all matters touching the governing and managing of the public weal, which could be achieved through administrative action; but in the improvement of the economy and of household management, as matters demanding a fundamental change in popular customs and habits, it is proper to act with caution. The present generation is incapable of rational and rapid innovation, and therefore, with complete indifference to momentary and flimsy successes, I have striven to gain the attention of the rural proprietors and to stir them to action by examples, persuasion, and encouragement. I tried, so to speak, to prepare the ground on which future workers will find all the facilities and means to successfully continue what has been begun.

Continuing, Kiselev proudly pointed out that on only three occasions had it been necessary to be "severe" with the peasants.[111] The maintenance of order was essential and close administrative control of all changes was necessary. If positive direction could not be achieved for lack of competent staff, the alternative was not to encourage peasant initiative but to be content with less progress.

[111] Ministerstvo gosudarstvennykh imushchestv, "Obozrenie upravleniia," p. 494.

Monetary reform, the start of railroad construction, and Kiselev's peasant program were the three "great events" in economic policy during the reign of Nicholas I. They all began in his second decade on the throne (1835–1845), yet they were almost entirely unrelated to each other and seem to tell us nothing about the general economic policy of the state.

The activity of these years was the result of specific problems that faced the nation and of the changed relationship between the Tsar and his minister of finance. In earlier years, all authority for economic affairs had been delegated entirely to Kankrin. By 1835, the Tsar had become more confident of his own judgment, and when an increasingly discouraged and pessimistic Kankrin refused to act on important issues, the Tsar listened more attentively to the advice of others or took matters into his own hands. Kankrin, however, was never really replaced by any influential adviser, not even after his retirement in 1844 and his death one year later. Nicholas remained true to the spirit of Kankrin's administration. And it was the attitude of the tired, pessimistic Kankrin of the early thirties that retained its influence in subsequent years. The cautious yet still imaginative and forward-looking policies of the late twenties were forgotten. It is true that in those early years Kankrin established the basic features of his administration—strict fiscal restraint, no additions to the money supply, credit for the gentry and the state but not for urban manufacturers—but these features were tempered then by his interest in urban growth and the series of measures to increase what he so aptly called the "capital of knowledge."

The divergence in views between Kankrin and the Tsar, which might have had a major effect on the overall direction of state policy, produced only limited and unrelated efforts. Had Nicholas been more inclined to change his advisers or had Kankrin been less prone to accept without question the Tsar's decision once it had been made, these limited differences on specific issues could have produced a dismissal or a resignation. Both the personal inclination of the Tsar and a basic principle of autocracy acted to reduce the likelihood of an overall change in economic policy. Monetary reform improved the currency system but did not create a more flexible arrangement that could provide additional credit. Railroad construction was started but no general network planned. The program for the state peasants had broad goals but was restricted by the means it chose to achieve them. Within the government, there was not even any discussion of the economy as a whole that was important enough to be recorded. No official in an influential position looked at the problems that faced the state with the whole economy in mind.

CHAPTER V

Monetary Problems and the Reform of the Currency

The role of currency problems and monetary reform in overall economic policy under Nicholas I is a complex and somewhat technical subject. Problems connected with the currency were the most widely discussed economic issues in Russia during the first half of the nineteenth century. They were the most conspicuous, and they were also important. Everybody who mattered used money, and if it changed in value, in shape, or in name there could be no secret about it. Other aspects of economic policy were wholly or partly hidden from public view. The state budget and credit operations were entirely secret. Discussion of questions involving the peasantry was drastically limited by censorship. Industry, railroads, guilds, and technical education were of interest to only a limited number of people. On monetary matters the state had to give thought to public opinion because the value of currency depended, in large measure, on what individual Russian citizens felt it was worth. Metal money with some intrinsic value could be used, hoarded, sent abroad, or melted as people saw fit, but its value was always partly independent both of public opinion and state policy. Paper money was far more sensitive. The state controlled the amount issued and decided whether it was freely convertible and at what rate.

But the Tsar could not control what people thought a paper ruble was worth and what they expected it to be worth in the future. It was the sum of these individual judgments, however, that determined its value, not the words printed on each bill.

Paper money was relatively new to Russia in the early nineteenth century. It was first issued in 1769 by Catherine the Great, but until the reigns of Paul and Alexander I it was used in limited amounts and caused no difficulties. As Russia became involved in the European wars that followed the French Revolution, more and more was issued to meet state expenses and its value declined. By 1810, it took 3.24 paper rubles to equal one silver ruble (see Table 11).[1] The restoration of the paper ruble, usually called an assignat, to its face value was one of the major goals of Speransky's financial plan of 1810. He proposed that the assignats be declared a form of state debt and be gradually redeemed with the proceeds of an internal loan and the sale of state lands. Few buyers for the lands were found, but the internal loan was successfully floated and five million rubles in assignats were retired in 1811. Napoleon's invasion of Russia in the following year forced the government to stop the program and issue additional millions in paper. In 1812, the government attempted to prevent a further decline in the value of the assignat. The assignat was made legal tender for all transactions, but at the current bourse rate, not at face value. Taxes were henceforth set and collected in assignats only.[2] These measures amounted to a legal recognition of the devaluation of the assignat, and they created the system of two currencies (assignats and metal coin), with fluctuating relative values, that caused trouble until the reforms of 1839–1843.

During the war with France, silver coins ceased circulating in Russia, and the assignat was the only form of currency

---

[1] There are 100 kopeks to a ruble and a Russian source would usually write 3 rubles 24 kopeks. Decimals are used in this chapter.

[2] Russia, Ministerstvo finansov, *Ministerstvo finansov, 1802–1902* (St. Petersburg, 1902), I, 66.

Table 11. Assignats issued and withdrawn (in thousands of assignat rubles)
and the bourse rate (in assignat kopeks per silver ruble), 1769–1840*

Year	Issued	Withdrawn	Total in circulation	Bourse rate
1769–1800	213,989	1,299		
1769–1787				101–103
1788–1800				109–153
1801	8,799	0	221,488	151
1802	8,976	0	230,464	138
1803	19,556	20	250,000	125
1804	10,658	0	260,658	126
1805	31,541	0	292,199	130
1806	27,041	0	319,240	134
1807	63,089	0	382,329	149
1808	95,039	0	477,369	187
1809	55,833	0	533,201	225
1810	46,173	0	579,374	324
1811	7,020	5,000	581,394	394
1812	64,500	0	645,894	388
1813	103,440	0	749,334	397
1814	48,791	0	798,126	396
1815	30,198	2,500	825,824	421
1816	5,600	0	831,424	404
1817	4,576	0	836,000	384
1818	0	38,024	797,976	379
1819	1,578	80,229	719,326	372
1820	1,461	35,614	685,172	374
1821	3,755	37,242	651,685	378
1822	0	44,968	606,777	375
1823	0	10,941	595,776	373
1824	0	0	595,776	374
1825	0	0	595,776	372
1826	0	0	595,776	372
1827	0	0	595,776	373
1828	0	0	595,776	371
1829	0	0	595,776	369
1830	0	0	595,776	369
1831	0	0	595,776	372
1832	0	0	595,776	366
1833	0	0	595,776	361
1834	0	0	595,776	359
1835	0	0	595,776	358
1836	0	0	595,776	357
1837	0	0	595,776	355
1838	0	0	595,776	354
1839	0	0	595,776	350
1840	0	0	595,776	350

* 100 Kopeks equal 1 ruble.
Source: P. A. Shtorkh, "Materialy dlia istorii gosudarstvennykh denezhnykh
znakov v Rossii s 1653 po 1840 god," *Zhurnal Ministerstvo narodnogo prosveshcheniia*,
CXXXVII (1868), 822–823.

generally available, aside from small change in copper. Between January 1, 1812, and December 31, 1817, some 254.6 million assignats were issued (Table 11). At the same time, 250 to 300 million silver and gold rubles went out of circulation, either into hoards or abroad.[3] Since each silver ruble was worth almost four assignat rubles, the actual stock of money in use was reduced. Local shortages of currency, particularly in small denominations, were reported in some areas immediately after the assignats' first sharp fall in value.[4]

The victory over Napoleon restored public confidence, and silver and gold coins began to reappear in circulation to such an extent that by 1818 the problem of the relationship between them and the assignats was discussed at length in the State Council. Part of the metal reappearing in circulation was old Russian coinage that had been hoarded during the years of uncertainty. Probably much more important was another source of metal: between 1811 and 1815 the mint issued as 35.4 million rubles in gold and silver, and between 1816 and 1820, 62.8 million—a total of 98.2 million between 1811 and 1820.[5] Since domestic production of precious metals was small at this time, most of this metal must have come from abroad, from England's wartime subsidies and the positive balance of payments that Russia enjoyed between 1812 and 1819.[6]

In the years immediately following the end of the war, the government had three main alternatives it could follow with respect to the currency situation. First, it could leave things

---

[3] Ilarion I. Kaufman, *Serebrianyi rubl' v Rossii ot ego vozniknoveniia do kontsa XIX veka* (St. Petersburg, 1910), p. 190.

[4] *AGS*, IV, pt. 1, 580.

[5] *Ibid.*, pp. 579–583; Kaufman, *Serebrianyi rubl'*, p. 191.

[6] Shtorkh estimates the total amount of money in circulation in 1835 at 515,743,000 silver rubles. He includes assignats, silver, gold, platinum, copper, and foreign coins, all in terms of silver rubles. The assignats represented just about one-third of the total (P. A. Shtorkh, "Materialy dlia istorii gosudarstvennykh denezhnykh znakov v Rossii s 1653 po 1840 god," *Zhurnal Ministerstvo narodnogo prosveshcheniia*, CXXXVII [1868], 796).

as they were. The disadvantage in this plan, of course, was that there were two currencies, silver rubles and assignats, and the rate of exchange between the two fluctuated constantly, even though within a narrow range, and stimulated speculation and fraud, generally at the expense of poorer, less commercially sophisticated people.

The second alternative was to recognize the devaluation of the assignats as permanent and to stabilize their value at the depreciated rate either by exchanging all of them for metal or by making them convertible into metal on demand. Several prominent figures advocated this policy, notably Nicholas Turgenev and L. H. von Jakob, professor of political economy at Kharkov University. It had earlier been espoused by Karamzin in his then unpublished "Memoir on Ancient and Modern Russia." [7]

The third alternative was a program designed to restore the assignats to their original value by reducing the number in circulation. Speransky's attempt to do this in 1810 had been halted by the war. In 1816, the minister of finance, Count Gurev, proposed to try again by gradually withdrawing the assignats from circulation with the proceeds of internal loans. The plan was approved and began in 1817. In exchange for assignats, the holder received interest-bearing bonds which, if the program achieved its aim, would be eventually redeemed in assignats fully equal to silver rubles. During the

[7] Nikolai I. Turgenev, *Opyt teorii nalogov* (St. Petersburg, 1818), pp. 359–360; Ludwig H. von Jakob, *Über Russlands Papiergeld* (Halle, 1817), p. 63, cited by Georg Sacke, "Ludwig Heinrich von Jakob und die russische Finanzkrise am Anfang des 19. Jahrhunderts," *Jahrbücher für Geschichte Osteuropas*, no. 3 (1938), p. 615. In 1810, Jakob had advised Speransky to restore the assignats to their full face value. In 1811, Karamzin advocated a policy strikingly similar to that followed by Kankrin in 1823: "Great breaks are dangerous. It is just as harmful suddenly to decrease the quantity of paper money as it is suddenly to increase it. What then is to be done? Suspend all further emission of assignats! . . . This is enough" (*Karamzin's Memoir on Ancient and Modern Russia: A Translation and Analysis,* ed. and trans. Richard Pipes [Cambridge, Mass., 1959], pp. 94–95, 177).

same year that the internal loans specifically earmarked for the retirement of assignats were being floated, two large loans were negotiated abroad to cover budget deficits, so in effect the retirement of assignats was actually being financed by foreign borrowing.[8] A total of 246.9 million assignats were withdrawn between 1818 and 1823, leaving 595.8 million in circulation, a decrease of almost 30 per cent. The effect on the rate at which assignats exchanged for silver was negligible. The 1817 bourse rate of 384 assignat kopeks per silver ruble had dropped to 373 in 1823, an improvement of 2.8 per cent.

Russia was not alone in facing currency problems at this time. In Great Britain, Bank of England notes had depreciated 20 per cent during the war, but in 1821 their full value was restored when they were made convertible on demand into gold. In Russia, immediate redemption at face value was not considered, for it was obviously beyond the financial resources of the state. The Speransky and Gurev programs were, of course, intended to make this possible eventually when the number of assignats had been sufficiently reduced and the market rate had risen of its own accord. Austria followed the alternative policy that Russia scorned and recognized the devaluation of the florin to permit the immediate restoration of convertibility into silver. The paper florin had fallen far more drastically than the assignat in Russia. In 1820, the notes were redeemed at 40 per cent of their face value, but these notes themselves had been issued in a previous devaluation in 1811, so the total depreciation amounted to about 92 per cent. In a later period, American experience with the greenbacks issued during the Civil War was initially quite similar to Russia's with the assignats. After the end of the war they circulated with a discount of 30 per cent. A reduction of 26 per cent in the amount outstanding, accomplished by 1868, made no impression on the rate. It was only with the rapid expansion of the economy and the inflow of capital

---

[8] *Ministerstvo finansov*, I, 59.

from Europe that they rose in value and sufficient reserves were accumulated to permit the renewal of specie payments in 1879.[9]

The failure of the assignats to increase in value between 1818 and 1822, and similarly of the greenbacks to rise while their number was being reduced, simply shows that the value of a paper currency in relation to metal money depends on many factors, not only on the amount outstanding. The amount of metal circulating, the volume of business transactions, and public confidence are all involved. In Russia the amount of metal circulating was rapidly increasing while the assignats were being withdrawn, so that the total stock of money was not reduced significantly and may even have increased. The assignat had become widely accepted as one quarter of a silver ruble and prices were set correspondingly. As long as assignats were not redeemable at face value and nobody expected that they would soon be, there was no real reason for them to rise rapidly in value.

THE KANKRIN POLICY

By the time Kankrin replaced Gurev in the spring of 1823, the withdrawal of assignats had largely stopped, although the attempt to raise their value had not been formally abandoned. The monetary policy adopted in the first year of the new administration remained unchanged until 1839, and serious consideration of reforms did not begin until 1837. The situation that Kankrin faced demanded a decision, but there was no crisis. The history of the Russian assignat had not followed the course of the assignat of revolutionary France. There paper had been issued in astronomical amounts and had eventually become completely worthless. The Russian assignat did fall in value from virtual parity

[9] R. G. Hawtrey, *Currency and Credit* (3rd ed.; London, 1927), pp. 335–345, 356–357, 370–371; J. Lawrence Laughlin, *A New Exposition of Money, Credit, and Prices* (Chicago, 1931), II, 190–200.

with the silver ruble (100 assignat kopeks per silver ruble) to a low point of 421 assignat kopeks per silver ruble in 1815. Nevertheless, it was still good money. One silver ruble was a substantial sum, in fact it was sometimes criticized for being awkwardly large. An assignat, worth about one quarter of a silver ruble, was not to be scorned. Furthermore, it was required in payments to the state after 1812.

Kankrin had made his position clear on what should be done about the assignats in his *Weltreichthum,* published in 1821, two years before he became minister of finance. He advocated a policy of "fixation," not "reduction," for depreciated paper currencies. This view is very close to devaluation, but he did not take the final step by advocating that the state acknowledge the depreciation as permanent and take steps to make the currency convertible at the devalued rate. Redemption at full face value remained the eventual but remote goal.[10]

A policy of doing nothing not only appealed to Kankrin's cautious nature, but in this case had the additional attraction of providing a substantial windfall of cash. In 1823, thirty-two million assignat rubles on hand had been earmarked for destruction, but the Finance Committee of the Department of the Economy of the State Council approved Kankrin's plan to use these funds to retire internal debt. This action amounted to a complete reversal of the Gurev program of redeeming assignats with borrowed money and destroying them. The committee agreed with Kankrin that too rapid a rise in the value of the assignats would bankrupt debtors and introduce confusion into the government accounts.[11] The formal end of the withdrawal of assignats from circulation did not come until April 25, 1824, but the new policy was actually in effect throughout most of 1823. Only

[10] *Weltreichthum, Nationalreichthum, und Staatswirtschaft, oder Versuch neurer Ansichten der politischen Oekonomie* (Munich, 1821), pp. 63–66.

[11] TsGIAL, f. 560, op. 22, d. 24, "Zhurnal Komiteta finansov i zapiska Ministra finansov," pp. 4–6, 20–21.

10.9 million assignats were withdrawn from circulation in that year, compared to 45.0 million in 1822 and similar numbers in previous years back to 1818.[12]

The final decision on what was the proper monetary policy was made early in 1824, when a new plan, submitted by former Minister of Finance Gurev, was rejected. Although he did not directly admit it, Gurev abandoned the idea of reducing the number of assignats until they should rise to their full face value. He now proposed an involved scheme to replace the existing assignats with notes based on silver over a period of twelve years. The two important features of the plan were the establishment of a new bank, replacing the existing State Loan Bank and Commercial Bank, which would issue notes based on silver, and the proposed conversion of the assignats at a rate below their face value, that is, the achievement of convertibility by devaluation.[13] This second feature is of particular significance; it proves that the basic feature of the eventual reform, official devaluation, was already being formally considered by the state early in the 1820's.[14] Kankrin's comments show that he had not given up the hope of restoring the assignats to their full face value, but he had no definite plan of his own for monetary reform. The basic assumption of Gurev's plan was that the assignats could not be allowed to remain as they were. Kankrin rejected this

[12] *Ministerstvo finansov,* I, 71.

[13] TsGIAL, f. 560, op. 22, d. 24, "Zhurnal Komiteta finansov po obsuzhdeniiu proekta . . . ," pp. 24–29. According to Speransky, Gurev turned to this idea in 1822. Writing in 1839, Speransky approved of it, and it is quite possible that Gurev prepared his 1823–1824 project under Speransky's influence, just as his original plan closely followed Speransky's plan of 1810. Speransky had returned to St. Petersburg in 1821 (M. M. Speransky, "O monetnom obrashchenii," *Chteniia,* LXXXIII [1872], 168 n.).

[14] Kaufman states that the Gurev plan was similar to one submitted to Alexander I by an Englishman, Alexander Grant, and quotes from a published version of this plan, *Observations sur le papier monnaie de la Russie* (London, 1823), which I have been unable to locate (I. I. Kaufman, *Iz istorii bumazhnykh deneg v Rossii* [St. Petersburg, 1909], pp. 52–55).

assumption and maintained that the current situation was stable and that small fluctuations did no harm. Nevertheless, Kankrin also criticized Gurev for advocating the exchange of assignats for less than face value. Such a step, he said, would abolish all hope of the improvement for which the government had already sacrificed so much. It would also betray those who were counting on restoration of the assignats to full face value.[15] In 1827, four years after he established the policy of leaving the assignats as they were, Kankrin pointed with pride to its success and claimed that it had produced a gradual increase in the value of the assignats without cost to the state. Echoing Nicholas Turgenev, he said that the rapid rise of the assignats to their old level would have produced the same distress as their original fall.[16]

The situation, however, was far from ideal. Two types of currency continued to circulate, metal money (gold, silver, and copper coins) and assignats, and there was no fixed relationship between them. Prices were normally stated in assignats, but according to the law, payment had to be accepted in either currency according to the current rate on the St. Petersburg bourse. The rate varied slightly from day to day even though the general tendency was for assignats to rise slowly in value. Because the country was large, communication poor, and the level of monetary sophistication low, there were persistent and surprisingly large regional variations in the relative value of assignats and metal money. In the late 1820's and particularly in the 1830's, the complexity of the monetary system was compounded by the spontaneous appearance of the "popular exchange rates" (*prostonarodnye kursy*), a peculiar set of discounts and premiums combined with prices set in a hypothetical currency unit.[17] But in the 1820's, the system, however awkward, worked reasonably

[15] TsGIAL, f. 560, op. 22, d. 24, "Ob"iasnitel'naia zapiska E. F. Kankrina . . . ," pp. 149, 156–158.

[16] *Zhurnal manufaktur i torgovli*, no. 7 (1827), pp. 155–157.

[17] For a detailed discussion of this complex development see the Appendix.

well, and the only issue debated within the government was whether or not the state should accept its own gold and silver coins in payment of taxes.

The acceptance of Russian coins for tax payments is not, in itself, an important issue. The interesting aspect of the question is the amount of attention it got from statesmen of the day. The hesitation with which they undertook even the slightest change in the monetary system is clear evidence of their almost obsessive fear of taking a step that might undermine the value of the assignat. The memory of their fall in value nearly twenty years before, and of the earlier catastrophe in France, was still strong and exerted a powerful influence on all aspects of policy involving money. As early as 1818, the question of the acceptance of metal money in tax payments was discussed at the highest governmental level. Count Gurev reported that metal money was circulating so widely and in such large amounts that many people in certain areas found it extremely difficult to accumulate the assignats required for the payment of taxes. The problem was not general and did not produce a significant change in the value of the assignat, but in some localities it was serious. The obvious solution of the difficulty, Gurev said, was to permit taxes to be paid in coin as well as with assignats, but, he believed, such action was unwise because even acceptance of one-half of tax payments in coin would so reduce the demand for assignats that their value would fall, thus nullifying the effect of the government's program to increase their value. Instead, Gurev proposed to accept coins at the rate of 3.6 assignats to one silver ruble in the sale of spirits from the state stocks to retail dealers. Since the receipts of these dealers were largely in silver, it was difficult for them to purchase their supplies with assignats. After considerable debate, which emphasized the danger of weakening the assignats, the Finance Minister's proposal was accepted by the State Council and subsequently confirmed by the Tsar.[18]

Gurev's palliative measure did not solve the problem, and

18 *AGS*, IV, pt. 1, 584–590.

his program of reducing the number of assignats in circulation tended to make it worse. The situation was particularly bad in the case of small payments to the state, because the smallest assignat was a five-ruble note and these bills were in extremely short supply.[19] Taxpayers holding silver were frequently forced to pay a premium to get the assignats they needed to pay their taxes. Since the assignats were slowly rising in value, and Gurev's announced policy was to stimulate their rise, it was natural for speculators to accumulate assignats and to part with them only at an advantageous rate.[20] The masses of the population were poorly informed in monetary matters, so that the alert trader was able to make considerable profit.

There was no change of policy when Kankrin took over. In 1824, the military governor of the Ukraine forwarded the request of a local marshal of the nobility for permission to pay taxes in silver. The new finance minister refused to agree on the ground that any such step might seriously threaten the value of the assignats.[21] Such requests soon became so frequent, however, that the local treasury offices in seventeen provinces were permitted to exchange assignats for silver coin to the extent necessary to enable citizens to pay their taxes. Since the assignats that the treasury offices paid out for coins were immediately paid in as taxes, then paid out again to the next taxpayer for coin, and so on, the result was the same as if the state had taken coin directly.[22] In 1827, this formality was abandoned, and coin was accepted for certain specific taxes in all provinces. Only in 1830 did Kankrin

[19] Shtorkh, "Materialy," p. 825. Copper coins were also in short supply because of a steady increase in the price of copper. For details see Alfred Schmidt, "Das russische Geldwesen während der Finanzverwaltung des Grafen Cancrin (1823–1844)," *Russische Revue, Monatsschrift für die Kunde Russlands,* VII (1875), 37–41; and Shtorkh, "Materialy," pp. 792–795.

[20] *AGS,* IV, pt. 1, 584.

[21] Quoted in Kaufman, *Iz istorii,* pp. 58–60.

[22] TsGIAL, f. 1152, op. T. II, d. 89, 1830, "O prieme v podati zvonkoi monety . . . ," p. 1; Kaufman, *Iz istorii,* p. 61.

finally decide that the general acceptance of coin was inevitable. The requirement to pay in assignats was no longer necessary, because "trials show that the value of assignats is so established here and the opinion of the public about them is so confirmed, that the permission to accept metal money not only will not be injurious, but on the contrary will satisfy the wishes of the public, and the more the public is satisfied, the more it has faith in artificial tokens of value." [23] The final decree of December 11, 1830, provided that only silver coin was to be accepted. It was not until May 1833 that Russian gold coins as well as silver were made fully acceptable for tax payments.[24]

The government's nervousness about anything connected with the monetary system had more important consequences than the reluctance to accept its own coins. In the 1830's, the confusion resulting from the spread of the "popular rates" reached serious dimensions, but for years nothing was done. The ironic aspect of the situation is that the government's inaction made what was actually a very stable monetary situation appear to be highly unsettled, yet sound money was the thing most highly valued by the Ministry of Finance. The peculiar phenomenon of the "popular rates" had existed as early as the mid-twenties, but the first serious complaints to the government came from a group of Moscow merchants in 1833.[25]

The primary concern of this chapter is with the state's general attitude toward monetary questions and the way it reached the decision to undertake a reform. The full discussion of the highly complex question of how "popular rates" worked and the reasons for their appearance has therefore been placed in an appendix. Briefly stated, the "popular rates" were not exchange rates at all, but discounts or pre-

[23] TsGIAL, f. 1152, op. T. II, d. 89, "O prieme v podati zvonkoi monety . . . ," pp. 4–10.

[24] Kaufman, *Iz istorii,* pp. 66–67.

[25] TsGIAL, f. 583, op. 4, d. 228, 1833, "Vsepoddanneishie dokladnye zapiski," pp. 247–250.

miums given by merchants to customers when goods were bought and sold The size of the discount or premium was the "rate" for the type of money used. The "popular rates" were not used when one type of currency was exchanged for another, and there was normally no possibility of arbitrage, although the way in which they were quoted gives the impression that there was. The instability of the situation was produced by competitive pressures that tended to force merchants to give the impression of offering a better "rate" to an unsophisticated public when in fact they were not. The situation was made even more complex by the fact that both the actual rate of exchange between assignats and silver rubles and the "popular rates" varied significantly in different parts of the country.

In July 1834, at the Tsar's request, the question of changes in the currency system was considered by a special committee and referred to the Finance Committee of the State Council. Two proposals designed to fix the value of the assignat in terms of silver were put forward. Both plans contemplated official devaluation and the convertibility of the assignat into silver. The measure that was finally adopted, however, merely forbade the conclusion of written agreements that provided for payment according to the "popular agio or rate of exchange." [26] It was, almost certainly, Kankrin who blocked more drastic action. He was convinced that the matter was not a serious one and wrote in his annual report at the end of 1834:

This calculation [the popular exchange rate] does not amount to anything substantive, for when giving a higher price to silver it adds a percentage to the assignats in such proportion that actually no important difference from the bourse rate results.[27]

A year later, however, he admitted that the law of October 8, 1834, had not solved the problem. "It is very difficult, . . .

[26] Kaufman, *Iz istorii,* pp. 97–98.
[27] TsGIAL, f. 560, op. 38, d. 336, "Obshchii otchet . . . za 1834," p. 15.

to correct this strange phenomenon, based on the one hand on ignorance and dreams, and on the other on craftiness and fraud." There was no concession, however, that any change in the monetary system might be needed.[28]

REFORM BEGINS

Complaints about the confusion and difficulty caused by the existence of the "popular rates" and by the difference in rates from place to place and from day to day continued to come, not only from merchants, but in the reports of the Tsar's officials in the provinces. Nicholas always read these documents with care, making many short marginal notes. On one such report, from the military governor of Kursk province, the Emperor wrote: "This subject of general complaint urgently demands the consideration of the Minister of Finance." Kankrin dutifully reported back to the Tsar that he was in constant contact with the provincial authorities regarding the problem and "that the time has come to take determined measures for the elimination of this evil, and I am busy with the final consideration of this matter." [29]

On July 29, 1837, the Finance Minister presented two proposals to the State Council for consideration. One was called "On the necessity of stopping the valuation of coin and assignats according to the popular rates" and the other, "On the establishment of deposit offices for silver deposits in the State Commercial Bank." In the proposal on the "popular rates," Kankrin repeated his earlier suggestions. Nothing, he said, was fundamentally wrong with the money system, and the current problems were the result of fraud, speculation, and confusion and therefore could be eliminated by a combination of punitive and educational measures. He urged that the existing prohibition of the use of the "popular rates" in

[28] *Ibid.*, d. 354, "Obshchii otchet . . . za 1835."

[29] *Materialy,* pp. 8–9. Kaufman notes the significance of the Tsar's initiative in *Iz istorii,* pp. 98–99.

written agreements be extended to oral agreements and that
all payments be made at either the bourse rate or the rate
used in tax collections. The new law was to be read in all
churches and the local police were to be responsible for its
enforcement. Kankrin emphasized that the existing assignats
should be left as they were because it was impossible to fore-
see the results of a change in the money supply.[30]

The second proposal, on the establishment of silver-deposit
offices, was entirely new and eventually became law as the
first step in the monetary reform, but it was presented as an
almost petty administrative measure. The increased circulation of metal money and its receipt in tax payments, Kankrin
said, had caused a transport problem for the state that could
be solved by establishing special offices in the branches of the
State Commercial Bank to exchange coin for new "deposit
office notes." There would be no charge for the safekeeping
service; the deposit notes would be full legal tender, equal
to silver in all respects, and always exchangeable for silver on
demand. The bank was to hold the coins deposited separately
from their regular deposits and to maintain 100 per cent
metal backing of the notes issued.[31]

Certainly this proposal, sensible though it was, would not
warrant attention except for the fact that Kankrin added, almost as an afterthought:

The introduction of such notes must have another, still more
important, use of a different sort. It would serve as a preparatory
measure to the introduction of silver assignats, if the government
in due course finds it necessary to change those now existing.

Such a change, he continued, would be much easier if the
public were already accustomed to the use of paper notes
based on silver, for it would then be possible to proceed to
a gradual destruction of the existing assignats and to the
establishment of an exchange office to redeem them for silver.
However, in view of the present amount of paper money,

[30] *Materialy,* pp. 1–7.
[31] *Ibid.,* pp. 10–12.

Kankrin concluded, such an office would require far too great a sum.[32] The stubborn old Minister of Finance was under pressure, from the Tsar and some of his colleagues, to institute changes in the monetary system and this proposal was his way of yielding very slowly, without ever admitting that his position had changed at all.

The reference to the gradual destruction of the assignats shows that the Finance Minister was still thinking of reduction and eventual redemption at face value, the kind of program that Speransky had proposed in 1810 and Gurev had attempted in 1817. A few months later, Kankrin rejected a suggestion that assignats be exchanged for silver on demand at the current bourse rate and insisted that the deposit offices were a first step toward ultimate exchange at face value.[33] To restore the full value of the assignats was, of course, a much more difficult task than simply to make them convertible at the current bourse rate. The economic impact of such a sharp deflation would undoubtedly have been severe. Kankrin had never favored the rapid restoration of the assignats to face value, and he certainly did not contemplate any immediate action that would upset the *status quo* that he had maintained so carefully since 1823.[34]

The plan to establish deposit offices to exchange silver coin for deposit notes redeemable on demand met little opposition, but there was fundamental disagreement between the majority of the State Council and the Minister of Finance on the problem of the "popular rates" and what to do about the monetary situation in general. The Department of the Economy of the State Council rejected Kankrin's theory that punitive measures would eliminate the "popular rates" and suggested that they were the result both of a shortage of

[32] *Ibid.*, pp. 14–15.
[33] *Ibid.*, pp. 10–14, 25–28.
[34] Kankrin, *Weltreichthum*, pp. 64–65, shows his awareness of the problems of restoring the assignats to full face value by reducing the number in circulation.

assignats and small coins and of public uncertainty as to whether or not taxes could be paid in metal. The department urged the opening of exchange offices in areas where the problem was most severe and the "establishment" of assignats equal to silver at the current bourse rate. The new assignats would be issued in amounts equal to state receipts of silver and the old assignats gradually withdrawn. This plan amounted to a proposal for official devaluation of the assignat to the current bourse rate and is the first reference in official documents since the Gurev Plan of 1824 to the possibility of recognizing the devaluation of the assignats as permanent. The record does not indicate who submitted the idea, but the majority of the members of the Department of the Economy approved and sent it to the Minister of Finance for comment.[35]

Kankrin's comments were sharp. He rejected the contention that there was any shortage of assignats or small silver coin. The immediate exchange of assignats for metal at face value was completely impossible and to exchange them at the current bourse rate would not eliminate the "popular rates" because these were produced by fraud and illegal dealings and demanded police action. Kankrin concluded this argument by saying that the only result of the council's proposal would be an increase in the number of assignats. The available documents, however, do not support any such conclusion. The State Council plan was simply that the government should put its silver receipts in the deposit offices, spend deposit notes, and gradually replace the assignats with deposit notes backed by a reserve. Such a program would not increase the stock of money. Kankrin feared, nevertheless, that any change in the monetary system might threaten the current value of the assignat, and he had not yet given up the notion of redemption at full value in the remote future. The State Council, at a full meeting of all its sections, refused to alter its stand that extensive reform of the monetary

[35] *Materialy,* pp. 16–19.

system was needed to eliminate the "popular rates," and on November 29, 1837, it requested the submission of formal proposals on the problem by council members.[36]

Drafts were received from Admiral Greig, Admiral Mordvinov, Prince Drutskii-Liubetskii, Count Speransky, and finally from Kankrin himself. The presentation and consideration of these five proposals occupied an entire year and a half, from November 1837 through May 1839. Greig's plan arrived promptly in December 1837; Mordvinov's was written in November 1837, but not considered until February 1838; and Drutskii-Liubetskii's lengthy document followed in April 1838. In January 1839, Speransky sent his proposal to Kankrin for comment, but it was not submitted to the State Council until March, shortly after Speransky's death. Finally, in May 1839, Kankrin presented his own version of Speransky's plan.

Greig suggested an alternative to redeeming the assignat at face value in silver, or reducing its face value to correspond to its actual value in terms of silver. This was to reduce the actual weight of the silver ruble so it would be equal to the current value of the assignat. Greig argued, with considerable justification, that, since prices were universally quoted in assignats, to reduce the face value of assignats to correspond to silver rubles would require general price reductions which would be difficult and confusing. The silver ruble was too valuable a coin to be convenient for ordinary transactions

---

[36] *Ibid.,* pp. 21–33. The record, or *zhurnal,* of the State Council meetings is not a verbatim transcript, but a relatively brief summary prepared by a secretary after the meeting. In some cases the *zhurnal* covers more than one meeting. It can be assumed that resolutions and conclusions formally agreed on by the council were recorded with reasonable accuracy, while summaries of discussion or the "sense of the meeting" depended to a greater degree on the memory and sympathy of the secretary. The item discussed above was part of a formal conclusion, but lacks supplementary material to clarify how the members of the council thought the proposal would work. Texts of documents submitted to the council, such as Kankrin's proposals, are available in full in *Materialy.*

and Greig's idea recognized that the assignat ruble was a more convenient unit, not merely in physical size but also in value. Greig called for some degree of convertibility of assignats into silver on demand. He also believed that the value of the assignats varied directly with the number in circulation, a theory that had been discredited by the experience during the withdrawals under Gurev from 1818 to 1823. The Greig project, of course, was a devaluation, since it did not attempt to restore the assignat to its original value in terms of silver.

Kankrin opposed Greig because he did not make provision for maintaining the new silver ruble equal to the assignat, because of the cost of reminting all the existing silver coins, and because of possible problems connected with foreign exchange. The first point was valid, and was accepted by the State Council. Greig attempted to refute Kankrin on the question of the cost of reminting by citing English experience for a comparable undertaking.[37] The council did not refer to this question in rejecting Greig's plan. It was not convinced that there would be no repercussions in foreign trade, and added the objection that the new silver coins would be too small for convenience. It is clear from another of Kankrin's comments on the Greig plan that he was still thinking in terms of an eventual redemption of the assignats at their full face value. He said proudly to the State Council, "Our money system is the best in Europe," and insisted that nothing needed to be done except to reduce the number of assignats until they were equal in value to the silver ruble. Kankrin did not specify when he felt that this could be done, but he did estimate that at the current rate of improvement it would take one hundred and eighty years for the assignats to regain their original face value. Despite the boastful asser-

[37] Greig was the son of a Scottish admiral who had been employed by Catherine II. He had been educated in England and presumably was well informed on British affairs. His son was minister of finance in the second half of the nineteenth century.

tions, these statements are the first in which Kankrin was willing to admit that some change in the monetary system might be in order.[38]

Mordvinov submitted only a few general observations which did not amount to a complete program for action. He was a very old man in 1837, and although the brief memorandum was treated with great formal respect, the suggestions in it were not actually given serious consideration. Mordvinov emphasized, as he had done so many times in previous years, the importance of increased economic activity, and favored an increased supply of money to be achieved by the stimulation of gold production and a "Labor Encouraging Bank."

Kankrin, writing in March 1838, of course rejected the idea of a bank with the power to issue currency as highly dangerous. He did, however, show signs of being somewhat reconciled to monetary reform when he insisted that the preparatory measures for the creation of "silver assignats" had already been taken. The deposit offices were what he had in mind, but that had not been the stated purpose when they had been first suggested. Then, reform had been mentioned as little more than a remote possibility.[39]

The third of the five proposals came from Prince Drutskii-Liubetskii, and it embodied the main features of the actual reform. Most of the lengthy document that the Prince submitted in late April 1838 was a detailed and confusing historical and theoretical treatise, but he concluded with a series of specific proposals for action. The silver ruble should be declared the basic currency of the realm and the rate used currently for tax payments (3.6 assignats per silver ruble) made permanent. A deposit office was to be set up to give out silver coin or the newly created silver assignat notes for all other types of metal. The new silver assignat note would be convertible on demand into coin. At the discretion of the minister of finance, some of the money in the deposit office was to be loaned out and the profits from these loans were to be

[38] *Materialy,* pp. 41–49, 57–60, 65–67, 197–198.
[39] *Ibid.,* pp. 74–76, 79–80, 197.

used to exchange the old assignats for the new silver assignats at a rate of 3.6 to 1. If it seemed desirable to hasten this process, borrowed funds could be used to enlarge the backing fund for the new silver assignats.[40]

Drutskii-Liubetskii's proposal was an elaboration of the State Council's outline of October 27, 1837 (see above), which he may well have helped to prepare. It contained all the basic elements of the reform as it was ultimately adopted: (1) the proclamation of the silver ruble as the main currency of the realm and the repeal of the law of 1812, which gave this position to the assignat; (2) the establishment of a fixed rate of exchange; (3) the use of the deposit office to put new silver-based currency into circulation; and (4) the ultimate exchange of the old assignats for new silver-based notes at a fixed, devalued rate. The only important part of the plan not adopted was the lending of deposit-office funds and the use of the resulting profit to retire the old assignats.

Kankrin had many objections, but the fundamental one was to the Prince's suggestion that the deposit-office funds could be used to create credit via the Commercial Bank, in effect to increase the money supply. This, in his view, would be a betrayal of public trust and would destroy the entire system. It was a notion fundamentally inconsistent with Kankrin's fierce devotion to monetary stability and mortal fear of any move that might be considered even potentially inflationary.[41] It would furthermore introduce an element of political control into the monetary system, something that Kankrin had always rejected as unsafe. The basis of Kankrin's fears was the experience of an earlier generation, and perhaps what he observed of more extreme developments in other countries. Within the Russian government there was no influential support for an inflationary policy. Not even Drutskii-Liubetskii was an easy-money man. He simply favored a somewhat more flexible currency and credit system. The benefit that the gentry debtor would derive from cheap

[40] *Ibid.*, pp. 113–118.
[41] *Ibid.*, pp. 129–132.

money was hardly mentioned in discussions of monetary policy. Since there was little pressure on the gentry to pay their debts to the state, their concern was probably much less active than that of similar groups in other countries.

For almost a year after the discussion of Drutskii-Liubetskii's plan, no further action was taken, although informal and unrecorded discussion must have continued among the very small group of men who knew that action was contemplated. In his annual report to the Tsar for 1838, Kankrin vigorously restated his conviction that the current monetary problems did not arise from substantive defects in the monetary system but solely from improper speculative activity and fraud.[42]

In January 1839, Speransky sent a plan for monetary reform directly to Kankrin for his consideration. Early in February, Kankrin replied with a cordial letter and enclosed his comments, but a few weeks later Speransky died without having replied to Kankrin's criticisms. Both documents were discussed by the State Council in March. Speransky's proposals did not differ greatly in substance from Drutskii-Liubetskii's, but they were presented so much more clearly and convincingly that they probably had a great influence on those who were undecided on the question. Moreover, it was relatively easy for Kankrin to accept proposals from Speransky, with whom his relations had been good, whereas to approve Drutskii-Liubetskii's would have forced the arrogant and stubborn Minister to admit that his most outspoken critic was right after all.

Speransky proposed, as had Drutskii-Liubetskii, the establishment of a deposit office to issue notes in exchange for metal and the proclamation of a fixed rate for assignats in terms of silver to be used in all transactions, public and private. He believed that these actions would eliminate the "popular rates." When the deposit notes and the fixed rate were firmly established, the assignats were to be exchanged

[42] TsGIAL, f. 560, op. 38, d. 402, "Obshchii otchet . . . za 1838 g.," p. 12.

gradually for deposit notes. The deposit-office funds were to remain untouched and money needed to back the newly issued deposit notes borrowed, either internally or abroad. The exchange process, Speransky estimated, would take ten years. The reform followed this outline exactly, and the final exchange of assignats for deposit notes was accomplished much more rapidly than predicted. Drutskii-Liubetskii's controversial plan to create a backing fund from profits on loans of deposit office money was omitted by Speransky.[43]

Kankrin's main disagreement with Speransky was on questions of timing, but he accepted without comment the principle of recognizing the devaluation of the assignat as permanent. He concluded the discussion of Speransky's plan by presenting his own concrete program.

The first step was to establish the deposit office, and that, Kankrin said, entailed no risk whatever. The "tax rate" for assignats was to be maintained close to the current bourse rate. Gradually taxes and state payments could be shifted to a silver basis to encourage the use of the deposit notes. Once this had been accomplished, the further course of action could be decided on. Kankrin felt, however, that it would probably only involve the shifting of remaining receipts and payments to a silver basis and the establishment of a backing fund of one-fifth or one-sixth to insure the convertibility of the notes issued in exchange for the assignats. The exchange would be carried out at the current bourse rate or at a special rate to be determined at the appropriate time. The funds of the deposit office were to be inviolate. Kankrin agreed that it would be permissible to borrow to establish the backing fund. At several points in his discussion, Kankrin repeated his conviction that none of these measures would eliminate the "popular rates" and that punitive measures would still be required.[44] Although he still clung tenaciously to his position on the "popular rates," Kankrin accepted the main elements of Drutskii-Liubetskii's and Speransky's plans. He in-

[43] Speransky, "O monetnom obrashchenii," pp. 166–174.
[44] *Materialy,* pp. 179–191.

sisted, nevertheless, that the only step to be taken at once was the establishment of the deposit offices, which he had proposed almost two years earlier.

In March, April, and May of 1839, the State Council, after quickly dismissing the plans of Greig and Mordvinov, considered the three main proposals. The council agreed early in the discussion that one of the initial steps in the reform should be the determination of a single rate at which assignats would be exchanged for silver. Kankrin thereupon abandoned his opposition to fixing the value of the assignats before the final exchange and proposed that all transactions should be put on a silver basis after January 1, 1840, and that the deposit offices should be opened at that time. On January 1, 1841, or later as circumstances permitted, the assignats would be exchanged for a silver-based note.[45]

Only two important matters now remained unsettled: the rate at which the assignats would be fixed and the nature of the backing fund for the notes issued to replace the assignats. Kankrin proposed a rate equal to the average bourse rate in recent months, which would be about 3.5 assignats per silver ruble. A majority of the State Council endorsed the current tax rate of 3.6, which had been in effect for many years. Kankrin's proposal favored those who held assignats or bank deposits (always in assignats), because in converting assignats into the silver rubles they would be divided by about 3.5 instead of 3.6. Kankrin was worried about the possibility of a run on the banks, particularly by foreigners. Conversely the State Council's proposed rate of 3.6 assignats per silver ruble would have favored those, mainly gentrymen, who owed assignats to the banks. The issue was much debated and was eventually settled only when the Tsar decided that the rate would be 3.5. This was essentially what Kankrin wanted, although he would have preferred that it be tied to the bourse rate rather than arbitrarily fixed. It was a decision that recognized the state's concern for fiscal stability as more important

[45] *Ibid.,* pp. 201–202, 213–220.

than the immediate interests of the gentry debtor.[46] The striking thing is, however, that only on this very minor issue did the interests of debtors versus creditors arise, so firmly accepted was the commitment to highly restrictive money and credit policy.

The other matter that remained to be decided in the spring of 1839 was the question of the backing fund for the notes replacing the assignats. If the new notes were to be convertible on demand into silver, there obviously had to be some assurance that the silver would be available when demanded. Speransky had not specified whether he felt that 100 per cent backing was needed. He merely said that money should be borrowed to provide the fund. Drutskii-Liubetskii wanted 100 per cent backing for the new currency and proposed to get it by accumulating the profits made by loaning out the funds of the deposit office, which meant the deposit notes would not have full backing. The State Council rejected that idea as too risky, but decided that it was impossible to consider borrowing enough to provide 100 per cent backing. Finally it accepted the Finance Minister's proposal of one-fifth to one-sixth backing.[47]

In May 1839, Kankrin submitted detailed proposals for the implementation of the monetary reform. The goal was formally stated as being to stop the further increase in the value of the assignat, "in many ways harmful," to exchange the assignats for silver, and to aid in the elimination of the "popular rates." That final phrase must have been a difficult concession for Kankrin to make in view of his repeated statements that such measures could not affect the "popular rates." In the State Council, Greig and Drutskii-Liubetskii made final pleas for their own plans. Greig said the old silver ruble was long unknown and that repricing of goods would cause great confusion. Drutskii-Liubetskii claimed that the deposit office would take the needed small silver out of circulation

[46] *Ibid.*, pp. 205–207, 259.
[47] *Ibid.*, pp. 210–211.

and insisted that a bank was required to issue notes needed to alleviate the shortage of money. Their criticisms went unheeded, and on July 1, 1839, two manifestoes were issued which inaugurated the first major change in the Russian money system since Catherine II had introduced the assignat.[48]

The major provisions of the first of the two laws were: (1) that the silver ruble was to be restored to the position it had held in 1810 as the basic currency of the realm; (2) that assignats were to be a supplementary token of value and were to circulate at a rate of 3.5 per silver ruble; (3) that all payments by and to the state were to be made at that rate, and after January 1, 1840, all transactions among private persons were to be in terms of silver; (4) that the district treasury offices were to exchange silver and assignats on demand insofar as their resources permitted; and (5) that the use of all other rates was forbidden. The second law set up the deposit offices almost exactly as Kankrin had originally suggested. They were to open on June 1, 1840, as parts of the Commercial Bank, but were to keep the coin received in exchange for deposit notes separate from other funds and were to redeem the notes on demand with no service charge. There was no mention of the planned exchange of the assignats for silver-based notes in either manifesto.[49]

It is difficult to assign responsibility to any one person for either the content or the actual initiation of the reform measures. It was certainly not "Kankrin's reform," as it was frequently called in later years. He was responsible for the idea of the deposit office to receive metal money and issue deposit notes in exchange, but he wanted to put off any further decisions until this step had been put into operation. The main elements of the eventual reform were elaborated by Prince Drutskii-Liubetskii in April 1838 and were revised and clarified by Count Speransky in January 1839. Only after those proposals had been submitted and received support from the State Council did Kankrin accept the major ele-

[48] *Ibid.*, pp. 244–255.
[49] *Ibid.*, pp. 262–265.

ments in them and submit his own version, which was then adopted with little change.

The role of the Tsar was undoubtedly very important. It was in response to his request that Kankrin's initial proposals were submitted in July 1837. If it had not been felt that Nicholas wanted a thoroughgoing reform of some sort, the State Council probably would not have insisted on a more extensive plan than that which Kankrin first submitted. On the other hand, the Tsar apparently did not exert much pressure for quick action, for the reform took over two years to reach the first stage of implementation.

Drutskii-Liubetskii's contribution was not an original idea by any means. The recognition of the devaluation of the assignat as permanent had been discussed by the State Council before his proposal was considered. It had also been suggested by Karamzin, Turgenev, and Jakob before Kankrin took office and was even formally pressed by Gurev within the government in 1824. Any statesman interested in the problem must have been familiar with the idea. Speransky deserves credit for his lucid exposition of the principles involved in the reform. His prestige and the fact that he and Kankrin were on good terms gave his memorandum greater weight than Drutskii-Liubetskii's. Without Speransky's plan to act as a catalyst the debate might well have lasted much longer.[50]

The deposit offices were opened on January 8, 1840, and by the end of the year 25,623,037 silver rubles had been deposited and an equal number of deposit notes issued. Over 70 per cent of this sum, 18,215,500 rubles, was silver deposited by state agencies, while only 7,407,537 had been deposited by private individuals. More important, however,

[50] Marc Raeff, in his excellent biography of Speransky, underestimates the importance of his subject's contribution to the monetary reform when he writes that "his views did not prevail against those of Finance Minister Count Kankrin" (*Michael Speransky, Statesman of Imperial Russia, 1772–1839* [The Hague, 1957], p. 350). Kaufman carefully summarizes the documents, giving due credit to both Drutskii-Liubetskii and Speransky (*Iz istorii*, pp. 98–125, esp. pp. 113–114.

was the fact that only about 5.5 per cent, 1,453,637 rubles, of the total notes issued had been redeemed for silver.[51] Since the state put the deposit notes it received into circulation by paying them out to meet its bills, it is of no particular significance that the bulk of the deposits were made by the state as long as the notes remained in circulation and were not redeemed. There were only a limited number of offices where deposits could be made and it is not surprising that private individuals did not deposit as much as the state.

The manifesto of July 1839 was successful in eliminating the troublesome "popular rates." Trade at the great Nizhni-Novgorod fair was slow after the announcement in July, but by the end of the season trading revived as the new system was accepted. In his report for the year 1840, Kankrin proudly claimed that the "popular rates" had "vanished from the memory of the people." [52] Although this is undoubtedly an exaggeration, there is no evidence that they continued to be a significant problem.[53]

There were complaints that, although prices were changed from assignats to silver rubles, they did not fall as much as people felt they should. Even if every price was adjusted with complete fairness and mathematical exactitude there would have been some gains and losses because exchange rates other than 350 to 100 prevailed in many areas. In Moscow it was about 336 to 100, so the new fixed rate of 350 to 100 meant a decline in the value of the assignats in terms of silver, and therefore a purchaser would have to expect to pay more than before the reform when using assignats. Insofar as the Mos-

[51] Kaufman, *Iz istorii*, p. 258.

[52] *Zhurnal manufaktur i torgovli*, no. 11 (1839), p. 291; P. A. Ostrou-khov, "Iz istorii russkago denezhnago obrashcheniia," *Zapiski, Russki svobodnyi universitet Prague, nauchno-issledovatel'skoe obedinyenia*, II (1941), 7; TsGIAL, f. 560, op. 38, d. 433, "Obshchii otchet za . . . 1840," p. 2.

[53] A. D. Druian, by no means sympathetic to Kankrin or the reform, states that reports from various cities throughout the empire indicate that the popular agio disappeared (*Ocherki po istorii denezhnogo obrashcheniia Rossii v XIX veke* [Moscow, 1941], p. 25).

cow situation prevailed throughout the country, as it did in many areas of central Russia, the reform proclamation had a mildly inflationary effect, since it recognized the assignat as representing slightly more monetary units than was currently the case, while the amount of silver in circulation was not affected. Persons who received their income in assignats therefore presumably lost purchasing power.[54]

The more sophisticated groups were undoubtedly able to avoid loss more readily than the less well informed, and the complex nature of the existing system must have provided many opportunities for making a final killing. But it was indeed a *final* killing. The rate of exchange of assignats and silver rubles was now fixed; and even though in some areas trade was conducted in terms of assignats for many years, there was no doubt about the relationship between the two currencies and no problem of constant repricing of goods to correspond to a fluctuating rate of exchange, or of seeking means to avoid such repricing.[55]

The results of the 1839 reform decrees prove that the Minister of Finance was mistaken when he claimed that there was nothing wrong with the monetary system and that the "popular rates" were only the result of fraud and speculation. The disappearance of the "popular rates" showed that it had been the lack of a stable relationship between the two currencies that had permitted them to develop and continue to exist. The reform proclamation established a fixed rate of exchange by decree, and, it should be noted, the government was willing to exchange assignats or silver at 350 to

[54] This reasoning is supported by the contemporary comment of Nikitenko, writing in his diary in July 1839, when he says that bureaucrats lost 7 per cent of their income (Aleksandr Vasilevich Nikitenko, "Dnevnik," *Russkaia starina,* LXIV [1889], 111), and similarly by an article in *Severnaia pchela,* which concluded that those who lost from the reform were persons whose income was in assignats and who bought in silver (S. Usov, "Razsmotreniia nekotorykh tolkov o novom denezhnom schete," *Severnaia pchela,* no. 238 [Oct. 21, 1839]).

[55] V. A. Kokorev, *Ekonomicheskie provaly po vospominaniam s 1837 goda* (St. Petersburg, 1887), pp. 22, 87–88.

100, although it did not guarantee unlimited exchange. This
final step was to come shortly and insured the permanency
of the fixed rate as long as the opportunity to convert paper
into metal was maintained. Some of the Kankrin's critics,
particularly Drutskii-Liubetskii and Mordvinov, where also
shown to have been mistaken in maintaining that the "popular rates" were the result of a shortage of money. The reform
measures did not significantly alter the quantity of money in
circulation, but the "popular rates" disappeared nevertheless.

All that remained to be done was to exchange the assignat
for a new type of note with a face value equal to a silver
ruble and redeemable in silver on demand. The details of
this final step were discussed at great length, but it was actually a secondary matter, for the 1839 reform had produced
a stable monetary system with a paper currency in practice,
though not formally, convertible into metal on demand. It was
the initial reform measures that achieved the primary goal
of the entire reform, the elimination of the "popular rates."

THE COMPLETION OF MONETARY REFORM

The reform plan submitted to the State Council on May
11, 1839, had called for the exchange of the old assignats
for silver based notes in 1841. The series of crop failures that
began late in 1839 produced a financial crisis that lasted into
1842 and delayed the final phases of the monetary reform.[56]
Money was needed for a reserve to back the new currency,
and an essential element in the contemplated exchange was
a high degree of public confidence in the state's credit.
Neither requirement could be satisfied during a time of
distress.

The introduction of the state credit note as an emergency
fiscal expedient during the financial crisis had no connection

[56] *Materialy*, pp. 226–230; TsGIAL, f. 560, op. 38, d. 433, "Obshchii
otchet . . . za 1840," p. 2.

with monetary reform.[57] It did, however, add another type of currency to an already complex situation. The decrees of 1839 had achieved the primary goal of fixing the relationship between assignats and silver rubles, but by mid-1841 there were three types of paper money in circulation: the assignats, whose number had not changed since 1823 and whose value was now set at 3.5 per silver ruble; the deposit notes given out in exchange for Russian silver coin, backed by 100 per cent reserves of silver and redeemable at face value on demand; and the new credit note, backed in fact by 100 per cent reserves during the first six months after the issue began and by progressively lower percentages in subsequent periods, reaching the publicly proclaimed one-sixth backing in January 1843.[58] The old interest-bearing state treasury notes also still circulated as money, although thay were not legal tender for private transactions. Of course there still remained Russian silver, gold, and copper coin, and many types of foreign coin. Russian gold coin had become increasingly common in the twenties and thirties as domestic gold production rose rapidly. It was not accepted by the deposit offices in exchange for deposit notes, although it was legal tender and accepted for payment of taxes with a slight premium over silver.[59]

Early in 1843, in response to the Tsar's request, Kankrin presented a plan to eliminate all the assignats and replace them with deposit notes, backed by a reserve of metal equal to one-sixth of the face value of the new notes issued. Nicholas was not satisfied and pointed out to the special committee

[57] See Chapter IV, pp. 127–130.

[58] Kaufman, *Iz istorii,* p. 133.

[59] In February 1841, Kankrin stated that gold coin was light and easy to transport and that therefore there was no reason to try to withdraw it from circulation. If his aim was to get the public accustomed to the deposit notes in preparation for the final exchange of the assignats, it is difficult to understand why he did not want Russian gold coin as well as silver accepted by the deposit offices. Apparently he was still thinking in terms of his original idea of making the shipment of funds easier and had not really adjusted to the idea of a full reorganization of the currency system. See Kaufman, *Iz istorii,* p. 260.

that there would then be two types of deposit notes, the original ones exchanged for metal and fully backed, and the new ones backed only to one-sixth of the total issue. This, he felt, could not be permitted, for it would undermine public faith in the deposit notes.

The Tsar then proceeded to read a plan he had prepared himself. It proposed that the emission of deposit notes be stopped, that those received by the state be destroyed, and that the 100 per cent metal reserve that backed these notes be used to form the one-sixth backing for the new credit notes. Credit notes would be issued in bills of small denomination, from one to twenty-five rubles, as well as the existing fifty-ruble note. Those who wished to exchange silver coin or bullion for credit notes could do so on the same basis as for deposit notes, except that full backing would not be provided. The backing fund for the new credit notes would be established with four million rubles silver from the military reserve fund and would be expanded with metal exchanged for credit notes or transferred from the deposit offices as the deposit notes received by the state were destroyed. The final replacement of the assignats would take place over a period of five years through the destruction of assignats received by the state and the use of credit notes for one-fifth of all payments by the state. According to Nicholas, there would be no risk of disturbance because nothing would really be changed. Those with deposit notes who wanted silver could get it. The backing fund would be formed without resort to borrowing.[60]

Kankrin believed that the public would be disturbed by the shift of the deposit-office metal reserves to the fund designated to back the credit notes. The Tsar rejected the criticism on the ground that deposit notes that were received and destroyed by the state automatically freed an equal quantity of metal in the deposit-office reserves which the state could use as it saw fit. With little further discussion the plan

[60] M. A. Korf, "Imperator Nikolai v soveshchatel'nykh sobraniiakh: (Iz sovremennykh zapisok stats-sekretaria barona Korfa)," *Sbornik IRIO*, XCVIII (1896), 178–180.

was adopted. During the final elaboration of the details, Kankrin continued to make objections on secondary points, but was overruled by Nicholas. [61]

The final decree was promulgated on July 9, 1843. The intention to gradually replace the existing assignats with their equivalent in silver credit notes was announced. The new notes were to be redeemable on demand in metal and backed initially by a fund of 28.5 million rubles, half from reserve capital and half from metal representing deposit notes that were on hand or that would come into state possession. The backing fund was not to be less than one-sixth of the total amount of credit notes exchanged for assignats. The deposit offices would cease to issue deposit notes, but would continue to redeem them for metal on demand. The main exchange office in St. Petersburg was to exchange any amount of credit notes for metal, the Moscow office up to three thousand rubles per person, and the district treasury offices in the provinces up to one hundred per person. The exchange offices were also authorized to receive silver and gold coin or bullion and issue credit notes in return. The state credit notes were to be issued in exchange for assignats received by the state from November 1, 1843, onward.[62]

In practice, the exchange proceeded much more smoothly and rapidly than the Tsar, Kankrin, and the other members of the special committee had expected. In only two years, 70 per cent of the old paper currencies (assignats and deposit notes) had been exchanged. By 1852, 166,916,951 silver rubles worth of assignats had been exchanged, leaving outstanding only 3,304,851 silver rubles' worth, about 2 per cent of the original total. The public demonstrated its confidence in the new currency by exchanging silver and gold coin for credit

[61] *Ibid.,* pp. 180–182, 186–194.

[62] For the full text of the law see Korf, "Imperator Nikolai," pp. 273–278. Kaufman correctly points out that the law is poorly worded and the decree actually guaranteed one-sixth backing only for the credit notes exchanged for assignats, leaving unclear the status of the credit notes issued to replace deposit notes or metal money (*Iz istorii,* pp. 141–142).

notes. Between September 1, 1843, and December 31, 1846,
182.4 million rubles in gold and silver were received for
credit notes and 97.4 million were redeemed, leaving a net
deposit of 85.0 million rubles silver.[63] The results of the
monetary reform may be summarized as follows:[64]

State credit notes in circulation, January 1, 1853

Issued between 1841 and 1843	10,952,300
Issued in exchange for assignats	166,916,951
Issued in exchange for deposit notes	48,548,976
Issued in exchange for silver and gold (net)	84,957,354
Total	311,375,581

The backing fund, January 1, 1853 (in silver rubles)

Deposited in exchange for deposit notes destroyed	48,548,976
Deposited on the issuance of credit notes exchanged for silver and gold	84,957,354
Deposited by the state to back credit notes issued	13,288,518[65]
Total	146,794,848

Of the 146.8 million silver rubles in the fund backing the
credit notes, only about 9 per cent had been supplied by the
state. The remainder was supplied by the public, either
through paying taxes with deposit notes or coin or by direct
exchanges of metal for credit notes. The operation was based
almost entirely on public confidence, not on the accumulation of large reserves by the state. In 1853, the total amount
of metal held in reserve amounted to 47 per cent of the credit
notes issued, far in excess of the one-sixth required by law,
but even this amount would not have sufficed for long had the
public tried to exchange their credit notes for metal as
quickly as they could.

Since all the credit notes were the same, the person who
had formerly held assignats had just as valid a claim on the
silver and gold in the backing fund as did the person who had
originally held deposit notes or coin. Thus the backing fund
for the credit notes was created by reducing the 100 per cent

---

[63] Kaufman, *Iz istorii*, pp. 142–145.

[64] *Ibid.*, pp. 143–144.

[65] This figure is calculated by Kaufman as a residual, subtracting the
other two known amounts from the known total. According to the
decree of 1843, this sum should have been 14.5 million.

reserve backing the deposit notes, but this was accomplished with the consent of the holders, since they had the option of keeping their deposit notes or of converting them into metal. The option of converting credit notes into coin was also open, but few chose to do this.

The final reform measures involved no increase in the amount of money in circulation. Assignats were exchanged for their equivalent in silver credit notes at 3.5 to 1, the rate established in 1839. Deposit notes and coins were exchanged at their face value for credit notes. The original credit notes that had been issued in accordance with the law of 1841 did, of course, represent a net increase in the supply of money to the extent that their face value exceeded the fund set aside to back them. By 1853, however, they amounted to only about eleven million silver rubles, or 3 per cent of the total of all credit notes. A little over one-third of the thirty million originally authorized had actually been issued in twelve years.

Although the various stages of the monetary reform of 1839–1843 were carried out with little more than the reluctant cooperation of the cautious Minister of Finance, it would be a mistake to regard them as a victory for a more forward-looking or expansionist position. Kankrin suffered personal defeats on minor questions, but there was no real change in the general policy of monetary restraint that he had established so firmly. The entire program was highly conservative and made no alteration in the total stock of money, nor were any new sources of credit developed. The proposals for a more flexible monetary system submitted by Prince Drutskii-Liubetskii were ignored by the Tsar, who was interested only in the technical problem of establishing a single monetary unit.[66] In a formal sense, the reform was no more than a recognition of the devaluation of the assignat, which had existed in fact since the Napoleonic Wars. It was, nevertheless, a significant achievement. It marked a shift from the passive and unnecessary acceptance of a confused situation to positive, though cautious control of the monetary system.

[66] Korf, "Imperator Nikolai," pp. 196–197.

When it acted to eliminate the "popular rates" and establish a single monetary unit, the state accepted a responsibility that it had shirked for twenty-five years.

The successful completion of the monetary reform was possible because of widespread public confidence in the state's fiscal policy; people were willing to accept the convenient credit notes and did not insist on turning them into metal. The formation of a large reserve fund through budgetary saving or borrowing was not necessary. The entire operation could have been carried out whenever there was sufficient public confidence to produce the voluntary deposits of coin in exchange for convertible notes that were essential to build up the reserve fund. In theory, then, the reform could have been started at almost any time, although there is no evidence that the Tsar, or Kankrin, gave the matter serious thought before 1834. The opening of deposit offices, as Kankrin himself pointed out, involved no risks; they simply exchanged paper for coin and vice versa, keeping a 100 per cent reserve at all times. The reputation for thrift that Kankrin created, at least partially through secret borrowing from the state banks, undoubtedly contributed to the high degree of public trust evident at the time of the reform.

Yet the reformed monetary system did not survive the Crimean War. To meet massive wartime deficits, large numbers of state credit notes were issued, convertibility had to be abandoned, and the value of the notes fell. The fault did not lie with the structure of the monetary system. Even a far larger metal reserve would not have lasted long in the face of the wartime pressures. The state's revenues, and indeed the economy as a whole, simply could not respond to major demands for additional funds. Only a sweeping and extensive program designed to develop the resources of the nation could conceivably have enabled the economy to meet the needs of a major war without serious inflation. In the 1820's, there had been signs of state interest in such a program, but the Ministry of Finance had quickly concluded that the obstacles were too formidable to permit significant progress.

CHAPTER VI

Russian Industry in a Changing World

Monetary reform, the state peasant program, and railroad construction all began in the late 1830's. Monetary reform was completed in 1843, but the other two programs went on, without significant changes in scope, goal, or method, until the Crimean War (1853–1856) and the death of Nicholas I in 1856. Limited though they were, these were the great and obvious events of the reign, as far as the economy was concerned. After these three programs had been started, the state made no more major decisions on economic matters except, it could be argued, the decision not to build more railroads than it did and not to attempt a more extensive program among the state peasantry. These, however, were not alternatives seriously considered. The existing projects were regarded as maximum programs.

The most interesting aspect of economic policy during the last fifteen years of Nicholas' reign is the state's hesitant and uncertain attitude toward industrial development. There was no important figure within the government who was interested in industry. Mordvinov was in virtual retirement by the late thirties. Yet the state was obliged to consider questions involving industry because of developments both in Russia and in western Europe. Within Russia, two industries grew rapidly, although the government was far from certain that it wanted them to grow at all. Another, however, attracted attention because it could not meet growing demands despite a long-established policy of state support. Beyond the borders of the empire, there were a series of revolutions and disturbances in 1848, and for the first time an important official called for strict regulation of industrial expansion.

Only one specific problem that was considered in the last years of Nicholas' long reign provided an opportunity for overall consideration of state policy toward industry. In 1850, a major revision of the tariff was enacted, the first that brought into question the basic principles of the existing tariff system established in 1822. Tariff policy would have been relatively simple to determine if it had been a matter of concern to industry alone, but of course it was not. The old problem of state revenue had a great deal to do with the nature of the tariff and therefore with the state's attitude toward the industries that were protected, either deliberately or inadvertently. The development of beet-sugar production, cotton spinning, and iron smelting in Russia demonstrates the complex problems that the state faced when it considered tariff revision.

THREE INDUSTRIES: SUGAR, COTTON, AND IRON

Beet-sugar production in Russia was almost entirely the result of the enterprise of a few energetic gentrymen. During the reign of Alexander I, the state had provided some limited encouragement to those who wished to experiment with the new crop on their estates. The attempts were unsuccessful. Sugar-beet technology was still at a very low level, the yield low and the costs high. When the tariff of 1822 was promulgated, sugar-beet production was negligible. The import of refined lump sugar was forbidden, and a duty had been placed on granulated cane sugar that had to undergo further refining in Russia. It was above all a revenue-producing tariff, but it also protected the St. Petersburg sugar refineries. There was no intention at the time of protecting beet-sugar production because the industry had not yet become technically feasible in Russia. In 1831 and in 1841, the duty on imported sugar was increased to provide additional revenue in periods of severe fiscal difficulty.[1] The increased duties also raised the level of protection for anyone who wanted to try his hand at making sugar from beets, but the state did not expect any significant growth of domestic production. In 1826, when private groups were already becoming enthusiastic about the possibilities of the new industry, the minister of the interior was skeptical and suspected that the promoters were more interested in distilling vodka from the left-over mash than in making sugar. Kankrin, in the Ministry of Finance, was equally skeptical in 1829. His subordinate Pel'chinskii, who was so enthusiastic about most industries, shared his chief's views on beet sugar. The Tsar himself believed that beets injured the land where they were grown.[2]

The rapid development of new techniques abroad, which were quickly borrowed by Russian entrepreneurs, and the existing high tariff enabled sugar-beet producers to make high profits, and output grew rapidly in the thirties and forties.[3] The attitude of the state remained indifferent and even unfriendly, but nothing was done to stop the growth of the new industry. In 1833, Kankrin remarked, "The beet-sugar industry is one of the most illfounded projects of the

[1] Konstantin Lodyzhenskii, *Istoriia russkago tamozhennago tarifa* (St. Petersburg, 1886), pp. 279–280, for data on tariff rates.

[2] K. G. Voblyi, *Opyt istorii sveklo-sakharnoi promyshlennosti S.S.S.R.,* I (Moscow, 1928), 100–102; Vikentii Pel'chinskii, *O sostoianii promyshlennykh sil Rossii do 1832 goda* (St. Petersburg, 1833), p. 39.

[3] Output grew as follows: in 1820, 5.5 thousand poods; in 1825, 15.0 thousand; in 1830, 32.0 thousand; in 1835, 90.0 thousand; in 1840, 130.0 thousand; in 1845, 350.0 thousand; in 1850, 1063.5 thousand. The average for 1851–1856 was 1405.2 thousand poods (P. A. Khromov, *Ekonomicheskoe razvitie Rossii v XIX–XX vekakh, 1800–1917* [Moscow, 1950], pp. 437–439, citing M. A. Tolpygin, *Sakharnaia promyshlennost' ot osnovaniia ee do nastoiashchego vremeni* [Kiev, 1894], pp. 11–13).

Russian gentryman." [4] When a branch of the State Commercial Bank was opened in Kiev, it was allowed to make loans for periods of three to nine months on most agricultural commodities, but not on sugar. Protests by the gentry producers against this limitation were of no avail until 1861.[5]

The unfriendly official attitude toward beet-sugar production had nothing to do with the social or political consequences of industrialization. Of all Russia's significant industries, beet-sugar refining was perhaps the least subject to such problems. The bulky and perishable nature of the sugar beet required that processing be carried out as close as possible to the fields where the plant was grown. The industry was scattered on estates in southwestern Russia and had no effect on the main centers of urban population located farther north. If the gentry could make money from sugar beets, why should there be any difficulty? For the state, of course, the problem was financial. Every pood of beet sugar sold meant one less pood of imported cane sugar that paid duty. In 1829, Kankrin still maintained that the sugar-beet industry would never succeed in Russia, but he predicted that if it did, an excise might someday be necessary to replace the lost tariff revenue.[6]

Despite the growth of domestic beet-sugar production, imports of cane sugar continued to rise steadily until 1840 in response to growing demand. Imports then leveled off and declined moderately in the late forties, but beet-sugar output continued to grow rapidly.[7] The excise tax on domestic production that Kankrin had envisioned in 1829 became a matter for serious discussion in the mid-forties. In 1844, twenty-two St. Petersburg refiners, who used imported cane sugar, com-

[4] Voblyi, *Opyt*, p. 390.

[5] *Ibid.*, pp. 279–281.

[6] TsGIAL, f. 560, op. 38, d. 116, "Vsepoddanneishie zapiski Ministra finansov," p. 59.

[7] Voblyi, *Opyt*, pp. 349–350; L. Tengoborskii, *Commentaries on the Productive Forces of Russia*, II (London, 1856), 227. Tengoborskii's name is given on the title page as M. L. De Tegoborski.

plained of the increasing competition from Ukrainian beet sugar. Their petition received a sympathetic reception from Minister of Finance Vronchenko because the St. Petersburg refiners used sugar that paid duty. In May 1845, the ministry proposed an excise tax on beet sugar. The Ministry of State Domains and the Department of the Economy of the State Council opposed the excise. The beet-sugar industry was called "a happy union of industry and agriculture," but Nicholas supported the interests of the state treasury and approved Vronchenko's plan. A moderate excise was enacted in February 1848, and a few months later a slight reduction was made in the duty on the lower grades of imported sugar.[8]

The state's action was so moderate that there was almost no measurable effect. Sugar-beet production continued to rise and cane-sugar imports went on falling. Discussion of more drastic measures continued throughout the fifties. The northern refiners continued to complain, and the Ministry of Finance proposed, in February 1854, to cut the duty on imported raw sugar in order to increase revenue. No action, however, was taken until after the Crimean War.[9] A Finance Ministry official observed rather sadly that it was impossible to destroy the beet-sugar industry by a radical reduction in import duties because the capital had been invested in good faith.[10]

Kankrin's policy of maintaining high duties on cane sugar to raise revenue had backfired because the domestic industry grew up under the protection of the revenue tariff, despite the old Minister's belief that it could not. The excise on beet sugar was expensive to collect, and it could not make up the full amount lost on cane-sugar duties. As the Finance Ministry itself recognized, the state had come to subsidize, through tariff protection, an industry it had never wanted. Other seg-

[8] Voblyi, *Opyt*, pp. 320–339, 355–357; *PSZ* II, statutes 22024, 22817.

[9] M. N. Sobolev, *Tamozhennaia politika Rossii, vo vtoroi polovine XIX veka* (Tomsk, 1911), pp. 86–93. For a detailed citation see the bibliography.

[10] Voblyi, *Opyt*, pp. 350–351; *PSZ* II, statute 30696.

ments of the state administration, particularly the Ministry of State Domains, looked with greater favor on beet sugar, but their influence had had nothing to do with the original high tariff on cane sugar or with its maintenance in the crucial years down to the mid-forties. The final increase in the tariff in 1841 was solely the responsibility of Kankrin.[11]

The other important industry that grew dramatically in the late years of Nicholas' reign was the spinning of raw cotton into thread. It was as dependent on tariff protection as the beet-sugar industry, but the state's attitude toward it was more complex. The spinning industry used American raw cotton.[12] Cotton was spun in good-sized factories located in St. Petersburg and, particularly, in and around Moscow. It did not provide a market for Russian agricultural products, but instead competed with domestic flax and wool. More than any other industry of the day, it brought large numbers of workers together in one place. It was the industry that embodied all the unpleasant aspects of the industrial revolution in England. If the state came to be seriously concerned about industry from the social or political standpoint, the cause must have been the growth of the cotton-spinning industry above all. The other "industries" of Russia, woolen and linen spinning and weaving, cotton weaving, leather goods, and so forth, were simple operations scattered throughout the countryside. The substantial but stagnant iron industry was located in the distant Urals.

The state, however, did nothing to prevent the growth of cotton spinning. The growth could easily have been stopped by permitting the free import of cheap English thread. Just as in the case of beet sugar, the cotton-spinning industry began to develop under the protection of a duty that had been imposed as a source of revenue. In 1822, the import of all

[11] Lodyzhenskii, *Istoriia*, p. 214.

[12] Small amounts of short-staple cotton were imported from Central Asia, but had no significance for the spinning industry (Grigorii Nebolsin, *Statisticheskoe obozrenie vneshnei torgovli Rossii* [St. Petersburg, 1850], II, 83–84).

types of cloth was either forbidden or subjected to high duties to protect the weaving industry. To raise revenue, cotton thread was subject to a substantial, but not prohibitive, duty.[13] Raw cotton was admitted free of duty. Imports of cotton thread for Russian weavers rose steadily until 1837 and then declined in the forties, and especially in the fifties. Imports of raw cotton rose as Russian-made thread replaced English thread on domestic looms. Until 1841, there was no change in tariff policy. Free import of raw cotton and a substantial duty on thread favored the domestic spinning industry, which made some slow progress, although it was greatly hampered by the difficulty of obtaining English machinery, which could not be legally exported until 1842.

The tariff of 1841 was a revenue measure, part of the scramble to find ways of meeting a crisis caused by successive poor harvests. Kankrin spoke of his "great reluctance" to increase customs duties, but saw no alternative because there were "compelling objections" to increases in other levies.[14] In the same year, he argued against the request submitted by the owners of Moscow spinning mills for increased duties on thread to protect them against falling English prices. In the mid-thirties, the Tsar had expressed concern about the social implications of concentrated factory industry, and he must have had cotton spinning in mind, because it was the most extreme example then known in Russia. Nevertheless, the tariff of 1841 raised the duty on thread 30 per cent. It also imposed a 25-kopek duty on each pood of raw cotton imported. The increased duty on thread did increase the amount of protection afforded domestic spinning, but the duty on raw cotton, formerly duty free, took away part of the gain. The overall intention was clearly to increase revenue. Domestic spinning was still quite small and thread imports were an important source of revenue.

[13] In 1822, 4.00 rubles per pood; 5.00 after 1824 (Lodyzhenskii, *Istoriia,* p. 290).

[14] Quoted in V. N. Storozhev, ed., *Istoriia Moskovskogo kupecheskogo obshchestva; 1863–1913* (Moscow, 1914–1916), II, pt. 1, 481.

Only after the British ban on the export of spinning machinery was lifted in 1842 did the Russian industry grow rapidly, behind the protective wall erected for fiscal reasons. Raw-cotton imports in 1852 were nearly five times the annual average for 1839–1841. Thread imports in 1852 were less than one-fifth of the average for 1842–1844.[15] The state would hardly have acted as it did in 1841 had such a rapid development been foreseen. Cotton spinning was a less serious threat to revenues than the beet-sugar industry because import duties for revenue purposes could be shifted to raw cotton. From every other standpoint, however, it was far less attractive. The industry provided no market for Russian agricultural products, and it produced what were coming to be considered by some to be undesirable concentrations of people.

Cotton spinning and beet sugar were new industries for Russia, the product of the rapidly changing technology of the early nineteenth century that made what was impossible in one decade profitable in the next. Iron, one of Russia's oldest and most firmly established industries, was also affected by changing technology and tariff policy, but in an entirely different way. Russia had been a leading producer and exporter of pig iron in the eighteenth century, but lost this position in the early nineteenth century, as English technique, notably the substitution of coke for charcoal, outstripped that of the Russians. By the mid-nineteenth century, the Russian industry, largely located in the Urals, could survive only if imports were almost entirely prohibited. The maintenance of a domestic iron industry, however inefficient, had obvious military value. For that reason alone, no govern-

[15] Tengoborskii, *Productive Forces,* II, 50. The growth of Russian cotton spinning and, later, mechanized cotton weaving in the period is closely tied to the activity of Ludwig Knoop, who was the link between the English machine builders and Russian entrepreneurs. He not only acted as an agent, but supplied credit, raw materials, and technical advice. For many years he dominated the Russian cotton-textile industry. See Gerhart von Schulze-Gävernitz, *Volkswirtschaftliche Studien aus Russland* (Leipzig, 1899), pp. 91–106.

ment could be expected to allow it to disappear, aside from the fact that the state itself and very influential members of the nobility were its major owners. The state even went beyond mere preservation of the *status quo* and actively attempted to encourage the use of Russian iron in the first railroads by supporting the domestic fabrication of rails and rolling stock, the only important instance of direct and conscious stimulation of factory industry by the government of Nicholas I.

During the early discussions of railroad projects in the late 1830's, Gerstner, the chief promoter, gave lip service to the possibility of using Russian-made rails. At one stage of the negotiations he proposed to build the first 100 versts of his first very ambitious project with Russian-made rails if he were given six instead of four years in which to do it.[16] Later he agreed to pay a 15 per cent premium for Russian rails if they were available.[17] With these exceptions, Gerstner proposed to use foreign equipment imported free of duty. The first official commission objected to the duty-free import of rails on the grounds that they could be made by the Ural industry. Nicholas, however, eventually approved the use of English rails for the short experimental line to Tsarskoe Selo when it became clear that Russian supplies would not be available in time for construction to proceed even if a 10 or 15 per cent premium were paid.[18]

The practical benefits for the Russian iron industry were

[16] M. Krutikov, ed., "Pervye zheleznye dorogi v Rossii" (Report by Tol', Feb. 17, 1835), *Krasnyi arkhiv*, LXXVI (1936), 92; hereafter cited as Krutikov, with a summary title of the document, in English.

[17] V. S. Virginskii, *Vozniknovenie zheleznykh dorog v Rossii do nachala 40–kh godov, XIX* (Moscow, 1949), pp. 145–146.

[18] Krutikov, Report by Tol', Feb. 17, 1835, pp. 94–95; P. P. Mel'nikov, "Svedeniia o russkikh zheleznykh dorogakh," *Krasnyi arkhiv*, XCIX (1940), p. 145; Krutikov, Application of Bobrinskii, Kramer, Gerstner, and Plitt to the President of the State Council, Novosil'tsev, for the right to form the Tsarskoe Selo Railway Company, Feb. 3, 1836, p. 103; Krutikov, Presentation of Kankrin in the Committee of Ministers, April 7, 1836, pp. 104–105; Virginskii, *Vozniknovenie,* p. 164.

nil, but Gerstner's gesture toward domestic production and the attitude of the first official commission make it clear what the prevailing assumption was. Whenever possible, even at higher cost, preference was to be given to domestic producers. In a sense, of course, this was simply the existing policy of protecting the home iron industry; permitting the free import of rails and rolling stock was an exception, but the future implications of a "buy Russian" policy were of major importance. If the domestic iron industry was to meet the vast new demands of railroad building, it would have to expand very rapidly. To continue the old policy of total protection and actually build railroads would require a drastic expansion of Russian industry with all the accompanying implications for society in general. The issue again became current when the decision to build the St. Petersburg–Moscow line was made in December 1841.

The project to connect the two capitals would demand huge quantities of rails, plus many locomotives and cars. The detailed report submitted to Nicholas in September of 1841, which strongly favored railroad construction, estimated the cost of Russian rails at one and a half times the cost of imported British rails, to give "Russian producers a chance." The authors doubted that Russia could supply the needed quantity and pointed out that the railroad would use an amount equal to one half the annual output of the Russian iron industry.[19] Apart from allowing for a 50 per cent premium on rails, the commission did not express any strong opinion on whether or not Russia should make a serious attempt to make its own equipment. Nicholas was strongly advised to do so by the engineer P. P. Mel'nikov, who argued that it was necessary to build locomotives and cars and even rails in order to create a force of trained workmen and avoid total dependence on foreign supplies. The Tsar's reply to

[19] Krutikov, Report to Nicholas I of the commission on the construction of a railroad between St. Petersburg and Moscow, Sept. 15, 1841, p. 129.

Mel'nikov was noncommittal, but in the main his advice was followed.[20]

With official encouragement, a group of prominent nobles, including Count Stroganov and Prince Beloselskii-Beloozerskii, organized a company to make rails at a state-owned iron foundry near St. Petersburg. Although the company received the order for all the required rails, it proved totally unable to produce the necessary quantity. In the end, it supplied only 50,000 poods of the total of 4,836,000 poods needed. The rest were imported from England.[21] In the building of rolling stock, the "buy Russian" policy was more successful. In 1844, the state-owned Aleksandrovsk factory in St. Petersburg was leased to the American entrepreneurs, Harrison and Winans. They successfully produced the required equipment, although it was really an assembly operation, putting together parts imported duty free, rather than full-fledged manufacturing.[22] Nevertheless, it was a major step in the development of modern heavy industry in Russia. It was the direct result of state encouragement, through guaranteed sales to the state at prices higher than those prevailing abroad and duty-free import of materials.

The iron industry was a special case, but so were the others already discussed. The traditional Russian industries were less affected by technological change and for the moment

[20] Virginskii, *Vozniknovenie,* pp. 225–226.

[21] *Ibid.,* pp. 228–230; N. A. Kislinskii, *Nasha zheleznodorozhnaia politika po dokumentam arkhiva Komiteta ministrov* (St. Petersburg, 1902), IV, 213.

[22] A. A. Brandt, *Ocherk istorii parovoi mashiny i primeneniia parovykh dvigatelei v Rossii* (St. Petersburg, 1892), II, 16–19; Kislinskii, *Nasha zheleznodorozhnaia politika,* IV, 214. The Aleksandrovsk factory that Harrison and Winans leased had been founded in 1789 and had been moved in 1801 and in 1824. It first was a foundry and later built various individual machines and even stationary steam engines for the state. It was important as an experimental workshop, but not as a producing operation (M. P. Viatkin, ed., *Ocherki istorii Leningrada,* I [Moscow and Leningrad, 1955], 469–471).

continued to exist as before, heavily protected by the tariff. The state gave no indication of formulating a general policy toward industry. It was surprised, and rather embarrassed, by two industries that grew up unnoticed, and it only tried to help a traditional operation when the state itself embarked on a venture that called for large quantities of the item it produced.

EDUCATION, URBAN GROWTH, AND THE FACTORY WORKER

In the twenties, the state expressed its concern for the development of the economy, as opposed to immediate fiscal problems, through its interest in technical education and urban growth. The possible disadvantages of a large city population were ignored entirely. In the thirties, the interest in technical education declined, and there were some signs that the problems associated with industrial growth had begun to be recognized, although there was no agreement as to what they were. In the forties and fifties, technical education was still ignored, despite the growing importance of technology throughout Europe, while the development of factories in Russia and political upheavals in western and central Europe produced some new legislation dealing with industry.

In this last decade and a half of Nicholas' reign, the Practical Technological Institute graduated about thirty students per year, an increase of ten or so over the average for the late thirties. At a more advanced level, at the Institute of Transport Engineers and at the Institute of Mining Engineers the number of graduates remained constant or even declined. Both of these institutions, the major centers of higher technical education in Russia, became increasingly military in orientation. The students were more and more frequently drawn from the gentry, the group least likely to be interested in industrial work. In the late twenties, about half the students at the Institute of Transport Engineers were nongentry; by 1843, they were greatly outnumbered by gentry; and the new statute of 1844 restricted entrance entirely to children of hereditary nobles. The Institute of Mining Engineers was less aristocratic, but in 1838 entrance was restricted to children of mining engineers and certain other state officials. In 1848, the number of state supported students was reduced and children of all gentrymen made eligible for entrance.[23]

Virtually the only positive step taken in advanced technical education in the last fifteen years of Nicholas' reign was the conversion of the Construction School of the Ministry of the Interior into the Institute of Civil Engineers in 1842.[24] At the secondary level, there were changes in the *gymnasium* curriculum in March 1849, introducing more practical courses in Russian, mathematics, and law for students planning to enter state service on graduation rather than continuing at a university.[25] Such changes in the training of lower-level bureaucrats, however, had little connection with technical education as an aid in economic development.

The St. Petersburg–Moscow railroad maintained thirty boarding students at the Practical Technological Institute from 1841 to 1847, but there was no other formal effort to train workers for the new railroad. Harrison and Winans, however, employed 1,500 workers to build rolling stock, and many of them must have learned the basic elements of factory

---

[23] [A. G. Nebolsin, ed.], *Istoriko-statisticheskii ocherk obshchago i spetsial'nago obrazovaniia v Rossii* (St. Petersburg, 1883), pp. 135–137; Russia, Institut inzhenerov putei soobshcheniia, *Spisok lits okonchivshikh kurs nauk v Institute inzhenerov putei soobshcheniia Imperatora Aleksandra I, s 1811 po 1882 g.* (St. Petersburg, 1883), pp. 34–36; Sergei M. Zhitkov, *Institut inzhenerov putei soobshcheniia, Imperatora Aleksandra I* (St. Petersburg, 1899), p. 70; Russia, Gornyi Institut, *Nauchnoistoricheskii sbornik* (St. Petersburg, 1873), pp. 106–122; Russia, Tekhnologicheskii Institut imeni Leningradskogo Soveta rabochikh, krest'ianskikh, i krasnoarmeiskikh deputatov, *Sto let (1828–1928)* (Leningrad, 1928), I, 46–57.

[24] Nebolsin, *Istoriko-statisticheskii ocherk*, p. 229.

[25] Russia, Ministerstvo narodnogo prosveshcheniia, *Istoricheskii obzor deiatel'nosti Ministerstva, 1802–1902* (St. Petersburg, 1902), pp. 277–278.

work and the use of simple machinery. It would not be un-
reasonable to date the origin of the famous St. Petersburg
class of skilled workers from Nicholas' decision to let two
American businessmen try their hand at making railroad engines and cars in Russia.

Technical education required positive support that was
not forthcoming. The broader problem of urban growth and
particularly the concentration of factories in the two capitals,
although not a pressing question, did get some attention because of developments beyond the control of the state. Despite
the Tsar's uneasiness in the mid-thirties about the concentration of workers at certain factories, nothing was done to limit
further factory growth. Kankrin was not worried about the
social consequences of industrial growth in Russia, and the
Tsar's other major adviser on economic affairs, Kiselev, favored the increase of factories as a way of helping agriculture:
"The success of agriculture in Russia, as a state primarily
agricultural, depends chiefly on the strengthening of foreign
trade and the increase of internal demand, that is, the increase of towns and factories." [26] In practice, Kiselev had no
authority over trade or industry, and he was fully occupied
with the immense tasks of his own Ministry of State Domains.

In the early forties, a few minor laws that involved industry
were enacted. One provided for the assignment of skilled
mechanics to eight provinces to provide technical help to
local manufacturers. The total annual appropriation was
12,000 rubles, and it was a straightforward attempt to spread
technical knowledge, the only new endeavor of that kind
in twenty years.[27] The two largest manufacturing centers, St.
Petersburg and Moscow, were not on the list of provinces,
and in that respect the law continued the policy of favoring
industrial development in the provinces which first appeared
in 1836 in connection with the preferential granting of exemptions from local taxes.[28]

[26] A. P. Zablotskii-Desiatovskii, *Graf P. D. Kiselev i ego vremia* (St.
Petersburg, 1882), II, 100, 200.
[27] *PSZ* II, statute 17379.
[28] See Chapter III, pp. 101–102.

The local tax exemptions were virtually abolished in 1845 in a measure that did not differentiate between central or provincial industry.[29] In August of the same year, a statute was issued that forbade night work in factories by children under twelve.[30] It was an overall restriction on all industry, but hardly one that was likely to be very limiting, even if it had been enforced. In fact, it contained no provisions to ensure compliance, was not included in the working law code (*svod zakonov*), and was soon forgotten.[31]

None of these measures suggest that the state was particularly concerned with either encouraging or limiting industrial growth. The European revolutions in 1848 seemed to change the situation, at least to some extent. One of the officials most directly concerned with the problem of maintaining public order, A. A. Zakrevskii, the military governor of Moscow, wrote to the Tsar:

For the preservation of calm and prosperity, which at the present time only Russia enjoys, the government must not permit the gathering of homeless and dissolute people, who will easily join every movement, destroying social or private peace.[32]

Nicholas took Zakrevskii's views seriously and the report was referred to the Committee of Ministers. Minister of Finance Vronchenko opposed the idea of restrictions on industry and maintained Kankrin's old position that, because of their close ties to their home villages, Russian workers differed from those of western Europe and were not dangerous.[33]

---

29 *PSZ* II, statutes 8575, 18868.

30 *Ibid.*, statute 19262. See above, Chapter III, pp. 99–101.

31 M. Tugan-Baranovskii, *Russkaia fabrika v proshlom i nastoiashchem* (3rd ed.; St. Petersburg, 1907), I, 175–176.

32 Quoted in *ibid.*, p. 179. See also the discussion in Sidney Monas, *The Third Section: Police and Society in Russia under Nicholas I* (Cambridge, Mass., 1961), pp. 277–279.

33 Tugan-Baranovskii, *Russkaia fabrika* p. 179. This same viewpoint had recently been expressed publicly by Baron Alexander von Meyendorff, an important official of the Ministry of Finance, first in the *Moskvitianin* and then in a German publication subsidized by the Russian treasury ("Über die Manufaktur-Betreibsamkeit Russlands in

Nevertheless, after prolonged discussion, a law was enacted in the summer of 1849 "on the limitation of the number of factories newly established in Moscow city district." According to the text, it was designed to deal with the increasing danger of fire, the pollution of streams, and the rising cost of food and fuel caused by large numbers of factory workers. It forbade the opening of new cotton- or woolen-spinning mills, iron foundries, and certain other industries in Moscow. Special permission from the military governor was required for other types of industrial activity, including weaving and dyeing.[34] In a sense it was merely an extension of the industrial zoning legislation that dated back to 1833.[35] It was, however, far more severe and was not limited to conventional restriction of nuisance industries. Some industries, notably cotton spinning, were entirely prohibited in Moscow. More was involved than moving the slaughterhouses to the edge of town. Zakrevskii was worried about the political danger involved in further concentration of workers in the city, and the law was intended to stop it or at least slow it down.

It would be mistaken to conclude that the revolutions of 1848 brought about a major change in the attitude of the Russian government toward industry on the basis of the law of 1849. The significance of the incident is not so much in the restrictive character of the law but in the fact that it remained the only regulation of that kind. As in the case of the regulation on child labor, the state seemed to be acting in a perfunctory way rather than from any feeling of urgency. Zakrevskii's further proposals for comprehensive legislation to control the daily life of the workers, their recruitment, and their relationship to employers were considered in a leisurely fashion for several years. They finally reached the State Council in 1854, but the outbreak of the Crimean War

---

Bezug auf die allgemeine Productivität und auf das häusliche Leben der neideren Volksklassen," *Archiv für Wissenschaftliche Kunde von Russland,* IV [1846], 565–566).

[34] *PSZ* II, statute 23358.

[35] See Chapter II, pp. 97–98.

caused them to be forgotten.[36] The diligent efforts of recent students have added nothing substantial to this limited evidence, first presented by Tugan-Baranovskii, of a strongly anti-industrial official attitude caused by fear of the proletariat.[37]

On the contrary, during the months when Zakrevskii's urgent appeal was being considered, a law was enacted on January 24, 1849, that was designed to make it easier for state peasants to move to the towns. Neither Moscow nor St. Petersburg were excluded. The sponsor of the measure was Kiselev, who saw migration from the land as one way of improving the condition of those who remained in the country. According to the new regulation, the village communal organizations could no longer prevent a peasant from leaving his village if his tax obligations had been met, nor could the town organization of the burghers or of the merchants refuse to admit state peasants if they paid the required entrance fee.[38] Many important barriers to the free movement of labor remained, but it is most significant that the state was willing to permit any relaxation at this particular time. Despite the revolutions of 1848, Zakrevskii's report, and the statute of 1849 limiting factory construction in Moscow, there was no general state policy designed to discourage urban growth or the development of industry, any more than there was a general program intended to encourage them.

THE TARIFF AND GENERAL STATE POLICY

The tariff of 1850 was the only legislation of the forties and fifties that required discussion and decisions on the level of

[36] Tugan-Baranovskii, *Russkaia fabrika*, pp. 179–184.

[37] See M. K. Rozhkova, "Ekonomicheskaia politika pravitel'stva," *Ocherki ekonomicheskoi istorii Rossii pervoi poloviny XIX veka: Sbornik statei,* ed. Rozhkova (Moscow, 1959), pp. 377–379; N. S. Kiniapina, "Promyshlennaia politika russkogo samoderzhaviia v gody krizisa feodal'noi sistemy," *Voprosy istorii,* no. 6 (1965), pp. 61–75.

[38] *PSZ* statute II, 22955; M. N. Druzhinin, *Gosudarstvenye krest'iane i reforma P. D. Kiseleva,* II (Moscow and Leningrad, 1958), 17.

general industrial policy. There had been no serious consideration of Russian tariff policy since the law of 1822, which had restored the prohibitive system that had been briefly relaxed in the post-Napoleonic period. Under Kankrin, high tariffs and import prohibitions were maintained to protect the existing manufacturing activities, not to stimulate further rapid development. The growth of beet-sugar making and cotton spinning were unexpected results of his general policy of maintaining the *status quo* whenever possible while maximizing revenue. He had tinkered with the tariff system on numerous occasions, but always with the limited goal of increasing revenues and reducing the incentives for smuggling. Import prohibitions were replaced by high duties on various goods that were not manufactured in Russia in any case. As a protective instrument, the tariff of the 1840's was no weaker than that of 1822, but produced more revenue.

In sharp contrast to the tariff revisions between 1822 and 1841, which were almost entirely determined by Kankrin, the tariff of 1850 was the product of prolonged and extensive debate within the government. The discussion began in 1844, when the memorandum of a prominent merchant named Popov attracted the attention of Count Orlov, president of the State Council.[39] The state received substantial numbers of such memoranda and in the normal course of affairs they were filed away along with the critical comments of the official to whom they were referred. The many suggestions of Admiral Mordvinov and several of the early projects for railroad building are typical and are of interest only for what they reveal of official attitudes on various questions. Popov's proposals fared somewhat better because they expressed a point of view that was shared by influential members of the government, and ultimately to some degree by Nicholas himself. Popov was primarily concerned with international trade and

[39] The exact circumstances of the submission of the Popov memorandum are not clear from the available sources. Presumably the original was addressed to the Tsar. Orlov may have been given a copy because he was known to be interested in the subject.

particularly with Russian exports, not with the protection of domestic industry or with state revenue. To this end he advocated the elimination of export duties, improved internal transport, storage, and shipping facilities, the reduction of duties on Asiatic goods imported only for re-export to Europe, and finally a complete review of import duties and prohibitions to eliminate those not essential to the protection of domestic agriculture and industry.[40]

There followed nearly six years of report writing and discussion by several high-level committees. There appear to have been two conflicting points of view. Vronchenko, the new minister of finance, aided by his subordinate, Baron Meyendorff, was primarily concerned with maintaining the *status quo* with respect to both revenue and protection. On the other side were Count Orlov and the economist Tengoborskii, who emphasized the importance of international trade, the full integration of Poland into the Russian empire, and the whole problem of what specific kinds of industry Russia really ought to try to encourage. At one point Vronchenko cited passages from List's *Das nationale System der politischen Oekonomie* to support his arguments for leaving the existing system virtually unchanged. Orlov quoted English free traders in reply, but in general the argument was not one between incompatible theoretical positions, but over the practical implications of specific changes that were proposed. All concerned accepted the idea that Russian industry needed substantial protection, and it was never suggested that existing Russian industry should be eliminated, either at once or gradually.

Count Orlov and the Tsar himself were undoubtedly influenced by diplomatic pressure from Great Britain in the middle and late forties for a relaxation of Russia's import prohibitions. Following the abolition of British restrictions on grain imports in 1846, Russia, as a major beneficiary, was under a moral obligation to reciprocate to some extent.

[40] Sobolev, *Tamozhennaia politika*, pp. 8–9; Lodyzhenskii, *Istoriia*, pp. 229–230.

Nicholas was anxious to maintain good relations with England. A limited set of reductions in the import duties (the most important on chinaware), made in 1846, was the direct result of diplomatic action.[41] There is no reason to doubt that the diplomatic aspect of the tariff question remained essentially unchanged between 1846 and 1850, although no detailed evidence is available.[42]

A question of internal politics was also involved in the tariff of 1850. Nicholas was determined to abolish the separate customs administration of Poland in order to further the total integration of Poland into the Russian empire. As long as there were differing tariffs there had to be border control and inspection that emphasized the separateness of Poland and, in the eyes of the Tsar at least, tended to encourage the nationalistic illusions of the Poles. Nationalism was a matter that easily aroused anxiety after the outbursts across Europe in 1848. The Tsar was so concerned that he ordered the new tariff to be ready by the end of 1850, despite complications involving existing contracts with Austria for the import of salt.[43] The desire for a common tariff with Poland created some pressure for lowering Russian rates and eliminating prohibitions, because the Polish tariff was far more liberal than the Russian. If excessive dislocation was to be avoided there had to be some compromise.

That some degree of relaxation was accepted from the start was evident when the minister of finance (Vronchenko) and the minister of foreign affairs (Nesselrode) agreed to give L. V. Tengoborskii the task of preparing proposals for a revised tariff. Tengoborskii was a Pole who had been associated

[41] Lodyzhenskii, *Istoriia*, pp. 235–238; Vernon John Puryear, *England, Russia, and the Straits Question, 1844–1856* (Berkeley, 1931), pp. 97–102.

[42] S. B. Okun', "K istorii tamozhennogo tarifa 1850 g.," in Leningradskii universitet, *Voprosy genezisa kapitalizma v Rossii, sbornik statei* (Leningrad, 1960), pp. 175–176. I have not had access to archival material on this question and published material provides little detail.

[43] Sobolev, *Tamozhennaia politika,* p. 21; Lodyzhenskii, *Istoriia,* pp. 245–246.

with Drutskii-Liubetskii, the energetic and imaginative Polish minister of finance in the 1820's. Later in his career, Tengoborskii represented Russia in commercial dealings with Austria. With the exception of Kankrin, he was the only official with an active role in shaping economic policy under Nicholas who was in any sense a scholar or a theoretician as well as a state servant.[44] Kankrin, of course, wrote two books on economic policy but they were not really contributions to economic thought, or like Tengoborskii's, valuable reference works. Tengoborskii never occupied a ministerial position and he was frequently overruled on specific items, but his ideas did provide the general framework for the tariff revisions of 1850 and 1857 as well.

Tengoborskii was, by Russian standards at least, a free trader. He thought every country, even England, was dependent on agriculture for the bulk of its wealth. This was particularly true of Russia, even though its agriculture could never be as productive as that of western Europe because of the natural handicaps of severe climate and poor soil.[45] Manufacturing, however, had its place in his view:

A great country like Russia, containing so many resources within herself, could not condemn herself to remain stationary in the development of her industry, and to refuse to profit by the new

[44] Tengoborskii's major work, *Études sur les forces productives de Russie,* was published in Paris in 1852–1855 and soon after in English and Russian editions. His general views, however, were already well known both from confidential memoranda and from published works dealing with economic affairs, such as *Des finances et du credit publique en Aufriche* (Paris, 1843; German ed., Vienna, 1845); *Essai sur les conséquences éventuelles de la décoverete des gites aufères en Californie et en Australie* (Paris, 1853; German ed., Weimar, 1853). In all these works his name is spelled Tegoborski.

[45] Tengoborskii, *Productive Forces,* I (1855), 216–219. The views of one of Tengoborskii's associates, Iu. A. Gagemeister, are also of some interest. He was a member of the commission that drafted the 1850 law, but did not play a leading role. He is discussed in Sobolev, *Tamozhennaia politika,* pp. 14–17; see also Gagemeister's article, "Vzgliad na promyshlennost' i torgovliu Rossii," *Russkii vestnik,* VII (1857), 5–52.

inventions, discoveries, and improvements with which the human mind had enriched itself in every branch of manufacture: but it does not follow that we were bound to enter the lists without taking into consideration the ensemble of our social economy, and to run the risk of all the inconveniences which over-excitement of industrial interests has produced in other countries. On the contrary our duty rather is to profit by the experience of others, keeping in view our own special situation and the nature of our resources. . . . In according protection to our manufacturing industry, we must not push it to the extreme of endeavoring to fabricate every thing for ourselves, and to reject every thing manufactured by others:—this is an object which no people can aim at without injury to itself. By concentrating our energy and resources upon the branches of industry most appropriate to the wants of the country, and the means at its disposal, we obtain surer and more durable results than we could obtain by dispersing them from a desire to do too much at a time.[46]

Tengoborskii clearly believed in the division of labor among nations to produce some degree of international specialization, a basic principle of classic free-trade doctrine. In two long volumes, he hardly mentions the problem of maintaining adequate manufacturing capacity for military purposes or the general connection of economic growth and national power, so important to List and his supporters.[47] The crucial question was, of course, what industries were "best suited" to Russia? Tengoborskii looked with favor on peasant craft work, which could usefully fill the long months of winter. It had, he said,

attained a considerable development without the aid of custom-houses or other forced and artificial means [nor did it] . . . carry in its train the present grave inconveniences, or the future fatal

[46] Tengoborskii, *Productive Forces*, I, 448.

[47] Gagemeister, whose views were generally similar to Tengoborskii's, explicitly rejected the security argument for protection both in general, since war was too infrequent to warrant great sacrifices, and specifically with respect to iron, which, he believed, could easily be stockpiled in sufficient quantity in peacetime ("Vzgliad na promyshlennost'," pp. 13, 35).

consequences of the concentration of the working classes in over-grown cities— . . . it is this village industry, we say, which above all others, ought to be most carefully preserved and most specially protected.[48]

That Tengoborskii had this view is not surprising. It was not an uncommon attitude in Russia at the time and, in various forms, continued to be popular among Russian intellectuals of widely different political convictions.[49] There was much that could be said for the position, particularly at this early date. Peasants certainly did need an opportunity for productive work in the winter months. Craft industries were already widespread and provided an important source of income for both peasants and their owners. Nor was it only the sentimental and the romantic who could find good reason to prefer the peasant working in his hut to life in the cotton-spinning mills of the early nineteenth century.

The important question is to what extent the pro-handicraft, moderately anti-industrial attitude of Tengoborskii actually affected the tariff policy that he helped to formulate. The extensive import prohibitions and the high duties of 1822 had certainly not been instituted to favor peasant crafts over large manufacturing establishments. The issue simply had not arisen at that time. The law of 1822 was in the long-standing mercantilist tradition of protecting indiscriminately virtually all domestic manufacturing. The subsequent changes made by Kankrin also had no relation whatever to the craft-versus-industry problem, and in fact his efforts to maximize revenue had made possible the growth of two definitely non-craft industries, beet sugar and cotton spinning. The issue was a new one, because concentrations of factory workers had only recently appeared on the Russian scene. The tariff re-

[48] Tengoborskii, *Productive Forces,* p. 446.
[49] Tugan-Baranovskii, *Russkaia fabrika,* ch. 8, esp. pp. 297–303; Alexander Gerschenkron, "The Problem of Economic Development in Russian Intellectual History of the Nineteenth Century," *Continuity and Change in Russian and Soviet Thought,* ed. Ernest J. Simmons (Cambridge, Mass., 1955), pp. 11–39.

vision of 1850 was the first occasion on which the problem
arose in connection with an important piece of economic
legislation.

The tariff of 1850, as it was finally promulgated, was a
lengthy document covering hundreds of items. The discussion of the kind of industry that Russia should encourage,
however, involved only a few key commodities: woolen and
cotton cloth, cotton thread, and iron. The rest of the new
tariff schedule reflected nothing more than an energetic and
thoroughgoing version of the kind of revision that Kankrin
had made several times, to increase revenue by increasing
legal imports. Regulations were simplified, most of the remaining prohibitions were removed, and duties were lowered
on a large number of manufactured luxuries and colonial
products that were not produced in Russia.[50]

In the textile industry there was a clear distinction between
the still largely unmechanized and decentralized weaving
operation and the highly concentrated mechanical spinning
industry that had experienced such rapid growth in the previous decade. In the case of the iron industry, the supposed
advantages of decentralized production in peasant villages
were not at issue, for the Russian iron industry was a relatively large-scale operation owned by a few great magnates
and the state itself. It had, however, made little technological
progress since the eighteenth century and was very vulnerable
to foreign competition.

Tengoborskii did not approve of the cotton-spinning industry, but he conceded the necessity of tolerating it: "We
would rather look upon a single spinster plying her industry
beneath the humble roof of her father's cottage than upon a

---

[50] The items remaining on the forbidden list were: dried mushrooms,
refined sugar, alcoholic beverages and honey in barrels, tea (via Europe), formed iron, cleaned saltpetre, gunpowder, beds and pillows
"not brought by passengers," and beaver pelts. The list reflects the
conglomeration of major and minor interests, plus perhaps pure ca-
price, that always is present in a law as complex as a tariff (Lodyzhenskii, *Istoriia*, p. 253).

thousand villagers imprisoned within four walls of a spin-
ning-mill." But, he continued, cotton goods had become so
necessary that Russia had only the choice of procuring them
abroad and becoming a "tributary to the industry of others"
or of manufacturing them at home.[51] Cotton weaving was
much more desirable than spinning because it was "best
adapted to the situation of our agricultural classes." They
could weave without "quitting their own firesides." Neither
cotton spinning nor weaving, he said, could hope to successfully withstand foreign competition in the foreseeable future.[52]

It was relatively easy to decide what line to take on the
protection of the Russian weaving industry. All were agreed
that it was a desirable form of activity. Tengoborskii proposed that the coarser grades of cloth (cotton and woolen),
which were the main product of Russian weavers, should
continue to receive substantial protection. For the finer
grades, not produced in Russia, he proposed much lower
duties to discourage smuggling and increase revenue-producing legal imports. The minister of finance, Vronchenko, accepted this approach, although he took a more timid position
about the extent of the reductions that would be possible.
The rates that Tengoborskii proposed were eventually approved by the State Council and the Tsar.

The issue of protection for the cotton-spinning industry
was more difficult to resolve. The State Council agreed with
Tengoborskii that weaving was preferable to spinning because it employed more people and kept them in their homes
instead of concentrating them in unhealthy factories.[53] The
issue was complicated by the problem of maintaining state
revenue. The Ministry of Finance insisted that instead of
cutting the tariff on thread, the duty on raw cotton should

[51] Tengoborskii, *Productive Forces,* II, 49.

[52] *Ibid.,* pp. 65, 81.

[53] Okun', "K istorii," p. 178; Sobolev, *Tamozhennaia politika,* p. 44.
Okun' quotes a paragraph from the archives of the State Council that
is apparently the same as that summarized by Sobolev.

be raised. Vronchenko feared that thread imports would continue to fall despite a reduced duty and receipts would suffer badly. The State Council, however, supported Tengoborskii, cut the thread duty as he requested, and left the levy on raw cotton unchanged. It was, in theory, a victory for the weaving industry and ultimately for the consumers, because the maximum cost of thread was lowered (English price plus transport and duty). In fact, the reduction proved to be too small to arrest the decline in thread imports and the expansion of the domestic spinning industry.[54] The motive for the change, however, was clear. It was felt that the socially undesirable spinning industry had been growing too fast. It was therefore to be discouraged, while the socially beneficial weaving industry was to be encouraged. These considerations overrode the traditionally dominant issue of state revenues. There was no thought of destroying, or even reducing, the size of the spinning operations; that would have been more upsetting than further growth. Nevertheless, this was the first, and the only, occasion during the reign of Nicholas when a really significant decision on industrial policy can be attributed to concern over the impact of industry on the social structure.[55]

In the discussion of the iron industry, the social-political issue never arose despite the long history of labor disputes in the Ural factories. The blast furnaces were far from the main centers of Russian life, and the state was accustomed to the sporadic outbreaks that had occurred there since the industry developed on a major scale early in the eighteenth century. Even though it was probably as unhealthy to work at a Ural blast furnace as in a Moscow spinning mill, there was no outcry against this traditional activity. Iron was accepted as a "good industry," and, as already noted, when railroad construction began, a serious effort was made to develop domestic fabricating capacity to meet the new demand for iron products. The debate was over the question of whether or not it

---

[54] See the table in Lodyzhenskii, *Istoriia*, p. 291.

[55] The only possible exception to this statement is Zakrevskii's antifactory law of 1849 (see above, pp. 235–237).

was possible to remove the total prohibition of iron imports without too great a risk of injuring the domestic industry. Tengoborskii argued strongly that it was possible because the cost of overland transport would protect the inland market for the Ural industry, while the areas nearer to ports would benefit greatly from lower prices. Peasants, he said, were forced to use wooden nails, spades, ploughs, and unbound cartwheels for lack of iron at a reasonable price. Iron fabrication of all kinds was likewise greatly handicapped by the high price of the basic raw material.[56]

At first Vronchenko was inclined to agree that the import of iron with a substantial duty would stimulate Russian machine and tool making without injuring the primary iron industry and the duties collected would increase state revenues. But he soon backed down and proposed further study after reading the statements of several leading iron producers, the director of the state-owned blast furnaces, and merchants from the Nizhni-Novgorod fair. All these men emphasized the serious damage that they felt was sure to result from foreign competition. The State Council agreed with them, and the import of iron remained totally forbidden.[57]

The successful maintenance of the prohibition on iron imports in 1850 was probably the result of the influence of the Ural iron producers and the officials within the state involved in iron production. The merits of Tengoborskii's argument were recognized and his proposal was actually put into effect in the tariff of 1857. The basic decision in this case was not between "good" and "bad" industries like weaving and spinning, but between excessive protection for one (crude iron) at the expense of others (iron fabrication) and at the expense of state revenue.

[56] Tengoborskii, *Productive Forces,* II, 121–122, 131–132.

[57] Actually it was import by sea that remained prohibited. Import by land had been possible subject to a high duty. This duty was substantially reduced, but was still high enough to protect the Russian market. The land tariff did permit Poland to import iron via Germany, since transport costs for Ural iron to Poland were prohibitive. A similar dif-

The controversial question of the duties on sugar and the unforeseen progress of the domestic beet-sugar industry were not raised in connection with the tariff of 1850 because the limited duty reductions and excise tax on beet sugar established in 1848 had not been evaluated.[58] Tengoborskii's position was that domestic beet-sugar production had far more protection than it needed and the state should not continue to sacrifice substantial revenues to protect it. Not until after the Crimean War, however, were reductions in sugar duties actually put into effect. Great care was taken not to risk real injury to either beet-sugar producers or the northern refiners of imported cane.[59]

The other provisions of the tariff of 1850 did not raise the issue of industrial development. The tariff remained primarily a way of levying excise taxes. With the important exception of sugar, most of the revenue came from items that were not, and could not be, produced in Russia. When Russia did produce the item, the protective policy remained unchanged except in the case of cotton spinning, where there was a moderate reaction against an industry that had grown very fast. For weaving, solid protection was continued. Spokesmen for the entrenched and backward domestic iron industry were just able to withstand demands that some foreign competition be permitted. The demand for import of foreign iron was not based on hostility to the domestic industry, but on the hope that lower costs for iron would benefit other industries and agriculture. In the case of sugar, the fiscal interests of the state were so compelling (sugar generated about one-quarter of total tariff revenue in 1851) that eventually this concern overcame the strong position of an agriculturally based industry in the hands of the gentry. It did not happen, however, until 1857, long after the industry was firmly established.

---

ferential of sea and land duties was established for certain textiles to make the abolition of the Russo-Polish tariff wall less difficult.

[58] See above, pp. 224–225.

[59] Sobolev, *Tamozhennaia politika*, pp. 86–93; Tengoborskii, *Productive Forces*, I, 465–468.

The discussion of the tariff of 1850 was the first occasion for a general reappraisal of the regime's attitude toward industry since Kankrin decided in the mid-twenties to stop virtually all direct financial assistance to industry and in general to maintain the *status quo* as best he could.[60] Tengoborskii was a man of imagination and knowledge and was in a position to make his influence felt, but as head of the Tariff Commission he did not have the extensive power and full responsibility that Kankrin had had as minister of finance. The results of the tariff revision show that the state had no uniform attitude toward industry as a whole; each one presented unique problems of greater importance than any common factor that united them as industries. Most important of all is the fact that none of them, not even all of them put together, were of crucial concern; Russia already had the minimum of industry it seemed to need for its armed forces. Never in the discussions of the tariff of 1850 nor during the entire reign of Nicholas was concern expressed about the need to meet the strategic requirements that had plagued Russia in the eighteenth and even the early nineteenth centuries.[61] Industry produced little revenue for the state, but, except in the case of beet sugar, neither did it cost the state much. The social and political problems connected with industry were not regarded as serious or urgent.

[60] This is, of course, an oversimplification. The exact nature of Kankrin's attitude and the extent to which it changed is discussed in Chapters I and II.

[61] Some of the factories established with state support and provided with serf labor during earlier reigns were no longer needed. On the problems presented by these "possessional factories" and particularly the labor force attached to them, see Tugan-Baranovskii, *Russkaia fabrika,* ch. 3. The problem was largely social and legal, not economic. But the abandonment of the factories does demonstrate that the state felt confident of the nation's ability to meet military needs without special state intervention.

Conclusions

Despite the well-established precedents in Russia for active government involvement in the economy, the reign of Nicholas was marked by unusual passivity, both toward the state's needs for individual products—iron, woolen cloth, and the like—and toward the economic development of the country as a whole. The specific needs were met in a more or less satisfactory way by the industries that had developed at the state's behest in the eighteenth and early nineteenth centuries. Intervention with the broader aim of furthering general economic development was regarded under Nicholas as beyond the means of the nation. The approach was always piecemeal, restricted to one or two aspects of the whole problem.

In the 1820's, there was interest in stimulating the growth of the towns to develop a larger domestic market for grain and thus produce higher prices. Technological education received considerable attention as a logical prerequisite for expanded manufacturing and commerce, but at the same time state credit policy discouraged investment in factories. In the 1830's, the interest in the urban sector of the economy vanished as it became clear that there were problems as well as advantages in urban growth: factories were dirty, sometimes they could not sell their output, and concentrations of workers were a potential, though still rather vaguely discerned, problem. At the same time the price of grain rose so that agrarian pressure for larger urban markets was no longer present.

In the 1830's, positive action was confined to projects directly involving agriculture. The entire sector of gentry-owned serf agriculture was virtually excluded, but the new emphasis is significant because it marked the first time in Russian history that the state began to take a serious interest in the welfare of a large portion of the population. It is a striking feature of Nicholas' reign that these reasonable and well-intentioned efforts to develop the agricultural economy relied almost entirely on positive state action, steps that required substantial expenditure and effective administrative implementation. No use was made of permissive measures designed to stimulate action by the peasants themselves. Poor though it was in physical resources and administrative talent, the state was unable to imagine any way of accomplishing the desired results other than direct state action. The conflict between Kankrin and Kiselev was between a man who believed that the state did not have the resources to effect the desired reforms and one who thought that it did. Neither saw any other alternative. Of the important officials of the day only Speransky seems to have had some sort of Stolypin-like vision of a sturdy peasantry prospering as a result of its own efforts.

The two major developments in economic policy outside the agricultural area, monetary reform and railroad construction, strangely enough were undertaken with no intention of changing the general economic situation. The monetary reform was considered a technical problem and was carried out in a manner that did not affect the total stock of money. It produced a simplified but essentially unchanged monetary system. The potentially momentous decision to begin the construction of railroads was made on the narrowest fiscal grounds and almost nothing was said of its possible impact on the economy. There was no feeling of urgency from the standpoint of military needs, although the potential strategic advantages were pointed out at an early stage in the discussions. Nicholas and his major advisers had no particular prejudice for or against private railroad building. They recognized with commendable realism that major construction would require large amounts of foreign capital, which would be forthcoming only with some sort of state participation, direct or indirect. The state itself finally did build the first major line, but the really important point is the length of time needed to make the decision and the failure to pursue plans for further development.

During Nicholas' thirty-year reign there were indeed a number of measures that can be described as "anti-industrial," such as Kankrin's refusal to make loans secured by factories and the law forbidding the construction of additional factories in Moscow. On the other hand, there were a number of modest efforts made to encourage industrial growth, particularly through the development of technical education. But the main weight of the evidence is that the men who ran the government did not consider the problem of industry to be very important. Kankrin would not make loans on factories because he felt the rural gentry had a better claim to the money, not because he was against industry. Zakrevskii was the only official who was really aroused by the concentration of workers in Moscow. Tariff policy was firmly protective throughout the period, but more from habit and a desire to preserve what was already there than from any interest in development of new industries. In fact, the two industries that were most successful in the period, cotton spinning and sugar-beet growing, grew up under the shelter of sections of the tariff that had originally been designed to produce revenue, not to protect. They were subject to criticism within the government as their spectacular success touched state interests on sensitive points. Both clearly threatened customs revenues, and cotton spinning seemed to some officials to be producing an at least potentially dangerous concentration of uprooted peasants in the cities, but no significant attempt was made to stop their growth.

To look at Nicholas' reign in terms of attitudes toward economic growth is, of course, to view it from a standpoint not shared by the Russian officials of the second quarter of the nineteenth century. There is nothing wrong in doing that. We now find certain phenomena more interesting and significant than they were thought to be a century ago, but it must not be forgotten that the primary concerns of Nicholas' ministers were different than those of present day statesmen. In the realm of economic policy the most striking characteristic of economic administration was the predominance of a short-range, essentially hand-to-mouth view of economic problems that was based on the belief that significant economic progress could only be achieved at such a very slow pace that it was virtually irrelevant to current policy. The most extreme adherent of this position was Kankrin, who was also the most influential of the Tsar's advisers on economic policy and who had primary operational responsibility until 1844. Kankrin, as minister of finance, knew perhaps better than anyone else how weak the economy actually was, if only because it consistently failed to supply the revenue the state needed for its operations. Like the more activist statesmen of the day, Speransky, Mordvinov, Kiselev, and a few others, he saw at least some of the possible long-run solutions to current problems. He frequently spoke favorably of the development of a prosperous urban middle class that would pay taxes. He knew full well that thriving commerce, industry, and agriculture needed trained men and argued that "the capital of knowledge" must precede the extension of financial support for industry. Despite his clear perception of the problems at hand and at least some idea of how to solve them, Kankrin believed that the state had to restrict its activities to the barest minimum; not because of any belief of his in the ideals of *laissez faire* economic theory, which he rejected vigorously, but because of his firm devotion to what he regarded as sound fiscal policy and the need to husband with great care the state's limited supply of money and administrative talent.

The pessimistic nature of Kankrin's position from the start and his increasing rigidity and opposition to virtually all forms of change made it almost inevitable that he would eventually be overruled on some important questions by the Tsar. It was not in any sense a conflict between a conservative minister and a dynamic or progressive ruler; Nicholas was nothing of the sort. It is perhaps more correctly understood as a conflict of generations, between a relatively young ruler, more aware of changes taking place in the world and of the need for Russia to make some corresponding adjustment, and an old bureaucrat, accustomed to having his own way all the time, who refused to, or could not, recognize that policies that had maintained fiscal stability in the 1820's might lead to grave problems, if not the total collapse of the state, if maintained indefinitely.

Despite their disagreements and the criticism of Kankrin by other influential advisers, Nicholas kept him in office until 1844, when he was physically unable to carry out his duties any longer. During the last decade of the reign, it became clear that the Tsar's insistence that certain measures be carried out over the opposition of his minister of finance did not mean that he differed from him in fundamental outlook. Kankrin's role as primary adviser on economic matters remained unfilled. His successors, Vronchenko and Brok, introduced no innovations. The only important measure of the last decade, the tariff of 1850, came about when the Tsar delegated authority for that specific project to Tengoborskii.

The innovations of the thirties were not abandoned, but there was no increase in scale or significant additions to their number. The monetary system was established in what was viewed as its permanent form, Kiselev continued to labor at his immense task, and railroad construction, although begun, was not pursued with vigor. The changes in the tariff system of the fifties may have presaged future relaxation of extreme protection, but the significant changes made show a very hesitant and ambiguous attitude toward industrial development. Most important of all, the severely restrictive fiscal and credit policies that were the essential feature of Kankrin's administration were maintained, although with slightly less rigor. Nicholas proved in practice to be a basically loyal pupil of the man who had so long been his mentor in matters of economic policy. Perhaps by the late forties and early fifties

Nicholas had reached the same pessimistic conclusion that Kankrin had drawn a decade earlier, that the main problems of the world and of Russia were insoluble and that the best that could be done was to try to keep things going as they were. Actually Nicholas was fortunate because Russia was in a period when the compelling external pressures that had forced earlier sovereigns to intervene so actively in specific areas of the economy were gone or greatly reduced. The respite was, of course, brief and was really over by the end of Nicholas' reign, although the Tsar did not realize it. The pressure of external competition returned with force when the economic backwardness of Russia was exposed in the Crimean War and subsequent conflicts. Then, and only then, did the state hesitantly resume its role as the driving force in the economy, one that it has never relinquished.

The Problem of the "Popular Rates"

The "popular exchange rates" that Kankrin referred to in 1830 were a manifestation of a very troublesome monetary phenomenon of the period. This was the problem that eventually led to the reform of the late 1830's.[1] The difficulties were not simply those arising from the fluctuating value of two different types of money in a free market. Exactly what was happening is difficult to determine because most writers of the period assumed that their readers would be fully familiar with the way the system operated and they did not bother to describe it in detail.[2] The only careful contempo-

---

[1] The nomenclature relating to the problem is most confusing. Russian writers speak of the *prostonarodnyi lazh,* the *prostonarodnyi kurs,* and of *schet na monetu,* without clearly defining what they mean or differentiating between the various terms. Some use the foreign word "agio" (*azhio*) as the equivalent of the Russian term *lazh*; others use them in different senses. In this appendix, "agio" is used to mean simply a premium or a discount given because payment is made in a particular type of currency.

[2] The most detailed discussions of the question in the secondary literature are found in: Alfred Schmidt, "Das russische Geldwesen während der Finanzverwaltung des Grafen Cancrin (1823–1844)," *Russische Revue, Monatsschrift für die Kunde Russlands,* VII (1875), 115–138; Ilarion I. Kaufman, *Iz istorii bumazhnykh deneg v Rossii* (St. Petersburg, 1909), pp. 68–92; and A. D. Druian, "O nekotorykh osobennostiakh bumazhno-denezhnogo obrashcheniia v Rossii naka-

rary account of how the "popular rates" actually worked is
that written by Speransky in 1838 (or early in 1839) in connection with his proposals for monetary reform.[3]

According to Speransky, the bourse rate of exchange was
used exclusively for the exchange of one type of currency for
another, when no purchase of goods was involved. Presumably this was done largely by merchants and others who had
substantial sums. The "popular rates" were employed when
goods were bought and sold. Goods were normally priced in
terms of assignats. If a customer wished to pay in assignats,
the so-called "popular agio" was used. Speransky reports that,
if the "popular agio" was 6 per cent, an item priced at 100
rubles assignats would be sold for 94 rubles assignats. On
the other hand, if the customer wished to pay in silver, the
merchant would quote a rate of exchange more favorable
than the current bourse rate. Speransky says that when the
bourse rate was 352 assignat kopeks per silver ruble and
the agio (used for sales in assignats) was 6 per cent, merchants
in St. Petersburg accepted a silver ruble as equal to 375 paper
assignats. The rate at which silver was accepted in terms of
paper (375) was the "popular exchange rate." [4] This rate was
thus the number of assignat kopeks that would be allowed
per silver ruble when payment for goods was made in silver.
The "popular agio," on the other hand, was the discount
allowed on prices set in assignats when payment was made in
assignats.

It is certainly an unusual situation when an item priced
at 100 units of a particular currency is sold for 94 units of
that currency, while the price supposedly remains unchanged.
Speransky's description is confirmed in this respect by
Schmidt's first-hand report, and there seems to be no doubt
that this is what really happened.[5] Obviously, if 94 rubles

---

nune reformy 1839–1843," *Uchenye zapiski, Rostovskogo-na-Dony
finansovo-ekonomicheskogo instituta*, I (1941), 159–178.

[3] "O monetnom obrashchenii," *Chteniia*, no. 4 (1872), pp. 140–178.

[4] *Ibid.*, pp. 158–159, 176–177.

[5] Schmidt, "Das russische Geldwesen," p. 115.

assignats in the hand is worth 100 assignats on any price tag, there were then, in fact, two different "assignats," although the price-tag assignat existed on the price tag and nowhere else. It can be considered a hypothetical unit of value.

What apparently had happened was that between 1811 and 1816 assignats had become widely accepted at four hundred kopeks per one hundred silver kopeks, that is, as a quarter of a silver ruble. In contrast to the fall of the assignats from par value, which took place very rapidly, their rise after 1816 from the 400 rate was very gradual and marked by constant small fluctuations. If prices set in assignats remained unchanged while this occurred, the effect would be one of steadily increasing prices for those who paid in silver. Since most small-scale trade was conducted with coin, this would, of course, be extremely unpopular and, given a buyer's market, one could expect some concessions from the merchant. He could, of course, constantly reduce his prices in assignats as the value of assignats rose in terms of silver. This process, however, would have been inconvenient and difficult in view of the constant small fluctuations. Instead, the price-tag assignat (let it be called the "conventional assignat") was considered to be still equal to one-quarter of a silver ruble. The customer who paid in actual assignats was given a discount on the price, the "popular agio," in recognition of the increased value of the assignat with which he paid. It was not, however, as great a discount as that which would have been indicated by the difference between the conventional 400 to 100 rate and the current rate on the bourse (in Speransky's example 352 to 100), since, at the same time, a customer paying in silver was given a better rate for his silver than that current on the bourse. What the merchant was doing, in fact, was spreading the effect of the change in value of the currency among his customers, and actually favoring those paying in silver, who were presumably the majority.

If the merchant held prices in assignats constant as the value of assignats (in terms of silver) rose, and accepted silver only at the new lower rate, his total income would rise, if his volume of business did not fall; for the assignats received would be worth more. To avoid a decline in volume of business due to his rising prices in terms of silver, however, he would be under pressure to make some concessions to customers paying in silver, who now paid more for the goods priced in assignats. On the other hand, holders of assignats would feel cheated if they got no advantage. In the example that Speransky gives the difference has been neatly split. The bourse rate (352 to 100) is 12 per cent above the conventional rate (400 to 100). The "popular agio" is 6 per cent, while the "popular exchange rate" is 375 or about 6 per cent below the bourse rate.

The "popular agio" and the "popular exchange rate" operated only with the purchase and sale of goods. In Speransky's example taken from St. Petersburg, an item priced at 100 conventional assignats, subject to a 6 per cent "popular agio," cost 94 actual assignats. The same item would cost 26.7 silver rubles, since the "popular rate" was 375 to 100. Therefore, in exchange for goods, 94 current assignats equaled 26.7 silver rubles, a rate of about 352 to 100, or the same as the bourse rate.[6] If the system worked exactly in this way there would have been no possibility of arbitrage; in reality there were probably many imperfections and deviations from this description.

The "popular agio" and "popular exchange rate" aroused little complaint during the twenties, when they existed and operated with reasonable stability, approximating the bourse rate in their peculiar roundabout fashion. In January 1824, Kankrin quoted a provincial official's statement that "according to popular calculation the silver ruble circulates as four rubles, and the assignat with an agio" and noted that this amounted to exchange at the bourse rate.[7]

---

[6] Kaufman points out that for the calculation to be exact the popular rate must be the geometric mean between the bourse and conventional rates. In practice it is hardly likely that any such refined calculation was involved (*Iz istorii,* p. 79).

[7] Quoted in *ibid.,* pp. 59–60.

In 1830, when the state finally agreed to the acceptance of
silver rubles in tax payments, Kankrin expressed the hope
that this step would put an end to the "popular rates." Kankrin's hope was in vain, and instead the problem rapidly
became a serious one. In 1833, the merchants of Moscow
complained that assignats had risen 2.5 per cent in seven
months and the agio frequently changed, making commercial
transactions difficult. The merchants also emphasized that
foreign coin had virtually replaced Russian coin in the mar-
ketplace.[8] The government's efforts to publicize the true
value of foreign coins and its willingness to accept them for
payment of taxes at their intrinsic value had little effect, and
they continued to circulate on a par with the more valuable
Russian coins.[9]

During the thirties, the "popular agio" and "popular exchange rate" increased steadily, particularly outside St.
Petersburg. By 1838, the year of Speransky's description, the
"popular exchange rate" was 420 assignat kopeks per silver
ruble and the "popular agio" 20 per cent in Moscow and
at the annual market fairs. It was only 375 and 6 per cent
in St. Petersburg.[10] In 1837, according to Kankrin, the rate
was 6 per cent and 375 in St. Petersburg (the same as Speransky quoted a year later), 17 per cent and 420 in Moscow, 18 per cent and 420 in Nizhni-Novgorod and Iaroslavl',
10 per cent and 390 in Astrakhan, 10 per cent and 400 in
Viatka, 3.75 per cent and 375 in Mogilev, and 5 per cent and
380 in Pskov.[11]

In some cases, the "popular exchange rate" exceeded the
traditional rate of 400 to 100. This first occurred in the early

[8] TsGIAL, f. 583, op. 4, d. 228, 1833, "Vsepoddanneishie dokladnye
zapiski," pp. 247–250.

[9] *Ibid.*, f. 560, op. 38, d. 320, "Obshchii otchet . . . za 1833," pp. 10–
12; *ibid.*, d. 354, "Obshchii otchet . . . za 1835," p. 13; P. A. Ostroukhov, "Iz istorii russkago denezhnago obrashcheniia," *Zapiski, Russki svobodnyi universitet Prague, nauchno-issledovatel'skoe obedinyenia*, II
(1941), 7, 11.

[10] Speransky, "O monetnom obrashchenii," p. 159.

[11] *Materialy*, p. 3.

thirties, when the large influx of foreign coin began. The foreign coins were actually worth less than Russian coins, but the merchants were evidently forced by competitive pressure to accept them as equal to Russian coins.[12] The presence of large amounts of inferior coin in circulation reduced the average value of all coin, and it is surprising that this apparently produced an increase in the "popular exchange rate" to a point where it exceeded 400 in some cases. Why should coins averaging less metal content be worth more conventional assignats than before? (It must be remembered that the "popular exchange rate" refers to the value of coin used in the purchase of goods priced in conventional assignats.) The answer is that the "popular agio" on actual assignats also increased, with the result that the real exchange rate between actual assignats and coin rose in favor of actual assignats.

Take, for example, the rates Speransky gives for Moscow and the market fairs. The "popular agio" was 20 per cent and the "popular exchange rate" was 420 kopeks of conventional assignats per silver ruble. At the same time, the corresponding rates were 6 per cent and 375 in St. Petersburg. Under these circumstances an item priced in Moscow at 100 conventional assignats would cost 80 actual assignats or 23.8 silver rubles; therefore, the real exchange rate of assignats for silver was 336 to 100. Thus the value of silver in terms of actual assignats is lower, not higher, than in St. Petersburg, where the real rate corresponded to the bourse rate of 352. This is reasonable, since coin was more plentiful in the central provinces around Moscow than in the west nearer St. Petersburg, and assignats were relatively scarce.[13] Therefore, the real value of coin should be lower in Moscow.

The increase in both the "popular exchange rate" and the "popular agio" was probably the result of competitive pressure on the merchant. To avoid offending a customer paying

---

[12] Druian, "O nekotorykh osobennostiakh," p. 173, citing a report of the military governor of Moscow.

[13] *Severnaia pchela,* no. 84 (April 18, 1839), p. 3.

in foreign coin, the merchant increased the agio on actual assignats rather than reduce the rate on silver in conventional assignats. A competing merchant could increase both rates and thus give the appearance of offering a better bargain. The process could go on indefinitely except for the fact that increases in the "popular agio" cut the merchant's receipts if his prices remained unchanged. (In the example already given, with the agio at 6 per cent and the popular rate at 375, the merchant got 94 actual assignats or 26.7 silver rubles for goods priced at 100 conventional assignat rubles. With the agio at 20 per cent and the rate at 420, he would get only 80 actual assignats or 23.8 silver rubles.) To avoid losses he would either have to raise prices in conventional assignats or reduce his costs to the same or a greater extent by purchasing goods on the same basis that he sold them.

The pressure to increase prices in conventional assignats may actually have added to the incentive to increase the "popular agio" and the "popular exchange rate." As the price in conventional assignats was increased, the merchant could increase the agio and the rate a little so the buyer would feel he was not hurt by the increased price. In a competitive situation there would have been a tendency for both prices in conventional assignats and discounts to rise in spiral fashion, although there need not have been any rise in real prices. Unfortunately, price data with a clear indication as to the nature of the price quoted, which are needed to confirm this theory, are unavailable. Obviously, if everybody knew exactly how the game was played, it would make no difference— wholesale and retail prices, wages, and so forth would all be adjusted and everyone would be back where he started. But of course nothing of the sort occurred. Such an unstable and complex situation produced losses for some and gains for others.

Comment in contemporary journals emphasizes the difficulties caused the gentry, but this is probably more indicative of the nature of the journals than of the overall impact of the popular agio and exchange rate. For example, consider

the landlord with one hundred serfs who paid their dues
(*obrok*), set at 40 conventional assignat rubles, in silver coin.
When the "popular exchange rate" was 400 to 100, the landlord got 1,000 silver rubles; with the "popular exchange rate"
at 430 to 100, he got only 930 silver rubles. Rents could not
be raised fast enough to adjust for changes in the "popular
exchange rate," which was the accepted basis of payment,
since most prices were expressed in terms of conventional
assignats.[14] Similarly, a workman who contracted to work for
a year for 300 conventional assignats when the "popular agio"
was 20 per cent would expect to receive 240 actual assignats,
but if the agio rose to 24 per cent he would receive only 228,
or 12 rubles less. Nevertheless he would have to pay his taxes
and buy vodka without corresponding benefits of the increased agio.[15] Count Benkendorf reported to the State Council in the late thirties that it was the peasants and workmen
who suffered from the increase in the popular agio.[16] This is
hardly surprising, for the Russian peasant was uneducated
and did not deal with money very much. If he had any ideas
at all about exchange rates, it was presumably the fixed notion
that a silver ruble was four assignats.[17]

[14] P. Morozov, "O lazh na den'gi," *Zhurnal Ministerstva vnutrennikh del*, no. 2 (1839), p. 54, reprinted from the *Zemledel'cheskaia gazeta*.

[15] D. Shelekhov, "O lazhe ili promene na den'gi," *Biblioteka dlia chteniia*, XXXIII (1839), sec. 4, 44.

[16] Druian, "O nekotorykh osobennnostiakh," p. 176, citing archival sources.

[17] In trying to imagine the extent of fraud and chicanery that was undoubtedly prevalent, I am reminded of Ignazio Silone's vivid description of how some Italian peasants were persuaded to divide a disputed water supply into two equal shares, three-quarters for themselves and three-quarters for the landowner (*Fontamara* [New York, 1934], pp. 64–65). Certainly the Russian peasant of the 1830's was no more sophisticated than the Italian peasant of the 1930's and the situation was inherently more complex.

BIBLIOGRAPHY

In the absence of a substantial monograph or of a special bibliography treating state economic policy in the second quarter of the nineteenth century, the most fruitful sources of bibliographical information proved to be the secondary works on various aspects of the subject. General treatments of the reign of Nicholas I (Schilder, Schiemann, Polievktov) pay little attention to economic questions, and general economic histories (Khromov, Liashchenko, Wittschcwsky) do not provide a comprehensive discussion of state policy.

Prerevolutionary scholarship emphasized monetary and tariff policy. The best of the several studies in these fields are certainly those of I. I. Kaufman and M. N. Sobolev. M. Tugan-Baranovskii's classic *Russkaia fabrika* is the only prerevolutionary work to deal with the state's attitude toward industry. Soviet scholars have not produced many works dealing with government policy, but the quality of those that do is generally high. This study would have been far more difficult, if not impossible, to complete without the monographs of Borovoi, Druzhinin, Rozhkova, Ryndziunskii, and Voblyi.

Published documents are available in widely varying quantities for different subjects. The monetary reform of 1839–1843 is well covered in a volume published in 1896 (Gosudarstvennaia kantseliariia, *Materialy*). *Krasnyi arkhiv* contains a valuable selection edited by Krutikov on early discussions of railroads. Baron Korf's "Imperator Nikolai v soveshchatel'nykh sobraniiakh" is useful for both of these topics. The published *Arkhiv Gosudarstvennago soveta* is very important on the question of credit policy, but does not go beyond 1825. For other subjects, there are only isolated documents and memoirs scattered in historical journals and secondary works. The *Arkhiv grafov Mordvinovykh* is the only collection of private papers with substantial amounts of relevant material.

Government finance and almost all other aspects of economic policy were strictly confidential in the age of Nicholas and the censored press could neither speculate nor criticize. Contemporary published documents are therefore of very limited usefulness. The most important publications were the Ministry of Finance's *Zhurnal manufaktur i torgovli* and *Kommercheskaia gazeta,* which reflected to some extent the views of those within the government most concerned with economic development.

Unpublished documents in the Central State Historical Archive in Leningrad were consulted. The most useful material was found in the collections of the Chancery of the Ministry of Finance (*fond* 560), the Department of Manufacturing and Internal Trade (*fond* 18), and the State Council, Department of the Economy (*fond* 1152). Within these collections, the annual reports of the Ministry of Finance and its departments, the minister's comments on proposals submitted to the Tsar and referred to him, and the summaries of State Council deliberations were the best sources of information on matters of general policy. The limited time available did not permit the extensive use of archival material for every subject considered in this study. It was possible, however, to microfilm many of the documents cited, and a copy of this film has been deposited in the Harvard College Library.

The bibliography lists all published material cited in the text with the exception of general studies and reference works in Western languages. In addition, a selection of the more important specialized literature consulted but not cited has been included. No attempt, however, has been made to provide a comprehensive bibliography for the period or for the general economic history of Russia in the second quarter of the nineteenth century.

The listing is alphabetical by author. Government publications without an individual author or editor are listed under "Russia," followed by the transliterated name of the agency.

Barbashev, N. I. *K istorii morekhodnogo obrazovaniia v Rossii.* Moscow, 1959.

[Bartenev, Peter] P. B. "Graf Egor Frantsovich Kankrin," *Russkii arkhiv*, no. 1 (1866).

Benkendorf, A, Kh. "Iz zapisok Grafa A. Kh. Benkendorfa," *Istoricheskii vestnik*, XCI (1903).

Bezobrazov, V. P. *O nekotorykh iavleniiakh denezhnago obrashcheniia v Rossii*. Moscow, 1863.

——. *O vliianii ekonomicheskoi nauki na gosudarstvennuiu zhizn' v sovremennoi Evrope*. St. Petersburg, 1867.

Bliokh, I. S. *Finansy Rossii XIX stoletiia*. 4 vols. St. Petersburg, 1882. A superficial general survey; available in French translation.

Bliumin, I. G. *Ocherki ekonomicheskoi mysli v Rossii v pervoi polovine XIX veka*. Moscow and Leningrad, 1940.

Blum, Jerome. *Lord and Peasant in Russia from the Ninth to the Nineteenth Century*. Princeton, 1961.

Borovoi, S. Ia. "K istorii promyshlennoi politiki Rossii v 20–50kh godakh XIX v.," *Istoricheskie zapiski*, LXIX (1961).

——. *Kredit i banki Rossii (seredina XVII v.–1861 g.)*. Moscow, 1958. An extremely useful book both in itself and as a source of bibliographical and archival references.

Bozherianov, I. N. *Graf Egor Frantsevich Kankrin, ego zhizn', literaturnye trudy i dvadtsatiletniaia deiatel'nost' upravleniia Ministerstva finansov*. St. Petersburg, 1897. The only substantial biography of Kankrin. Sponsored by the family, it is highly sympathetic, but it cites critics as well as admirers and has valuable bibliographical notes.

Brandt, A. A. *Ocherk istorii parovoi mashiny i primeneniia parovykh dvigatelei v Rossii*. 2 vols. St. Petersburg, 1892.

Brzheskii, N. *Gosudarstvennye dolgi Rossii*. St. Petersburg, 1884. Contains valuable statistics.

Crisp, Olga. "The State Peasants under Nicholas I," *Slavonic and East European Review*, XXXVII (1959).

Curtiss, John S. *The Russian Army under Nicholas I, 1825–1855*. Durham, 1965.

De Tegoborski, M. L. See Tengoborskii, L.

Del'vig, A. I. *Polveka russkoi zhizni*. 2 vols. Moscow, 1930. Memoirs of a graduate of the Institute of Transport Engineers in the early years of Nicholas' reign.

Dolgorukov, P. V. *Peterburgskie ocherki*. Ed. P. E. Shchegolev. Moscow, 1934.

Druian, A. D. "Denezhnaia reforma Kankrina i bor'ba klassov,"
  Trudy Leningradskogo finansovo-ekonomischeskogo instituta,
  I (1940). This study by Druian, and the two following, are the
  only serious Soviet works on the monetary reform of 1839–
  1843.

———. "O nekotorykh osobennostiakh bumazhno-denezhnogo
  obrashcheniia v Rossii nakanune reformy 1839–1843," *Uchenye
  zapiski, Rostovskogo-na-Dony finansovo-ekonomicheskogo instituta,* I (1941).

———. *Ocherki po istorii denezhnogo obrashcheniia Rossii v XIX
  veke.* Moscow, 1941.

Drutskii-Liubetskii, K. "Mnenie ob otsenke i prodazhe imenii
  pomeshchikov," *Chteniia,* no. 3 (1863).

Druzhinin, M. N. *Gosudarstvennye krest'iane i reforma P. D.
  Kiseleva.* 2 vols. Moscow and Leningrad, 1946, 1958. An en-
  cyclopedic study of the state peasant under Nicholas I.

Edlitskii, Ezhi. "Gosudarstvennaia promyshlennost' v tsarstve
  pol'skom v XIX v.," in Akademiia Nauk, Institut istorii, *Genezis kapitalizma v promyshlennosti* (Moscow, 1963).

Ellison, Herbert J. *History of Russia.* New York, 1964.

Ermolov, A. P. Letter to A. A. Zakrevskii, dated Tiflis, June 8,
  1823, *Sbornik IRIO,* LXII (1890).

Ferguson, Alan D. "The Russian Military Settlements, 1825–
  1866," *Essays in Russian History: A Collection Dedicated to
  George Vernadsky,* ed. Alan D. Ferguson and Alfred Levin
  (Hamden, Conn., 1964).

Fester, Richard. *"Der Universitäts-Bereiser" Friedrich Gedike
  und sein Bericht an Friedrich Wilhelm II (Ergänzungs heft des
  Archives für Kulturgeschichte,* Vol. I.) Berlin, 1905.

Filimonov, D. "Kreditnye uchrezhdeniia Moskovskogo vospitatel'nogo doma," *Russkii arkhiv,* no. 1 (1876).

Fok, M. M. "Pis'ma M. M. Foka k A. Kh. Benkendorfu," *Russkaia starina,* XXXII (1881).

Fomin, Aleksandr. *O ponizhenii tsen na zemledel'cheskiia proizvedeniia v Rossii.* St. Petersburg, 1829.

Fon-Bradke, E. F. "Avtobiograficheskie zapiski Egora Fedorovicha Fon-Bradke," *Russkii arkhiv,* nos. 1–3 (1875).

Gagemeister, Iu. A. "Vzgliad na promyshlennost' i torgovliu
  Rossii," *Russkii vestnik,* VII (1857).

Gerschenkron, Alexander. "The Problem of Economic Development in Russian Intellectual History of the Nineteenth Century," *Continuity and Change in Russian and Soviet Thought,* ed. Ernest J. Simmons (Cambridge, Mass., 1955).

"Geschichte des Kartoffelbaues in Russland," *Archiv für Wissenschaftliche Kunde von Russland,* VII (1849).

Grech, N. I. *Zapiski o moei zhizni.* Moscow and Leningrad, 1930.

Grüning, Irene. "Graf Georg Kankrin," *Lebensbilder aus Kurhessen und Waldeck, 1830–1930,* Vol. III, ed. Ingeborg Schnack (*Veröffentlichungen der Historischen Kommission für Hessen und Waldeck,* Vol. XX) (Marburg, 1942). A thorough summary of the standard Russian sources.

Haxthausen, Baron von. *The Russian Empire, Its People, Institutions and Resources.* 2 vols. Trans. Robert Farie. London, 1856.

Iakovlev, B. "Vozniknovenie i etapy razvitiia kapitalisticheskogo uklada v Rossii," *Voprosy istorii,* no. 9 (1950).

Iasnopol'skii, L. N. *Ocherki russkago biudzhetnago prava,* Vol. I. (*Istoricheskii obzor sostavleniia nashikh gosudarstvennykh rospisei i biudzhetnaia reforma Tatarinova.*) Moscow, 1912. The only extensive study of budgetary practice.

Iatsunskii, V. K. "Krupnaia promyshlennost' Rossii v 1790–1860 gg.," *Ocherki ekonomicheskoi istorii Rossii pervoi poloviny XIX veka, sbornik statei,* ed. M. K. Rozhkova (Moscow, 1959).

Kabuzan, Vladimir Maksimovich. *Narodonaselenie Rossii v XVIII-pervoi polovine XIX v. (po materialam revizii).* Moscow, 1963.

Kahan, Arcadius. "Continuity in Economic Activity and Policy during the Post-Petrine Period in Russia," *Journal of Economic History,* XXV (1965).

——. "The Costs of Westernization, the Gentry and the Russian Economy in the Eighteenth Century," *Slavic Review,* XXV (1966).

Kankrin, Egor Frantsevich. *Aus den Reisetagebüchern des Grafen Georg Kankrin, ehemaligen kaiserlich russischen Finanzministers, aus den Jahren 1840–1845: Mit einer Lebensskizze Kankrin's nebst zwei Beilagen.* Ed. Alexander Graf Keyserling. 2 vols. Braunschweig, 1865. Appendix 2 is a translation of Kankrin's final report to the Tsar.

[——.] *Dagobert; eine Geschichte aus dem jetzigen Freiheit-*

skriege: Als Gegenstück zum Graf Donomar, eine Geschichte aus dem siebenjährigen Kriege. 2 vols. Altona, 1797–1798.

——. *Die Oekonomie der menschlichen Gesellschaften und das Finanzwesen—von einem ehemaligen Finanzminister.* Stuttgart, 1845. Unlike all the other works published during the author's lifetime, this book was not anonymous. The preface is signed "Graf Cancrin." Published in Russian translation, *Graf Kankrin i ego ocherki politicheskoi ekonomii i finansii* (St. Petersburg, 1894).

[——.] *Fragmente über die Kriegskunst, nach Gesichtspunkten der militärischen Philosophie.* St. Petersburg, 1809. Second edition, Braunschweig, 1815.

——. *Im Ural und Altai: Briefwechsel zwischen Alexander von Humboldt und Graf Georg von Kankrin aus den Jahren 1827–1832.* Leipzig, 1869.

——. "Kratkoe obozrenie rossiiskikh finansov, grafa E. F. Kankrina. 1838 god," *Sbornik IRIO,* XXXI (1881). Also published separately in St. Petersburg in 1880 with the same title. Kankrin's lectures on finance for the heir apparent to the throne.

——. "Nastavlenie: O predpolozheniiakh i vidakh po finansovoi chasti" [St. Petersburg, 1840]. This unpublished document, written to guide his deputy while Kankrin was on leave, is available in bound photo-copy in the Harvard College Library and the Cornell University Library. The original is in the TsGIAL with number f. 560, op. 22, d. 98.

[——.] *Über die Militairökonomie im Frieden und Krieg und ihr Wechselverhältniss zu den Operationen.* 3 vols. St. Petersburg, 1820–1823.

[——.] *Weltreichthum, Nationalreichthum, und Staatswirtschaft, oder Versuch neurer Ansichten der politischen Oekonomie.* Munich, 1821.

[——.] "Zapiska ob osvobozhdenii krest'ian v Rossii ot krepostnoi zavisimosti, sostavlennaia v 1818 godu," Trans. from French by S. A. Sobolevskii, *Russkii arkhiv,* nos. 10–11 (1865). The original remains unpublished.

Karamzin, Nikolai Mikhailovich. *Karamzin's Memoir on Ancient and Modern Russia: A Translation and Analysis.* Trans. with intro. by Richard Pipes. Cambridge, Mass., 1959.

Karataev, S. I. *Bibliografiia finansov, promyshlennosti i torgovli: So vremen Petra Velikago po nastoiashchee vremia (c 1714 po*

1879 god vkliuchitel'no). St. Petersburg, 1880. A guide to periodical literature.

Kaufman, Ilarion I. *Iz istorii bumazhnykh deneg v Rossii.* St. Petersburg, 1909. Kaufman's works are still the best for financial and monetary problems.

——. *Kankrinovskaia sistema tabachnago oblozheniia v Rossii.* St. Petersburg, 1912.

——. *Serebrianyi rubl' v Rossii ot ego vozniknoveniia do kontsa XIX veka.* St. Petersburg, 1910.

——. "Statistika russkikh bankov," pt. 1, *Statisticheskii vremennik rossiiskoi imperii,* ser. 2, no. 9 (1872).

Keyserling, Alexander. "Lebensskizze Kankrin's." See Kankrin, Egor F. *Aus den Reisetagebüchern.*

Khromov, P. A. *Ekonomicheskoe razvitie Rossii v XIX–XX vekakh, 1800–1917.* Moscow, 1950. Particularly useful for its extensive statistical appendix.

Kiniapina, N. S. "Promyshlennaia politika russkogo samoderzhaviia v gody krizisa feodal'noi sistemy," *Voprosy istorii,* no. 6 (1965).

——. "Voprosy promyshlennogo razvitiia Rossii vtoroi chetverti XIX v russkoi periodicheskoi pechati," *Vestnik Moskovskogo Universiteta—Istoriia,* no. 2 (1965).

Kislinskii, N. A. *Nasha zheleznodorozhnaia politika po dokumentam arkhiva Komiteta ministrov.* 4 vols. St. Petersburg, 1902. An important summary based on archival documents. Sometimes cataloged under "Komitet ministrov."

Kokorev, V. A. *Ekonomicheskie provaly po vospominaniam s 1837 goda.* St. Petersburg, 1887. Memoirs of a Russian merchant.

Korf, M. A. "Imperator Nikolai v soveshchatel'nykh sobraniiakh: (Iz sovremennykh zapisok stats-sekretaria barona Korfa)," *Sbornik IRIO,* XCVIII (1896). An important source for the later stages of the monetary reform and for the railroad question.

——. "Iz zapisok barona (vposledstvii grafa) M. A. Korfa," *Russkaia starina,* XCIX (1899).

Kornilov, Alexander. *Modern Russian History.* Trans. Alexander S. Kaun. New York, 1943.

Krutikov, M., ed. "Pervye zheleznye dorogi v Rossii," *Krasnyi arkhiv,* LXXVI (1936). The most important collection of published documents on the early discussions of railroad building.

Kutukov, A. P. "Svedeniia o biletakh gosudarstvennago kazna-cheistva (seriiakh) ," *Ezhegodnik ministerstva finansov,* IV (1873). A detailed study.

Lazhetnikov, I. I. "Neskol'ko zametok i vospominanii po povodu stat'i 'Materialy dlia biografii A. P. Ermolova,' " *Russkii vest-nik,* LI (1864).

Lodyzhenskii, Konstantin. *Istoriia russkago tamozhennago tarifa.* St. Petersburg, 1886. One of the few works covering prereform tariff history. It leaves many questions unanswered.

Longinov, N. M. Letter to S. R. Vorontsov, dated St. Petersburg, May 15, 1823, *Arkhiv kniazia Vorontsova,* ed. Peter Bartenev, XXIII (Moscow, 1882).

Maslov, Stepan. *Istoricheskoe obozrenie deistvii i trudov impera-torskago moskovskago obshchestva sel'skago khoziaistva so vre-meni ego osnovaniia do 1846 goda.* 2nd ed. Moscow, 1850.

Medynskii, E. N. *Istoriia russkoi pedagogiki do velikoi oktiabr'-skoi sotsialisticheskoi revoliutsii.* Moscow, 1938.

Mel'nikov, P. P. "Poezdka na Volgu," *Krasnyi arkhiv,* LXXXIX–XC (1938). An engineer's description of river transport in the 1840's.

———. "Svedeniia o russkikh zheleznykh dorogakh," *Krasnyi ar-khiv,* XCIX (1940). The memoirs of a leading figure of the early years of Russian railroad construction.

Meyendorff, Alexander von. "Über die Manufaktur-Betreibsam-keit Russlands in Bezug auf die allgemeine Productivität und das häusliche Leben der neideren Volksklassen," *Archiv für Wissenschaftliche Kunde von Russland,* IV (1846).

Mikhailovskii-Danilevskii, A. I. "Zapiski," *Istoricheskii vestnik,* XLIX (1892).

Monas, Sidney. *The Third Section, Police and Society in Russia under Nicholas I.* Cambridge, Mass., 1961.

Mordvinov (family). *Arkhiv grafov Mordvinoykh.* Ed. V. A. Bilbasov. 10 vols. St. Petersburg, 1901–1903. Primarily the papers of Admiral N. S. Mordvinov, who made innumerable well-informed comments on state policy. Fascinating and valuable.

Mordvinov, N. S. "Zapiska admirala Mordvinova o sredstvakh protiv neumerennogo upotrebleniia v narode vina," *Sbornik svedenii i materialov po vedomstvu Ministerstva finansov,* I

(1865). Kankrin's comments on Mordvinov's proposals are included.

Morozov, P. "O lazh na den'gi," *Zhurnal Ministerstva vnutrennikh del*, no. 2 (1839).

Moskovskoe kupecheskoe obshchestvo. "Predlozheniia Moskovskago kupecheskago obshchestva," *Sbornik svedenii i materialov po vedomstvu Ministerstva finansov*, III (1865). A document submitted to Gurev shortly before he was replaced by Kankrin.

Müller, Adam H. *Ausgewählte Abhandlungen*. Ed. Jakob Baxa. 2nd ed. Jena, 1931.

——. *Die Elemente der Staatskunst*. Berlin, 1809.

[Nebolsin, A. G., ed.]. *Istoriko-statisticheskii ocherk obshchago i spetsial'nago obrazovaniia v Rossii*. St. Petersburg, 1883.

Nebolsin, Grigorii. *Statisticheskoe obozrenie vneshnei torgovli Rossii*. 2 vols. St. Petersburg, 1850.

Nikitenko, Aleksandr Vasilevich. *Moia povest' o samom sebe i o tom "chemu svidetel' v zhizni byl", zapiski i dnevnik (1804–1877 gg.)*. 2nd ed. 2 vols. St. Petersburg, 1905. Also in *Russkaia starina*, LXIV (1889).

Nolcken, Michael Herman Freiherr von. *Der russische Finanzminister Graf Georg Kankrin und seine Handelspolitik*. Riga, 1909.

Normano, J. F. *The Spirit of Russian Economics*. New York, 1950. Brief but interesting. See also Normano's *Aktsionernye kommercheskie banki v Rossii* (Petrograd, 1917), published under the name Isaak I. Levin.

Novodvorskii, V. V. "Drutskii-Liubetskii, Kniaz' Frantsisk-Ksaverii (1779–1846)," *Russkii biograficheskii slovar'*, Vol. Dabelov-Diad'kovskii (St. Petersburg, 1905).

"O raznykh sposobakh dlia vzimaniia piteinogo dokhoda," *Sbornik svedeniia i materialov po vedomstvu Ministerstva finansov*, I (1866).

Okun', S. B. "K istorii tamozhennogo tarifa 1850 g.," in Leningradskii universitet, *Voprosy genezisa kapitalizma v Rossii, sbornik statei* (Leningrad, 1960).

——. *Ocherki istorii SSSR, vtoraia chetvert' XIX veka*. Leningrad, 1957.

Ostroukhov, P. A. "Iz istorii gosudarstvennykh kreditnykh ustanovlenii v Rossii," *Sbornik russkago instituta v Prage*, II (1932).

——. "Iz istorii russkago denezhnago obrashcheniia," *Zapiski*,

Russki svobodnyi universitet Prague, nauchno-issledovatel'skoe obedinyenia, II (1941). (Transliterated as in the original.)

———. "Koniunktura na nizhegorodskoi iarmarke s 1817 po 1867 god," *Zapiski russkago nauchno-issledovatel'skago obedineniia v Prage*, XI (1942).

Panaev, V. I. "Vospominaniia," *Vestnik Evropy*, IV (1867).

Pazhitnov, K. A. *Ocherki istorii tekstil'noi promyshlennosti dorevoliutsionnoi Rossii—khlopchatobumazhnaia, l'nopen'kovaia i shelkovaia promyshlennost'*. Moscow, 1958.

———. *Problema remeslennykh tsekhov v zakonodatel'stve russkogo absolutizma*. Moscow, 1952.

Pecherin, Ia. I. *Istoricheskii obzor rospisei gosudarstvennykh dokhodov i raskhodov s 1803 po 1843 god vkliuchitel'no*. St. Petersburg, 1896. An important collection of budget statistics.

Pel'chinskii, Vikentii. "O rasprostranenii sbyta rossiskikh manufakturnykh izdelii v Zakavkaze i Persii," *Zhurnal manufaktur i torgovli*, no. 1 (1831).

———. *O sostoianii promyshlennykh sil Rossii do 1832 goda*. St. Petersburg, 1833. The best example of industrial "propaganda" of the period.

Pfuel, [Ernest von]. "Kurze Darstellung der National Ökonomie, nach Adam Müller," *Archiv für Geografie, Historie, Staats- und Kriegskunst*, nos. 80–81 (July 5 and 8, 1811).

Pintner, Walter M. "Industry and Government during the Ministry of Count Kankrin, 1823–1844," *Slavic Review*, XXIII (1964).

———. "Inflation in Russia during the Crimean War Period," *American Slavic and East European Review*, XVIII (1959).

Pipes, Richard. "The Russian Military Colonies, 1810–1831," *Journal of Modern History*, XXII (1950).

———. ed. and trans. See Karamzin, Nikolai Mikhailovich.

Pokrovskii, V. I., ed. *Sbornik svedenii po istorii i statistike vneshnei torgovli Rossii*. Vol. I: *Ocherk po istorii vneshnei torgovli Rossii. Otpusk i privoz tovarov v XIX stoletii. Tablitsy otpuska, privoza i tamozhennykh dokhodov* (only one published). St. Petersburg, 1902. The standard collection of foreign trade statistics.

Polievktov, M. *Nikolai I*. Moscow, 1918.

Portal, Roger. "Das Problem einer industriellen Revolution in Russland im 19. Jh.," *Forschungen zur Osteuropäischen Geschichte*, I (1954).

——. "The Industrialization of Russia," *Cambridge Economic History of Europe*, Vol. IV, ed. H. J. Habakkuk and M. Postan (Cambridge, Eng., 1965).

Potekhin, Vladimir. "O gil'deiskom sbore v Rossii," *Promysh-lennost', zhurnal manufaktur i torgovli*, III (1861).

Predtechenskii, A. V. "Bor'ba protektsionistov s fritrederami v nachale XIX v.," *Uchenye zapiski Leningradskogo Gosu-darstvennogo Universiteta, seriia istoricheskikh nauk*, no. 5 (1939).

——. "Istoriia osnovaniia Manufakturnogo soveta," *Izvestiia Akademii Nauk, otdelenie obshchestvennykh nauk*, ser. 7, no. 5 (1932).

——. *Ocherki obshchestvenno-politicheskoi istorii Rossii v pervoi chetverti XIX veka*. Moscow and Leningrad, 1957.

Proshin, G. G. "Tamozhennyi tarif 1819 goda," *Nauchnye do-klady vyshei shkoly—Istoricheskie nauki*, no. 4 (1961).

Przhetslavskii, Osip Antonovich. "Beglye ocherki," *Russkaia sta-rina*, XXXIX (1883).

Puryear, Vernon John. *England, Russia, and the Straits Question, 1844–1856*. Berkeley, 1931.

Raeff, Marc. *Michael Speransky, Statesman of Imperial Russia, 1772–1839*. The Hague, 1957.

Rashin, Adol'f Grigorevich. *Naselenie Rossii za 100 let (1811–1913 gg.)*. Moscow, 1956.

Rastopchin, F. V. Letter to A. A. Zakrevskii, dated January 3, 1824, *Sbornik IRIO*, LXXIII (1891).

Reinbot, F. A. "Graf Egor Frantsovich Kankrin: Zametki odnogo iz sluzhivshikh pri nem chinovnikov," *Russkaia starina*, XXXIX (1883).

Repczuk, Helma. "Nicholas Mordvinov (1754–1845)." Unpub-lished Ph.D. diss., Columbia University, 1962. A fine study of a fascinating personality.

Riasanovsky, Nicholas V. *Nicholas I and Official Nationality in Russia, 1825–1855*. Berkeley and Los Angeles, 1959. The most useful book in English on the reign of Nicholas.

Riboper, Aleksandr Ivanovich. "Zapiski," *Russkii arkhiv*, no. 5 (1877).

Roscher, Wilhelm. *Geschichte der National-Oekonomik in Deutschland*. Munich, 1874. Includes a discussion of the "Ger-man-Russian school."

———. "Über die deutsch-russische Schule der Nationalökonomik," *Berichte über die Verhandlungen der königlichen sächsischen Gesellschaft der Wissenschaften zu Leipzig,* philologisch- historische Classe, XXII (1872).

Rozhkova, M. K. *Ekonomicheskaia politika tsarskogo pravitel'- stva na srednem vostoke vo vtoroi chetverti XIX veka i russkaia burzhuaziia.* Moscow and Leningrad, 1949.

———. "Razlozhenie feodal'no-krepostnicheskogo khoziaistva i razvitie kapitalisticheskikh otnoshenii v pervoi polovine XIX v.," ch. 24 of *Istoriia SSSR,* Vol. I (*S drevneishikh vremen do 1861 goda*), ed. M. V. Nechkina (Moscow, 1956).

———, ed. *Ocherki ekonomicheskoi istorii Rossii pervoi poloviny XIX veka: Sbornik statei.* Moscow, 1959. A useful collection, particularly Rozhkova's article on government policy.

Russia, *Polnoe sobranie zakonov rossiiskoi imperii.* 1st ser., from 1649 to Dec. 12, 1825 (St. Petersburg, 1830). 2nd ser., from Dec. 12, 1825 to Feb. 28, 1881 (St. Petersburg, 1830–1884).

Russia, Glavnoe upravlenie putei soobshcheniia i publichnykh zdanii. "Istoricheskoe obozrenie putei soobshcheniia i pu- blichnykh zdanii s 1825 po 1850 god," *Sbornik IRIO,* XCVII (1896).

Russia, Glavnoe upravlenie udelov. *Istoriia udelov za stoletie ikh sushchestvovaniia, 1797–1897.* 3 vols. St. Petersburg, 1902.

Russia, Gornyi Institut. *Nauchno-istoricheskii sbornik.* St. Petersburg, 1873.

Russia, Gosudarstvennaia kantseliariia. *Materialy po voprosu ob ustroistve denezhnoi sistemy (izvlechennye iz dela Gosu- darstvennogo soveta, 1837–1839 g.).* St. Petersburg, 1896. An extensive and invaluable collection of documents.

———. *Svedeniia o piteinykh sborakh v Rossii.* 3 vols. St. Peters- burg, 1860. A detailed study with many long excerpts from documents.

Russia, Gosudarstvennyi sovet. *Arkhiv Gosudarstvennago soveta, zhurnaly po delam departamenta gosudarstvennoi ekonomii.* Vol. IV, pts. 1–2: *Tsarstvovanie Imperatora Aleksandra I-go (s 1810 po 19 noiabria 1825 g.)* (St. Petersburg, 1881). Vol. V. pt. 1: *Tsarstvovanie Imperatora Nikolai I, (s 20 noiabria 1825 po konets 1826 g.)* (St. Petersburg, 1904). Published minutes of the State Council. Extremely useful. Volume V is very brief, and no further volumes for Nicholas I were issued. Cited in the notes as *AGS*.

Russia, Institut inzhenerov putei soobshcheniia. *Spisok lits okonchivshikh kurs nauk v Institute inzhenerov putei soobshcheniia Imperatora Aleksandra I, s 1811 po 1882 g.* St. Petersburg, 1883.

Russia, Komitet ministrov. See Kislinskii, N. A.

Russia, Komitet uchrezhdennago vysochaishim reskriptom 6 dekabria 1826 goda. "Zhurnaly Komiteta 6 dekabria 1826 goda," *Sbornik IRIO*, LXXIV (1891).

Russia, Lesnoi departament. *Stoletie uchrezhdeniia Lesnago departamenta, 1798–1898.* St. Petersburg, 1898.

Russia, Ministerstvo finansov. *Ministerstvo finansov, 1802–1902.* 2 vols. St. Petersburg, 1902. A most useful survey, but lacks source references.

Russia, Ministerstvo finansov, Departament torgovli i manufaktur. *Istoricheskii ocherk oblozheniia torgovli i promyslov v Rossii, s prilozheniem materialov po torgovo-promyshlennoi statistike.* St. Petersburg, 1893.

Russia, Ministerstvo gosudarstvennykh imushchestv. *Istoricheskoe obozrenie piatidesiatiletnei deiatel'nosti Ministerstva gosudarstvennykh imushchestv, 1837–1887.* 5 vols. St. Petersburg, 1888.

——. *Izvlechenie iz otcheta ministra gosudarstvennykh imushchestv za 18— god.* Annual vols. for 1842–1854. St. Petersburg, 1843–1855.

——. "Obozrenie upravleniia gosudarstvennykh imushchestv za posledniia 25 let s 20 noiabria 1825 po 20 noiabria 1850 g.," *Sbornik IRIO*, XCVIII (1896).

Russia, Ministerstvo narodnago prosveshcheniia. *Desiatiletie Ministerstva narodnago prosveshcheniia.* See Uvarov, Sergei.

——. *Istoricheskii obzor deiatel'nosti Ministerstva, 1802–1902.* St. Petersburg, 1902.

Russia, Ministerstvo vnutrennykh del. *MVD, Istoricheskii ocherk.* 1 vol. with 2 apps. bound separately. St. Petersburg, 1901.

Russia, Ministry of Crown Domains, Department of agriculture. *The Industries of Russia*, Vol. III. (*Agriculture and Forestry.*) Trans. John Martin Crawford. St. Petersburg, 1893. Contains little information on the first half of the century.

Russia, Tekhnologicheskii Institut imeni Leningradskogo soveta rabochikh, krest'ianskikh, i krasnoarmeiskikh deputatov. *Sto let (1828–1928)*. 2 vols. Leningrad, 1928.

Ryndziunskii, Pavel Grigor'evich. "Gil'deiskaia reforma Kankrina 1824 goda," *Istoricheskie zapiski*, no. 40 (1952).

——. *Gorodskoe grazhdanstvo doreformennoi Rossii*. Moscow, 1958. A most useful study.

Sacke, George. "Ludwig Heinrich von Jakob und die russische Finanzkrise am Anfang des 19. Jahrhunderts," *Jahrbücher für Geschichte Osteuropas*, no. 3 (1938).

Safonovich, V. I. "Vospominaniia," *Russkii arkhiv*, no. 4 (1903).

Salomon, Julius. "Die Warschau-Wiener Eisenbahn und ihre Verstaatlichung," *Archiv für Eisenbahnwesen*, XXXVII (1914).

Schaulis, Georg. *Graf Georg Kankrin in nationalökonomischer und finanzwirtschaftlicher Beziehung: Ein Beitrag zur Geschichte der N.-Ökonomie und der Finanzwissenschaft*. Tilsit, 1914.

Schiemann, Theodor. *Geschichte Russlands unter Kaiser Nikolaus I.* 4 vols. Berlin, 1904–1919.

Schilder, N. K. *Imperator Nikolai Pervyi; ego zhizn' i tsarstvovanie*. 2 vols. St. Petersburg, 1903.

Schmidt, Alfred. "Das russische Geldwesen während der Finanzverwaltung des Grafen Cancrin (1823–1844)," *Russische Revue, Monatsschrift für die Kunde Russlands*, VII (1875). Aside from Kaufman, the best discussion of monetary matters. Schmidt had firsthand knowledge of the prereform era. His treatment of the "popular rates" follows Speransky.

Schulze-Gävernitz, Gerhart von. *Volkswirtschaftliche Studien aus Russland*. Leipzig, 1899.

Semevskii, V. I. *Krest'ianskii vopros v Rossii v XVIII i pervoi polovine XIX veka*. 2 vols. St. Petersburg, 1888.

Seraphim, Hans-Jürgen. "Die Deutsch-russische Schule, eine kritische Studie," *Jahrbücher für Nationalökonomik und Statistik*, ser. 3, LXVII (1924).

Seredonin, S. M. *Istoricheskii obzor deiatel'nosti Komiteta ministrov*. 6 vols. St. Petersburg, 1902–1903. A very valuable survey of the work of the Committee of Ministers.

Shchlepnikov, M. *Mysli o russkoi promyshlennosti*. St. Petersburg, 1830. Published by the Ministry of Finance, Department of Manufacturing and Trade.

Shelekhov, D. "O lazhe ili promene na den'gi," *Biblioteka dlia chteniia*, XXXIII (1839), sec. 4.

Shil'der, N. K. See Schilder, N K

Shtorkh, P. A. "Materialy dlia istorii gosudarstvennykh denezhnykh znakov v Rossii s 1653 po 1840 god," *Zhurnal Ministerstvo narodnogo prosveshcheniia*, CXXXVII (1868). Contains useful statistics.

Shubin, I. A. *Volga i volzhskoe sudokhodstvo.* Moscow, 1927.

Sobolev, M. N. *Tamozhennaia politika Rossii, vo vtoroi polovine XIX veka.* Tomsk, 1911. This valuable and lengthy monograph comprises all of Vol. XLI of *Izvestiia Imperatorskago Tomskago universiteta* and is often cataloged under that heading.

Spann, Othmar. *The History of Economics.* Trans. Eden and Cedar Paul. New York, 1930. Includes a discussion of Adam Müller.

Speranskii, M. M. See Speransky, Mikhail Mikhailovich.

Speransky, Mikhail Mikhailovich. "Mysli o novykh biletakh kaznacheistva," *Russkaia starina*, VIII (1873).

——. "O monetnom obrashchenii," *Chteniia*, no. 4, (1872). Speransky's 1838 plan for monetary reform.

[——.] *V pamiat' grafa Mikhaila Mikhailovicha Speranskago, 1772–1872.* Ed. A. F. Bychkov. St. Petersburg, 1872. Collected letters of Speransky.

Steinwald, Arnuf Manfred. "Der Staatsbahngedanke in der russischen Eisenbahnpolitik," *Archiv für Eisenbahnwesen*, XLVIII (1925).

Stieda, Wilhelm, *Die Nationalökonomie als Universitätswissenschaft. (Abhandlungen der philologisch-historischen Klasse der königlichen sächsischen Gesellschaft der Wissenschaften,* Vol. XXV.) Leipzig, 1906.

Storozhev, V. N., ed. *Istoriia Moskovskogo kupecheskogo obshchestva; 1863–1913.* 2 vols. Moscow, 1914–1916.

Strumilin, S. G. *Istoriia chernoi metallurgii v SSSR.* Vol. I: *Feodal'nyi period (1500–1860)* (only one published). Moscow, 1954.

——. *Ocherki ekonomicheskoi istorii Rossii.* Moscow, 1960. Collected essays, including "Promyshlennyi perevorot v Rossii," first published in 1944.

Sumner, B. H. *Peter the Great and the Emergence of Russia.* London, 1950.

Tegoborski, Ludwik. See Tengoborskii, L.

Tengoborskii, L. *Commentaries on the Productive Forces of Russia.* 2 vols. London, 1855–1856.

Treadgold, Donald W. *The Great Siberian Migration.* Princeton, 1957.

Tugan-Baranovskii, M. *Russkaia fabrika v proshlom i nastoiashchem,* Vol. I(only one published). 3rd ed. St. Petersburg, 1907.

Turgenev, Nikolai I. *La Russie et les russes.* 3 vols. Paris, 1847.

———. *Opyt teorii nalogov.* St. Petersburg, 1818.

Urodkov, S. A. *Peterburgo-Moskovskaia zheleznaia doroga; istoriia stroitel'stva (1842–1851).* Leningrad, 1951.

Usov, S. "Razsmotreniia nekotorykh tolkov o novom denezhnom schete," *Severnaia pchela,* no. 238 (Oct. 21, 1839).

[Uvarov, Sergei]. *Desiatiletie Ministerstva narodnago prosveshcheniia, 1833–1843.* St. Petersburg, 1864. A summary of the ministry's work, signed by the minister, Uvarov.

Veselovskii, K. S. "Vospominaniia K. S. Veselovskago," *Russkaia starina,* CXVI (1903).

Veshniakov, V. "Komitet 1833 goda ob usovershenstvovanii zemledeliia," *Russkii vestnik,* LXXXII (1869).

Viatkin, M. P., ed. *Ocherki istorii Leningrada.* 4 vols. Moscow and Leningrad, 1955–1964.

Vigel', F. F. "Vospominaniia," *Russkii vestnik,* XLIX (1864). Also available in his *Zapiski* (2 vols.; Moscow, 1928).

Virginskii, V. S. *Tvortsy novoi tekhniki v krepostnoi Rossii.* Moscow, 1947.

———. *Vozniknovenie zheleznykh dorog v Rossii do nachala 40-kh godov, XIX.* Moscow, 1949. The major secondary work on the subject. Despite its highly nationalistic tone, a serious and useful study using much archival material.

———. "Zheleznodorozhnyi vopros v Rossii do 1835 goda," *Istoricheskie zapiski,* XXV (1948).

Voblyi, K. G. *Opyt istorii sveklo-sakharnoi promyshlennosti S.S.S.R.* Vol. I: *Do osvobozhdeniia krest'ian* (only one published). Moscow, 1928. A comprehensive study of all possible aspects of the problem. A model for industrial histories.

Westwood, J. N. *A History of Russian Railways.* London, 1964.

Wittschewsky, Valentin. *Russlands Handels-, Zoll-, und Industrie-politik, von Potor dom Grossen bis auf die Gegenwart.* Berlin, 1905.

Zablotskii-Desiatovskii, A. P. *Graf P. D. Kiselev i ego vremia.* 4 vols. St. Petersburg, 1882. Written by one of Kiselev's associates.

Zhitkov, Sergei M. *Institut inzhenerov putei soobshcheniia, Imperatora Aleksandra I.* St. Petersburg, 1899.

Zlotnikov, M. "Ot manufaktury k fabrike," *Voprosy istorii,* nos. 11-12 (1946).

INDEX